Grill Power

Grill Power

Everything you need to know

to make delicious, healthy meals

with your indoor electric grill

Holly Rudin-Braschi

QVC Publishing, Inc.

QVC Publishing, Inc.
Jill Cohen, Vice President and Publisher
Ellen Bruzelius, General Manager
Sarah Butterworth, Editorial Director
Cassandra Reynolds, Publishing Assistant

Produced in association with Patrick Filley Associates, Inc.
Design by Marjorie Anderson
Jacket photography by Lou Manna
Author photo by Jeff Kan Lee

Q Publishing and colophon are trademarks of QVC Publishing, Inc.

Published by QVC Publishing, Inc., 50 Main Street, Mt. Kisco, New York 10549

Manufactured in the United States of America

ISBN: 1-928998-37-2

First Edition

10 9 8 7 6 5 4 3 2 1

Contents

Acknowledgments

This book could not have been written without the help, confidence and love of a lot of wonderful people. Sincere thanks to my publisher, Jill Cohen at QVC Books for her confidence in the project and belief in my talent. Much appreciation to her hardworking staff Ellen Bruzelius, Sarah Butterworth, and Cassandra Reynolds for helping get this book out in record time. Special thanks to Patrick Filley for his superb attention to detail and positive attitude.

Much love and appreciation to my husband John for taste testing every recipe I created for this book (both winners and rejects!) and cleaning a multitude of grills afterwards. Love and hugs to my mom, Jean Rudin, for her recipe and menu ideas, and to my father Dr. Bernard D. Rudin, whose off-the-wall wit is reflected in many of the clever titles in the book.

Food lovers cross all walks of life and that goes for my terrific family and friends who tested all the menus in this book (several times!) in their home kitchens. Sincerest thanks to my aunt Vicci Rudin, retired city planner; my sister, Emilie Smith, medical technician; LuAnne Center, legal administrator; Fiera Leibovich, retired Russian physician and clinical lab scientist; Richard Bell, landscape architect, and his wife Lynne Bell, graphic designer; Joyce Vollmer, dry cleaner; Cheryl Branson, office man-ager, and her husband Everett Branson, fine printing papers salesman; Rae Swanson, retired special education teacher and her husband Kay Swanson, retired clothing salesman; Lesley Gordon Mountian, Senior Bank Officer. Special thanks to Metthea Baker, the professional recipe tester, who retested all the menus after the the home cooks tried them. And special thanks to all the people who made sure that I had the proper grills and ther-mometers to accurately complete this book.

I also sincerely thank all of my food industry colleagues and friends, professionials who answered my questions so that I could give you accurate information: Nathalie Dupree, authority on Southern cuisine; Chef Bruce Aidells, authority on meat; Chef Martin Yan, authority on Asian cui-sine; Chef Paul Prudhomme, authority on Southern cuisine; Chef Rafih Benjelloun, authori-ty on Moroccan and Middle Eastern cuisine; Betty Fussell, authority on corn; Harold McGee, food scientist; Arch Corriher, food researcher and Shirley Corriher, food scientist; Randy Rice, Seafood Technical Program Director, Alaska Seafood Institute; Wilfred Sumner, USDA Food Safety Consultant and Technical Director for NutriClean; Diane Van, supervisor of the USDA Meat and Poultry Hotline, and her exceptional staff; Randy Duranceau, Marketing Director of the Petaluma Poultry Processors.

The Making of an Electric Grill Goddess

My love affair with grilling began the summer I was six years old during a visit to my Uncle Mannie and Aunt Ruth's house in Los Angeles. That was when I realized how much I adored watching my Uncle Mannie grill dinner each night on his charcoal barbecue. I'll never forget the first time he let me help him use his long handled tongs to turn the sizzling chicken breasts for his famous grilled chicken sandwiches (see page 193 for the recipe). But my biggest thrill was tasting the chicken that I helped grill—I was a potential grill goddess standing at the brink of grill heaven.

It is not surprising that watching Uncle Mannie grill fascinated me. From the time I could stand on a stool at the kitchen counter, I have been passionate about cooking. This delighted my mother, Jean, who encouraged me to help her cook everything from her pungent chili stews to her luscious French apricot pies. But it was my mother's mother, Grandma Jenny, who taught me to love a good cut of meat and burgers. Grandma Jenny, who grew up at the turn of the 20th century, believed her petite granddaughter needed a daily dose of meat for proper growth. "Eat, eat, my child!" she would say as she fed me. I will always be indebted to my father's mother, Grandma Lil, for sparking my life-long interest in international cuisine. In 1970, at the age of 72, she took my younger sister Emilie and me on a trip around the world. One of her goals during that trip was to expose her 11 and 16 year-old granddaughters to world cuisine. She made sure we sampled smoked salmon in Norway,

coq au vin in France, creamy polenta in Italy, green coconut curry sauce in Thailand, tart lemon chicken in Hong Kong, and tofu in Japan.

In the days BIEG (Before Indoor Electric Grills), I moved to New York City to attend graduate school. I regularly fired up my small charcoal hibachi in my 4th floor apartment's most appropriate place...the fire escape off of my kitchen window! Spring, summer, autumn, even on stormy winter nights, I leaned out my kitchen window over the hot hibachi fending off ravenous New York pigeons with my long handled fork to feed my cravings. I also fed my boyfriend John, who still jokes that my unique grilling technique clinched his decision to ask me to marry him.

I continued to grill in my apartment with gusto, but it was convenience cooking appliances that gave me my start as a professional cooking instructor. To help pay for grad school and for my summer studies in Europe, I took a part time job as a food processor demonstrator in department stores. My enthusiasm for these gourmet time-savers and my cooking expertise landed me my first professional teaching job at the New School for Social Research in Manhattan. I discovered after the first semester that I loved teaching and I was offered jobs teaching both adults and children at other cooking schools throughout the city. My repertoire quickly expanded to classes ranging from microwave, low-fat, chocolate, bread, and vegetarian to Mexican and northern Italian cuisine!

In 1986, John and I moved back to California, our home state. I was ecstatic because we now owned a house where I could fire up a large kettle barbecue in the backyard. My friend, Chef Martin Yan, helped me resume my teaching career in the west and also gave me my first taste of food television as his assistant during tapings of the *Yan Can Cook Show* in San Francisco.

My career took another leap forward when it dawned on me that every original recipe and menu I created for both my adult and children's classes were based on sound nutrition. I went back to college and became certified through the American College of Sports Medicine as a health and fitness instructor. Shortly afterwards, I took my healthy cooking message to corporate America through my Feasting in the Fast Lane® classes in which I teach employees how to fit healthy, fast, gourmet-quality cooking into busy lives.

In 1995 indoor electric grills first came on the market. I gave one a try and was hooked. I found them faster and easier than traditional charcoal grilling because I could preheat in 10 minutes, get very similar results without the smoke, and cleanup was a snap. Electric indoor grilling became such fun that I purchased all four styles available, then started using them in my corporate classes. They were an immediate hit.

I knew that electric indoor grills were here to stay when I took my passion to television. The first time I appeared on QVC, I sold over 30,000 electric grills in a 12-hour period. Since then, I have sold over 100,000 grills on TV.

Why I Love Electric Tabletop Grills

My first electric tabletop grill was and still is a revelation to me. I've used just about every model on the market and I love each for the same reasons:
- Year-Round Grilling: Electric tabletop grills allow you to grill to your heart's content year-round, rain or shine without ever having to mess with charcoal, fire, or lighter fluid.
- Fast Food: Electric tabletop grills help get food

on the table fast because they reach cooking temperature within 10 to 15 minutes.
- High Heat: Food looks and tastes as good as if it has been grilled over hot coals because electric tabletop grills get good and hot.
- Portability: Electric tabletop grills are portable and can be used on just about any surface.
- Cleanup is easy because most grills feature nonstick grilling surfaces and dishwasher-safe parts.
- Health: Electric tabletop grills make eating healthy easy because you don't have to use excess fat to grill on a nonstick surface. Plus, all grills on the market are designed so that fat drips away from the food as it cooks.

What This Book Will Do for You

Grill Power is the first book written especially for electric grills. It's a handbook packed full of information, tips, and solutions specific to electric grills that you won't find in the operational manuals that come with your grill or in traditional grilling books. Get ready for:
- An in-depth discussion and comparison of all grill types on the market and special techniques for using each one.
- Techniques for using and cleaning electric grills your manufacturer doesn't tell you about.
- Grilling charts created expressly for electric grills.
- Choreographed menus designed around your electric tabletop grill and other convenience cooking appliances to help you put a hot and healthy gourmet-style meal on the table within 45 minutes to one hour.
- Recipes that include instructions for each type of grill.
- Recipes and menus that won't bust your daily fat budget.

So, no matter which brand or model electric indoor grill you own, I designed this book to help you make the most of a great appliance and to give you the power to become a grill goddess (or god) too!

Grill Power Basics

Meet Your Electric Grill

When I received my first electric grill, I thought "Great! Instead of using messy charcoal and lighter fluid, all I have to do is power up this baby and boogie with my burgers." I was both right and wrong. Heating an electric grill is certainly as easy as plugging it in. But to get food grilled just the way you like it, I found that you have to learn the steps before you can begin to boogie. In other words, you must know exactly how your grill works before cooking with it. To write this book, I used just about every electric grill available and discovered that there are four basic styles:

1. Two-Sided Contact Grill
2. Hibachi-Style Grill
3. Combination Grill
4. Infusion Grill

Each style has a completely different design, and operates differently. To learn more about style you own, match your grill up with one of my descriptions below. Make sure to check out the "Special Tips" for your grill. These are pearls of wisdom that I learned the hard way and can make the difference between a great meal and one that you are forced to feed to the dog!

Two-Sided Contact Grill

I like contact grills because they cook food in half the time it takes with any other grill—electric, gas, or charcoal. Many models are extremely compact and store easily in a closed, upright position, which makes them perfect for small kitchens with limited counter or cabinet space.

How It Works

Two heated grilling plates cook opposite sides of the food at the same time by making direct contact with it. A floating hinge connects the two plates so that the grill opens and closes like a book and adjusts to fit food of all sizes and shapes.

Size and Capacity

A variety of manufacturers make oval, rectangular, or square shapes. Grilling surfaces range from a small (one steak) 6 inch oval up to a large (6 to 8 steaks) 9 x 15-inch rectangle. One two-sided grill offers a bun warmer attached to the upper half of the grill.

Grill Plates

All contact grills manufactured feature easy-to-clean nonstick ridged plates. The ridges put grill marks on the cooked food. Some contact grills have fixed grill plates that are embedded with the heating element. Other models feature removable, dishwasher-safe grill plates that fit above a coiled heating element. Many models offer reversible grilling plates with raised grilling ridges on one side and a flat griddle for pancakes or grilled cheese sandwiches on the other side. Some models come with two sets of removable plates: one grilling set, and one griddle. Any grill with fixed grilling plates that is not immersible must be washed after each use with a hot, soapy sponge to thoroughly kill bacteria. See the Conduct Germ Warfare section on page 25 for more detailed cleaning instructions.

Catching the Fat

Many contact grills have cooking surfaces that have no openings or holes for the fat to drip through. Instead, special channels or spouts allow excess fat to drip off of the grill plate and into a heatproof bowl or drip tray. A couple contact grills on the market are angled to move the fat away from the food faster and more efficiently into a drip tray.

One model is designed with two different grilling surfaces. The bottom grilling surface is like a traditional hibachi-style grill with openings between the ridges and embedded coils within the grilling ridges. The fat drips between the ridges and into a large removable tray. The upper cooking surface is a solid plate with grilling ridges. When open to 180° (Position 2 below) the fat is channeled to a

well around the edge of the plate and then pours into the fat tray under the bottom grilling surface through a fixed spout.

Grill Opening

A few models open only to a 90° angle. Others are designed with the following three options:

Position 1, known as the right-angle or 90° opening option, enables you to easily place food on the grill before closing it for contact grilling.

Position 2, known as the flat or 180° opening option, doubles the cooking surface of the grill. In this position, you are cooking one side of your food at a time, like on an open-hearth electric grill. Some manufactures call this the "barbecue or party" position because you can grill enough food for four to 10 people, depending on the size of the grill and the type of food you are cooking.

Position 3, called the toasting or browning option, keeps the upper griddle plate above but not touching the food grilling on the bottom plate. This position can be used for making toasted garlic bread, melting cheese on top of a burger after the burger is cooked or heating individual slices of pizza.

Special Tips

Time your grilling carefully. It's easy to overcook food on contact grills because they grill in half the time it takes on other types of grills, electric or traditional.

If your grill plates are removable, make sure they are securely in place before turning on the grill. Make sure the drip pan is in place before starting to grill any fatty meat. You could end up with fat and juices on your counter without it.

Hibachi Style or Open Hearth Style Electric Grill

Open-hearth grills are fun to use because they are the closest things to grilling on a traditional charcoal grill...only better. You don't have to mess with charcoal, there's no smoke, low splatter, and a fairly large grilling surface.

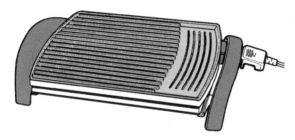

for sautéing small vegetables or fruit pieces that might otherwise slip through the drip openings.

These two surfaces allow two types of cooking at the same time. For example, while you are grilling burgers you can sauté onions on the griddle section to top them. Or, if you are using your grill to make your morning bacon or sausage, you can heat up frozen French toast or frozen pancakes on the griddle section.

How It Works

Hibachi or open-hearth style electric grills are smokeless versions of traditional charcoal hibachi grills. Like hibachis, open-hearth electric grills have no cover and have open grilling racks that allow the fat and juices to drip down from the food.

But that is where the similarity ends. Hibachis and other traditional grills create smoke because the food drippings fall directly onto the heat source (hot coals). In open-hearth electric grills, an electric heating coil is either fully embedded within the grilling rack or is a separate part sheathed by the grilling rack so that the top and sides of the coil are covered and the bottom is exposed. Whether embedded or sheathed, the heating coil heats the grilling rack and never comes in direct contact with food. This design eliminates smoke because the fat drips down through the grill rack openings, away from the heating coil, and into a shallow basin usually in the housing or base of the grill.

Size and Capacity

Hibachi-style electric grills are either rectangular or round in shape with cooking surfaces ranging from 14 inches in diameter to a generous 12 x 17-inches. The larger models offer enough space to grill 16 small steaks.

Grill Surface Design

Most hibachi-style grills have a grilling rack that is divided into two cooking surfaces. About 3/4 of the rack is a traditional grilling surface with openings. The remaining 1/4 is a flat griddle surface perfect

Catching the Fat and Preventing Smoke

The basins in hibachi-style electric grills are designed to catch and hold the fat and juices dripping off the grilling rack. Some basins are made of heatproof plastic while some are metal.

Grills with sheathed heating elements usually require 1 to 2 quarts of water in the basin. Without water, the reflected heat from the exposed heating coil would turn the basin into a smoking fry pan. Water helps the grill do 3 things:
- Prevents the grill from overheating by regulating the temperature of the basins.
- Eliminates fat splatter and smoke.
- Makes clean up easy because the fat and juices float in the water and don't bake onto the basin.

Most models of this type are designed with a safety feature that shuts the grill off if the water evaporates completely.

Hibachi-style grills with embedded heating coils don't require water because the heating element is not exposed and is far enough away from the catch basin to prevent smoking.

Special Tips

For hibachi-style grills that don't require water in the catch basin: Before turning the grill on, line the drip pan with aluminum foil. After grilling, carefully remove the foil and discard it. The drip tray will be clean.

For hibachi-style grills that require water in the basin: Never turn your grill on without the proper amount of water in the basin. Check your user's manual for the exact amount your model requires. Keep the water level stable. When grilling for a long period of time, check the water level every five to 10 minutes, adding more as needed. If you let all the water evaporate, the heat from the grill will build up and overheat the basin. Not only will this create smoke from dripping juices and fats falling on the hot basin bottom, but overheating will turn it off (if your grill has an automatic safety shutoff feature). Or, if your grill doesn't shut itself off, it could get hot enough to damage the counter or tabletop it is placed on.

Follow these steps to reheating a grill that has shutdown. Give it time to cool down: 10 to 15 minutes or more depending on the model. If you had food on the grill when it overheated, take it off, and don't put it back on until the grill is reheated to the same temperature. If you leave food on the grill while it reheats, it may dry out and become overcooked.

Combination Grill/Skillet

I love this style grill because it is so versatile. I originally got my first one to use just as a grill. But I soon learned that because it can hold liquid and it comes with a lid, I could use it to cook just about anything I would normally cook in an electric fry pan, such as meatballs in pasta sauce, Asian-style stir-fry, chili stew, lightly fried falafel, or potato pancakes. In addition to grilling, you can use this appliance to pan-fry, sauté, simmer, steam, and keep food warm.

How it Works

This grill is a combination grill and shallow electric fry pan. It comes with a 1- or 2-inch-deep nonstick grill pan without holes or outlets so all the food, juices, and fat remain in the pan as the food cooks. But the fat is still carried away from the food, thanks to tall, evenly spaced grilling ridges that lift the food off of the bottom of the pan and create deep channels that carry excess fat to the outer 1-inch space around the edge of the pan.

Like a traditional electric fry pan, combination grills come with lids, which prevent splatter. Lids

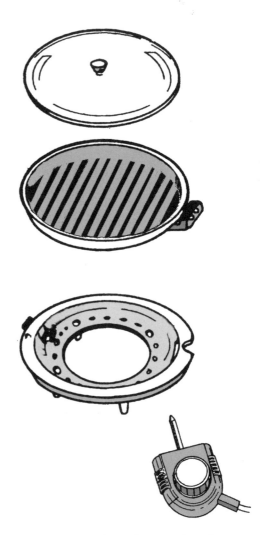

also help food cook faster because heat becomes concentrated and trapped under the top and is then reflected back down to the food, almost like a convection oven. To let steam escape during cooking, the lids are loose fitting. Stay-cool handles make lifting during cooking easy. Combination grills also have variable temperature controls that adjust from warm to about 425°F. Two models are available:

The fixed-pan model features a 1-inch-deep grill pan and heating coils as a single unit. This unit fits into a removable stay-cool housing, which is immersible in a sink of water for cleaning when the temperature control is removed.

The interchangeable-pan model features 2 interchangeable 2-inch-deep nonstick cooking pans: a grilling pan and a griddle pan. The cooking pans sit in a stay-cool base. The heating coils in this model are housed within the base instead of attached to the cooking pans. The cooking pans are dishwasher safe.

Size and Capacity

Combination grills are either round (11 to 14 inches in diameter) or oval (15 x 18-inch). Models currently on the market are big enough to hold 12 hamburgers or small steaks, or make a complete dinner for 2 to 6 people, including meat and vegetables. At a 1- to 2-inch depth, they can hold up to 8 to 10 cups of liquid stew, chili, or meatballs and sauce.

Special Tips

Do not preheat with the lid on the grill. You may damage it.

If the electrical heating unit is attached to the back of the grill pan, don't let the grill soak in sink water when you are cleaning it. Even though this style combination grill is immersible, it is not submersible. If the electrical outlet sits in water longer than a few minutes, your grill may not operate the next time you turn it on.

Never start cooking with the lid on the grill unless you want to steam your food. If you put the lid on when you begin grilling, the natural moisture in the food will gather as steam under the lid and no browning will occur. You have to let some of the moisture evaporate from the food to help the natural sugars caramelize into grill marks. Instead, put the lid on the grill halfway through the grilling time after you have turned your food or toward the end. When you put the lid on after the grill marks are deeply seared onto one or both sides of the food, it prevents further evaporation of the natural liquids and keeps food tender and juicy.

Infusion Grill

The infusion grill gives you the best of two cooking techniques…grilling and steaming. The surfaces of these grills put distinct grill marks on the outside of the food while the steam that comes from liquids in the infusion cup infuses the food with moisture and flavor.

How It Works

There are 2 types of infusion grills. One style is circular with a lid, the other looks like a hibachi-style grill.

Infusion grill with a lid. I call this grill my volcano of flavor because its unique design allows two types of grilling. You can grill traditionally with the cover off or you can grill with the lid on for steam grilling. The slanting, cone-shaped grilling surface is topped with an "fusion" cup, which, when filled with a flavoring liquid, steams as the grill heats, making it resemble a mini volcano. When you cover the grill with the glass lid, the steam creates a "rainforest" basting effect and infuses the cooking food with the aroma and flavor of the liquids in the infusion cup.

Even though steam is created by the liquids in the infusion cup, crispy grill marks still form on the food because the grill is designed to circulate the hot steam instead of trapping it under the lid. The lid sits loosely on top of scalloped vents on the lip of the grill pan to prevent steam buildup and enhance air circulation. There are also holes in the stay-cool housing under the grill pan. When the glass lid is in place, the heat of the grill creates air currents that circulate the steam created by the liquid in the infusion cup. Instead of staying under the lid, the heated steamy air evaporates through the air vents both at the sides of the pan and underneath it in the housing, so the food browns as it steams.

Hibachi-style infusion grill. On the outside, this grill looks exactly like a hibachi-style grill, but on the inside, it hides an infusion cup directly under the center of the grilling grid. The liquid inside the infusion cup is heated by an extension from the bottom of the grilling grid. When the liquid inside the cup gets hot, it creates a fine mist that filters up

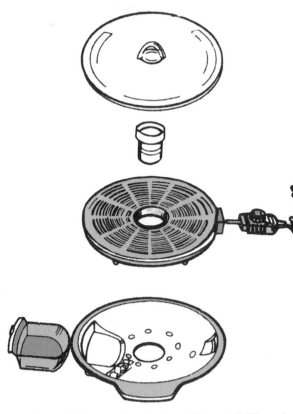

attached to the back of the grilling surface and are completely enclosed, making them immersible and easy-to-clean.

Catching the Fat

The infusion grill with a lid has a sloped cone-shaped, nonstick grill pan that allows fat and excess juices to roll down and away from the food and out through a small outlet into a separate grease tray in the removable base. The base of the hibachi-style infusion grill is deep, designed to catch fat that falls through the openings in the grilling grid.

Special Tips

Using the infusion cup for both styles of infusion grill:
• Even if you aren't filling the infusion cup with liquid, always have it in place when heating the grill and grilling.
• Never put more than 1/2-cup liquid in the infusion cup.
• If you are grilling over a long period of time (15 to 20 minutes or more) and your infusion cup is filled, keep checking to make sure that the liquid doesn't evaporate. Evaporated sauces tend to smoke and burn onto the bottom of the infusion cup instead of steam.

For the infusion grill with a lid:
• If your infusion cup is filled with liquid, grill with the cover on. If your infusion cup is empty, you can grill with the cover off.

through the openings in the grilling grid. The mist keeps everything on the grill moist and flavorful, yet allows crisp grill marks to form on the food because the moisture evaporates quickly.

Size and Capacity

The infusion grill with the lid offers a 14-inch diameter grilling surface. The hibachi-style has an equally generous 10 x 14-inch grilling surface. Either style is big enough to hold 12 hamburgers or small steaks or to make a complete dinner for 4 to 6 people, including meat and vegetables.

Grilling Surface Design

The infusion grill with a lid has concentric ridges on the grilling surface. These create grill marks and prevent the food from slipping off the cone-shaped surface. The hibachi-style infusion grill has a traditional grilling surface of ridges alternating with openings. The heating coils in both grills are

BONUS SECTION
Infusion Cup Recipes

The liquids you use to infuse your grilled food with flavor can be as simple as water mixed with fresh garlic or a more complex, homemade marinade. Here are a few tips for making my favorite infusion flavoring recipes opposite:
• Fresh herbs will give you the strongest flavors. Their natural oils are more pungent than dried herbs. Fresh garlic and fresh gingerroot are rich

with volatile oils, which will flavor your food more intensely than garlic or ginger purée from a jar.

- To intensify the flavors of the infusion liquid, you can rub some of the same ingredients you put into the infusion cup directly onto the food. For example, if you are infusing lamb chops with lemon-rosemary-garlic infusion, rubbing some extra garlic on the meat will give it added punch.
- Many of the infusion recipes can double as a heated dipping sauce after the food has been grilled (such as Asian Aromas or Salsa Sunrise).

Smokey Joe

⅓   cup water or steak sauce

1   tablespoon Worcestershire sauce

1   tablespoon pressed garlic

1   tablespoon liquid smoke

Hickory Heaven

¼   cup hickory barbecue wood chips soaked in water

1   tablespoon liquid smoke

Place the wood chips in the infusion cup. Add the liquid smoke and enough boiling water to fill the cup.

Lemon-Rosemary-Garlic

¼   cup lemon juice, fresh or bottled

2   tablespoons fresh chopped rosemary leaves or 1 tablespoon dried

2   tablespoons pressed garlic

Asian Aromas

¼   cup soy sauce

2   tablespoons freshly grated gingerroot

2   tablespoons pressed garlic

½   teaspoon Thai-style red or green curry paste (optional)

Salsa Sunrise

¼   cup salsa, mild or hot

2   tablespoons tequila

2   tablespoons finely chopped fresh cilantro

Tarragon Citrus Surprise

⅓   cup orange juice

2   tablespoons finely chopped tarragon or 1 tablespoon dried

2   tablespoons finely chopped fresh basil or 1 tablespoon dried

1   tablespoon pressed garlic

Caribbean Caper

⅓   cup pineapple juice

2   tablespoons dry or wet jerk seasoning (see page 54 for recipe if you can't find either in your grocery store)

3   tablespoons pressed garlic

1   tablespoon freshly grated gingerroot

Cajun Classic

⅓   cup spicy vegetable or tomato juice

2   tablespoons pressed garlic

1   tablespoon hot pepper sauce such as Tabasco

1   tablespoon Cajun spice mix (see page 54 for a recipe if you can't find a mix in your grocery store)

Texas BBQ

⅓   cup barbecue sauce

2   tablespoons finely chopped jalapeño pepper

Dilly Dijon

⅓   cup white wine

2   tablespoons Dijon-style mustard

2   tablespoons chopped fresh dill or 1 tablespoon dried

Japanese Sake to Me

¼ cup teriyaki sauce

¼ cup sake

Power of Performance

As I grilled my way through every electric grill on the market, I noticed a large variation in how efficiently each grill performed. Some are ready to rock-and-roll in 10 minutes, while others take up to 20 minutes to preheat. Some grills make my steaks continuously sizzle, while others make them alternately sizzle and go silent. If I put two steaks of equal weight and thickness on some grills, they cook to medium at the same time, while on other grills some of the meat gets overcooked while I wait for the rest to catch up. Some grills charred the outside of foods and left the inside undercooked, while others let me grill everything to perfection.

Lots of Heat Makes for Speedy Grilling

How fast does your grill cook food? That depends on the amount of your grill's wattage, plus the length of the heating coils and their arrangement under the grill rack or grill plate.

Wattage is the amount of electrical energy that powers your grill. All of the recipes in this book were developed and tested on the hottest electric grills available, ranging between 1,200 and 1,700 watts. Some manufacturers offer grills that range between 800 to 1,000 watts. Lower wattage increases grilling time, so if you own a lower-wattage grill, add a few more minutes to the total cooking time for each grill recipe in this book. High wattage grills (1,200 to 1,700 watts) are your best bet because they offer:

- **Quick preheating.** These grills get hot fast, reaching 420°F or higher within 10 minutes. That means you can cook fast and get food on the table even faster.
- **Stable temperatures and fast heat recovery.** Have you ever loaded a sizzling hot pan with food but it just wouldn't cook because the pan temperature immediately dropped? This doesn't

happen with high-wattage electric grills. Internal thermostats constantly cycle to keep temperatures stable no matter how much food you load on the grill.

- **Food that looks and tastes grilled.** High-wattage grills mimic the constant intense heat of a charcoal fire. This uniform, concentrated heat triggers a chemical reaction between the natural protein and sugars on the outer surface of the food and creates the same delicious crispy brown grill marks that are created on a traditional grill.

Heating Coils, their length and the way they are arranged under the grill plate, can make the difference between a calm or hectic meal. Grill racks heated by long, evenly arranged grilling coils (making at least 2 loops or 4 rows) are the most efficient because every spot on the grilling surface heats to the same temperature. This means if you load up the grill with food of equal thickness and weight, everything will cook at the same speed enabling you to make one trip to the grill to take everything off when it is done. Shorter heating coils with fewer bends cover less area under the grill rack and may have hot and cool spots. This type of grill may keep you running back and forth from table to grill to remove cooked food because not everything will grill at the same time. That's because food placed over hot spots cooks faster than food placed on slightly cooler spots.

Temperature Controls for Versatile Grilling

Electric tabletop grills offer either variable temperature controls or a fixed temperature. Grills with variable temperature controls allow you to do everything from searing the outside of a tender tuna steak for a rare grilled sashimi effect, or keep a batch of sausages warm for a breakfast buffet. These grills can have 4 or more settings depending on the model and manufacturer. The temperature setting indications on the control dial may also differ. Some temperature controls show dots (e.g., • means low, and • • • • means high or max). Others say, "0-Low-Med-Max." Some manufacturers give numbers (e.g., 1 to 5 or 1 to 6 where 1 means low and 5 or 6 means high), while others include the actual grill surface temperature (e.g., warm/simmer-250-300-350-400-420°F).

You'll use the highest setting (High, Max, 440°F, or setting number 6) for vegetables and meat no thicker than 1¹/₂ inches. You will use medium-high (1 or 2 steps below high) or to about 350° to 400°F for grilling fish and poultry. Intermediate temperature settings (3 or 4, Medium, or 325° to 350°F) allow you to grill thicker cuts of meat, poultry or fish (more than 1¹/₂ inches thick) more slowly and at a lower temperature so that the outside doesn't burn before the inside gets cooked. Low settings (1 or 2, Low, Warm, or 200° to 300°F) allow you to keep food warm on the grill after it has been cooked.

Grills with fixed temperature controls usually have just one setting (High) that reaches between 350°F to 450°F depending on the amount of wattage that powers the grill. (See previous section.) Many don't have on and off switches and begin preheating the moment you plug the grill in. Since you can't adjust the temperature, you have to be careful not to overcook your food on fixed-temperature grills. Nor is it a good idea to grill food thicker than 1¹/₂ inches on these grills because the outside will burn before the inside cooks.

Indicator Lights Can Take the Guesswork Out of Grilling

Most grills have one of two types of indicator lights:

On/Off indicator lights let you know the power is working. They go on as soon as the grill is plugged in or the on-off switch is set and stay on throughout the cooking time.

Thermostatically controlled indicator lights, available on some models with variable temperature controls, take the guesswork out of preheating and grilling. They illuminate when the grill begins heating and turn off when it reaches the desired temperature. This type of indicator light will cycle on and off throughout the grilling time so don't worry that your grill is not working correctly. To prevent the grill from overheating, these lights illuminate when the internal thermostat lowers the temperature, then go off again when the grill reaches the set temperature again.

Nonstick Grill Surfaces Make For Easy Clean Up

One of the reasons I love cooking with electric grills is the ease of clean up. Most offer nonstick surfaces on the grilling rack or pan. A few manufacturers make grills with uncoated stainless steel grill surfaces, though. If you have the latter, make sure you spray the cooking grid with nonstick cooking spray before you preheat it. If the spray from an aerosol can hits a super-hot heating coil you can start a fire or seriously burn yourself and those standing nearby.

Divine Secrets of the Grill Power Goddess

Did this chapter title catch your attention? I figured that if I gave it an intriguing one, you'd read it through. That way you wouldn't make the same mistakes I did learning how to perfect my electric-grilling technique. And who has time for mistakes when it's dinnertime and family members are hungry? I "divined" the following secrets after grilling literally hundreds of meals on every type of electric grill on the market.

Secret # 1: Use Your Indoor Grill under the Exhaust Fan over Your Stove

Even though many of the electric grills are "smokeless," the smell will still permeate your kitchen and your house if you are not using it in a ventilated area. To prevent smelling dinner the next morning, set your grill on top of your stove directly under the exhaust fan. To make sure that the grill is level, put a thin glass counter saver (about 1/4 x 14 x 20-inches) over a couple of the burners, then set your grill on top of it so the cord will easily reach a nearby electrical outlet.

Make sure all of the burners on your stove are turned off before you place your grill on the stovetop. Depending on the configuration of your stovetop, you may be able to place your electric grill over one-half of the stove top and use the burners on the other half at the same time to simultaneously cook things such as pasta or rice. Just make sure that the heat from the burners you are using is far enough away to not melt the plastic housing on your electric grill.

Secret # 2: Preheat, Preheat, Preheat!

Just as you wouldn't bake a cake without preheating your oven, you shouldn't cook on your electric tabletop grill without fully preheating it. Putting food on the grill during preheating tends to overcook and dry it out. That's because you inadvertently increase the total grilling time with the extra time it takes for the grill to reach the set temperature. Most electric tabletop grills take approximately 10 minutes to fully preheat. That's just enough time to prepare a salad while you wait to throw your steak on the grill.

So make a habit of powering up your grill before you begin any other preparation so that it will be ready to cook when you are. It's easy to forget to plug it in once you get involved in creating your meal.

Secret # 3: Never Oil Your Grilling Surface

Don't spray or brush the grilling surface with oil or nonstick spray. Most surfaces are already nonstick, so why bother? Even if the grilling surface is a wire stainless-steel grid, it's still not a good idea. Excess fat on a hot grilling surface smokes and will make your kitchen a mess. In addition, after grilling, your grill surface will be covered with sticky-brown baked-on fat that is hard to remove. To help your food quickly form distinct grill marks and to make sure it releases readily from the grill, spray the food with fat-free cooking spray, olive oil spray, or canola oil spray.

Secret # 4: Time Your Grilling

Hungry kids, telephone calls and a million other things only you can think of–can mean over- or undercooked grilled food. My solution: Carefully time each grilling step with a digital timer. I use either the timer on my microwave oven or a small digital kitchen timer.

Secret # 5: Make One Good Turn

Once you put food on the hot grill, your goal is to move it as little as possible. Less handling cooks food more efficiently, keeps it tender and juicy, and makes distinct, deep grill marks for a beautiful presentation.

Secret # 6: Use a Digital Thermometer

How do you test your grilled meat, poultry or fish to see if it is done? Do you just give it the old eye-ball test to see if the color looks right, or do you touch the surface to see if it springs back? Or do you slice into it so many times with the tip of a sharp knife that your food no longer looks nice enough to serve to anyone but yourself? Take the guesswork out of grilling–it's time you considered using a digital thermometer to test for doneness.

Why bother, you say, since professional chefs and home cooks have been doing without them for centuries? First, consider the safety factor. Let's face it. Unless you live in an area where you can purchase fresh meat, poultry and fish from local farms and fishermen, you can't always be sure where your food comes from, how fresh it is, or how it was processed and packaged. Of course, I am not saying that every piece of meat, chicken or fish you purchase is contaminated with health-threatening microorganisms such as salmonella or *E. coli*. But color, aroma, and texture are not the most accurate ways to determine whether food is contaminated before you cook it, or whether, after cooking, your food has reached an internal temperature high enough to kill harmful bacteria. It's a lot better to make sure your food is not undercooked by using an instant-read thermometer than to suffer unpleasant symptoms after eating.

Second, consider preferences and aesthetics. Checking the internal temperature of grilled meat, poultry or fish with a digital instant-read thermometer is the most accurate way to make sure food is cooked just the way you like it when it comes off the grill. And a small puncture from the thermometer's thin temperature probe won't destroy the way your food looks the way a knife tip will.

Third, consider convenience. Digital instant-read thermometers save you time and aggravation. Have you ever had a guest slice into a grilled steak that looked cooked on the outside, only to find that it was still cold and raw in the very middle? Then you had to throw it back on the grill and stay to watch it while everyone else continued eating. Since I started using digital instant-read thermometers, no one ever complains of their food being undercooked or overcooked, and I always eat at the same time my family and guests do.

I have 2 favorite types of digital instant-read thermometers. A watch/camera battery powers both types, so getting an accurate reading is quick. The heat sensor in both types of thermometers is a high-tech semiconductor in the tip of the probe.

Pen-type digital instant-read thermometers are about the length of a pen and have liquid-crystal temperature displays on top of a 1/8-inch diameter probe. Once inserted, the temperature reading appears in about 10 seconds.

Free-standing digital instant-read thermometers look like 3-inch square mini-computers and have a large pop-up liquid crystal display. This type of thermometer has a lot of easy-to-use bells and whistles that enable you to use it for cooking on the grill as well as in your oven. First, instead of being attached directly to the temperature probe like the pen-type thermometers, freestanding models are connected to the probe via a thin, detachable, stay-cool metal cable. This allows you to insert the thermometer at the start of grilling and leave it in the food until it reaches the exact temperature you choose because you don't have to worry that the plastic display will melt. (If, for example, you are using this type of thermometer to cook a roast in your oven, the connecting wire is thin and long enough to allow you to close the oven door on it and place the monitor outside on a cool counter.)

Second, it allows you to constantly monitor the exact internal temperature of whatever you are cooking so you can take the food off of the grill just at the right time. Third, freestanding models give the most accurate readings because you can program them to alert you with a beep when the food reaches the internal temperature you desire. Most models also come with timers that can be used simultaneously with the internal temperature reading. That means you can time your food on the grill to let you know when it is halfway cooked before turning it over and keep the probe in place the entire time.

Secret # 7: Choose the Best Grilling Equipment

Grill Surface Savers To save the nonstick surfaces on your electric tabletop grill, I recommend nylon tools designed to withstand high heat. If you use metal or stainless utensils with any regularity, you can kiss the nonstick surface of your grill good bye. My favorites are:
• Two nylon spatulas for turning and serving delicate fish steaks, fish fillets and large pieces of meat. I slip one spatula underneath the fillet and hold it in place with the second spatula on top before turning. This technique helps prevent delicate foods from falling apart.
• Nylon cooking tongs for turning small items such as vegetables and sausages.
• Two-pronged nylon forks for lifting larger cuts of meat to check the underside for doneness.
• Wooden skewers for kabobs. Wood won't scratch nonstick surfaces. In addition, since you are cooking with electricity instead of fire, wooden skewers don't require soaking in water because electric heat will not cause dry skewers to burn.

Keep Cooked Food Hot with Universal Plate Covers These are handy for keeping food hot between grilling and serving time. They are usually sized to fit over dinner plates. I particularly like the plastic plate covers designed for microwave ovens because they have a small hole at the top to let steam escape so your grilled food stays warm and doesn't get soggy.

Secret # 8: Store Your Grill Properly

Worried about your grilling surface getting scratched when you are not using your appliance? Here are my suggestions:
• Two-Sided Contact Grills: Before storing, put a piece of thick plastic (such as a gallon-sized freezer bag or air-filled packing material) between the grill plates to prevent them from rubbing together.
• Hibachi Style Grill: Store in a plastic bag, or, if you want to store a piece of equipment on top of it, place an old plastic placemat on top of the grill surface.
• Combination Grill or Fusion Grill: Always store them with the lid on. You can also put a plastic bag between the grilling surface and the lid before storing for extra protection.

Secret # 9: Conduct Germ Warfare

Ever wonder why you sometimes feel you have the flu just after you ate but can't figure out how you got exposed? In most cases, a flu bug isn't bothering your digestive tract; it's a mild case of food poisoning caused by not-so-careful cooking practices. The way you handle your food before, during and after you prepare it for the grill can either result in rave reviews for a delicious meal or someone feeling quite sick.

Does all this mean you should become paranoid about food and cooking? Absolutely not. Microscopic organisms have always been and will always be a risk. But you must store foods properly, cook them thoroughly and keep your hands and work areas clean to stay healthy. When it comes to those invisible little bugs, what you can't see can hurt you.

Clean Hands Are the Best Defense Listen to your mother! When she told you, way back when, to wash your hands before touching food, she was right. This simple habit can prevent everything from colds to fatal salmonella poisoning. Research proves that bacteria can remain active on a surface for more than 72 hours.

When should you wash your hands?
• Just before you begin handling food. Don't think that if you washed your hands a few minutes before coming into the kitchen they are still clean. Without thinking, you probably touched a number of things that were touched by other people (door handles, pencils or pens, countertops, etc.), who unknowingly left harmful but invisible bacteria on those surfaces.
• While you are cooking, after touching your face or any other part of your body. You can spread harmful bacteria just by unconsciously scratching the side of your nose and then making a fresh salad.
• After handling raw meat, fish or poultry, and particularly after using your hands to spread a marinade or put raw food on the grill. If you handle any food that will be served raw (such as salad) or food that is already cooked (such as French fries) after handling raw meat, fish, or poultry without washing your hands, you run the risk of contaminating the raw ingredients with salmonella.

Keep Your Grill Germ-Free Do you use paper towel or a damp sponge to wipe down your dirty grill because you saw it done that way on a TV advertisement? These demonstrations are designed to show the quality of the nonstick surfaces, not how to clean your machine.

Here's the bottom line: Whether your grill is immersable, has dishwasher-safe grilling surfaces, or the grilling surfaces on your machine are not removable (such as those on some contact grills), any part of your grill that touches raw or cooked foods must be sanitized after cooking to prevent food poisoning. To kill salmonellosis and other bacteria present in meat and poultry, experts suggest washing all surfaces with hot soapy water for at least 20 seconds. I sometimes use a paper towel to wipe food particles from the surfaces of the grill before washing. But I always follow with a shampoo of very hot soapy water to completely sanitize all of the cooking surfaces.

If you own a grill with a surface that is dishwasher safe, you still have to remove any stubborn dirt by hand before sanitizing it in the dishwasher.

For best results when cleaning your grill surface:
• Choose a liquid dish soap that breaks up grease.
• Use a soft-bristled dish brush or sponge made especially for nonstick cooking surfaces to clean all surfaces.
• Use the small bristle end of a baby bottle brush for removing stubborn baked-on food stuck in the openings of grilling racks.

Combination Grill Cleaning Tip: If you made the mistake of spraying or wiping oil onto your grill surface and now have a sticky baked-on mess, don't use an abrasive cleaning utensil or abrasive liquid cleansers to remove it. They will damage the nonstick surface of your grill. A simple homemade mixture will help remove the sticky stuff. Fill your grill with 4 to 5 cups of hot water mixed with 1/4 cup vinegar (any type) or 1/4 cup baking soda. Open all your windows for ventilation. Turn the grill on high and bring the water mixture to a boil. Let it boil for 3 to 4 minutes. This should loosen some or all of the baked on fat and grime. Let the pan cool then put it in the sink and wash the surface with a grease removing liquid dish soap and a nylon dish brush or sponge designed for cleaning nonstick surfaces. Repeat the process for stubborn dirt.

Secret # 10: Practice Food Safety

Keep Everything Cool Letting your meat, fish or poultry get warmer than 40° F, even for just a little while, can make the difference between a culinary success and a disaster that can send diners to the emergency room. So please keep perishables in the refrigerator just until grilling time.

Defrost Your Meat and Poultry Properly
• Completely thaw meat or poultry before grilling so it cooks more evenly.

- Use the refrigerator for slow, safe overnight thawing. It takes about 3 to 9 hours to thaw cut-up meat and poultry parts in the refrigerator.
- Foods defrosted in the refrigerator can be refrozen after cooking.
- Defrost in the microwave only if the food will be placed immediately on the grill or in the oven.
- Meat in airtight packaging can be defrosted in a bowl of cold tap water if you change the water every 30 minutes.
- Foods defrosted in the microwave or by the cold-water method should be cooked before refreezing because they may have been exposed to temperatures above 40°F, allowing harmful bacteria to grow.
- Chicken may be safely thawed in cold water. Place chicken in its original wrap or a watertight plastic bag in cold water. Change water often. It takes about an hour to thaw chicken parts.

Marinate Safely

- Always marinate food in the refrigerator, not on the counter.
- If some of the marinade is to be used for basting during cooking or as a sauce on the cooked food, reserve a portion of the marinade. Don't put raw meat and poultry in it.
- Don't reuse the marinade from raw meat, poultry or fish on cooked or partially cooked food unless it's boiled first to destroy any bacteria. After just a few seconds, a liquid marinade will pick up salmonella or other bacteria that is present on the outside of meat, poultry or fish. If you baste partially grilled food with leftover marinade, it may not cook long enough to kill the bacteria imparted to it from the raw meat.

Special Marinade Safety Tip for Fusion Grills

If after marinating meat, fish, or poultry you decide to put the leftover marinade in the fusion cup, do not baste with it. Use it only for steamed flavor.

Take Care When Carving Meat

Grilled foods should never be carved on a cutting board that was just used for cutting up raw meat and poultry. The board will still have some raw meat juices on it, which could contain bacteria; it must be thoroughly cleaned with hot, soapy water before using again.

Keep Grilled Meat Hot If you are not serving your grilled food within 15 minutes, keep it hot on the low or warm setting of your grill, in a 200°F oven, a chafing dish or on an electric hot tray. Keep hot, cooked food at 140°F or warmer.

Serve Grilled Food Safely When taking food off the grill, don't put the cooked items on the same platter that held raw meat. Any bacteria present in the raw meat juices could contaminate the safely cooked meat or other grilled foods. In hot weather (90°F and above), food should never sit out for more than 1 hour.

Handle Leftovers Safely Store leftovers in the refrigerator or freezer within 2 hours of taking food off the grill. Discard any food left out more than 2 hours (1 hour in hot weather–90°F or above).

Holly's Pantry

You just brought home the most beautiful piece of tuna you have ever purchased. Yasu! You could go Greek and make a grilled masterpiece in a marinade of oregano, dill, lemon juice and olive oil. Or maybe Japanese teriyaki tuna tickles your taste buds? But wait, *ma cher*! You can celebrate Mardi Gras off-season by giving that tuna a hefty rub of Cajun spices before throwing it on the grill. What about the side dish? You definitely want one that goes well with the meal's international theme but will cook fast enough to be ready when your fish comes off of the grill. How can you cater to your momentary gastronomic whims in record time? Be prepared! A pantry filled with an international variety of bottled sauces, condiments, seasonings and quick cooking grains and starches will give you a kaleidoscope of possibilities for reinventing mealtime every time you grill. What should you have in your pantry? Take a look at my International Pantry Solutions chart. I categorized it by international cuisine to take the guesswork out of shopping. But please don't panic when you look at the length of the list. I am not expecting you to purchase everything I suggest. Use it as a guide for choosing those ingredients you like. You can also use it to arrange your pantry like I do…by international cuisine. That way when you have to put a meal on the table fast, you can find all of your Asian ingredients in one place, your Italian in another, your Southwest in another, etc.

Notes about the Chart

•I did not include fresh garlic, onions and scallions in the chart because they are common to every international cuisine. These ingredients should have a permanent place on your shopping list for a well-stocked pantry.

•The alcohol suggested is used to spike marinades and homemade sauces.

•I like to use fresh herbs whenever possible because the flavor is more pungent and pronounced. If the herb is out of season, or if you are in a hurry, don't hesitate to use dried.

•You can mix dried and fresh herbs for "dry" seasoning rubs.

Cuisine	Prepared Sauces, Condiments & Sides	Dried or Fresh Herbs and Spices
Cajun/ Creole	Chili sauce, hot pepper sauce, ketchup, tomato sauce, hot sauce, canned chilies **Alcohol:** whisky or gin **Oil:** olive oil, corn, canola **Vinegar:** red or white wine **Quick Sides:** long grain white rice mixed with canned red or black beans, instant mashed potatoes	Cajun or Creole spice mixture (To make your own mixture stock: allspice, bay leaf, cayenne, chili pepper, white pepper, dehydrated garlic and onion, oregano, paprika, thyme, cumin, dry mustard, nutmeg, parsley)
Caribbean	Prepared jerk sauce or paste, ketchup, tomato sauce, chili sauce **Alcohol:** Rum **Oil:** canola, corn **Vinegars:** red or white wine **Quick Sides:** long grain white rice, steamed sweet potatoes	Dry Jerk seasoning mixture, chilies, ginger (To make your own mixture stock: bay leaf, paprika, cinnamon, nutmeg, allspice, onion and garlic powder, ground ginger, black pepper, cayenne pepper, thyme)
Chinese	Peanut sauce, soy, hot pepper sauce, ketchup, hoisin sauce, oyster sauce, black bean sauce, plum sauce, sweet and sour sauce, char siu (Chinese barbecue sauce) **Alcohol:** Sherry (dry or sweet), rice wine (Shao Hsing) **Oil:** chili, peanut, sesame **Vinegar:** seasoned rice **Quick Sides:** long grain white rice, cellophane noodles	Cilantro, chilies, ginger, sesame seeds
French	Dijon-style mustard, sweet hot mustard, cornichon (petite pickles), capers, cured black or green olives **Alcohol:** red or white wine, vermouth, Grand Marnier (orange brandy), Calvados (apple brandy) **Oil:** olive oil, walnut oil **Vinegar:** white and red wine, tarragon, sherry, champagne **Quick Sides:** microwave or steamed potatoes, oven baked fries, instant mashed potatoes	Chives, bay leaf, fines herbes mixture, Herbes de Provence, dill, green pepper corns, marjoram, tarragon, thyme, nutmeg, paprika, rosemary, basil, sage, lavender
Greek	Tomato sauce and paste, Kalamata olives, roasted marinated red peppers, fresh lemon juice **Alcohol:** red or white wine, ouzo (anise flavored liquor) **Oil:** Olive **Vinegar:** red and white wine **Quick Sides:** long grain white rice, orzo pasta, instant mashed potatoes	Cinnamon, dill, oregano, parsley, mint

Cuisine	Prepared Sauces, Condiments & Sides	Dried or Fresh Herbs and Spices
Indian	Yogurt, chutney, lemon juice, light coconut milk **Oil:** peanut or any light vegetable oil like safflower, or canola **Quick Sides:** Basmati rice, steamed potatoes	Curry powder, ginger, allspice, cardamom, chilies, cilantro, cinnamon, cayenne, cloves, cumin, mint, nutmeg, tumeric
Italian	Prepared pasta sauce, pesto **Optional Condiments:** sun dried tomatoes **Alcohol:** red or white cooking wine; Marsala wine (sweet) **Oil:** Olive **Vinegar:** red or white wine, balsamic **Quick Sides:** pasta (any type), polenta, or instant grits	Italian herb mixture, basil, oregano, sage, rosemary, dehydrated garlic and onion, black pepper, parsley, bay leaf, marjoram
Japanese	Teriyaki, low-sodium soy **Alcohol:** sherry (dry or sweet), sake, Mirin (sweet rice cooking wine) **Oils:** sesame, peanut, canola **Vinegar:** seasoned rice vinegar **Quick Sides:** short grain sticky rice	Chives, ginger, wasabi (powdered Japanese mustard), sesame seeds
Mexican/ Southwest	Green or red salsa, tomato sauce, enchilada sauce, mole sauce (savory chocolate sauce) **Alcohol:** tequila **Oil:** olive **Vinegar:** red or white wine **Quick Sides:** long grain white rice, canned refried beans, canned chili seasoned beans, instant grits	Chili powder blend, chilies any variety, coriander (cilantro), cinnamon, oregano, cumin
Middle Eastern	Tahini (sesame butter), tomato sauce, yogurt, lemon juice **Oil:** olive **Vinegar:** white **Quick Sides:** instant tabouli, couscous	Allspice, cayenne pepper, cinnamon, ground coriander, cumin, ground ginger, parsley, mint, black pepper, tumeric, cardamom
South East Asian: Thai, Vietnamese, Korean	Soy sauce, liquid chili sauce, coconut milk, kim chee (Korean pickled cabbage), lime and lemon juice **Alcohol:** Sherry (dry or sweet) **Oil:** chili, peanut, sesame **Quick Sides:** jasmine rice, short grain sticky rice, long grain rice	Basil, cardamom, chilies (any variety), coriander (cilantro), cumin, curry powder, ginger, black and white peppercorns, tumeric, cayenne pepper, mint, lemon grass

How many times did you pass-up a recipe because you were too tired, or just didn't want to take the time to wash, tear, shred, or cut up the vegetables? If you are not including fresh vegetables in your menus because of the preparation factor, try some bagged prepared vegetables or raid your supermarket salad bar. Bagged prepared, ready-to-eat shredded carrots, baby carrots, broccoli and cauliflower fleurettes, broccoli slaw, prepared coleslaw cabbage, washed and torn variety lettuce, are all available in the produce section of most supermarkets. Although they are more expensive than purchasing whole vegetables, I suggest using these wonderful time-savers because they make cooking with vegetables easy and fun. If your recipe calls for vegetables that are not available in bags, like sliced bell pepper, cucumber, celery, etc., you can usually find these ingredients in your supermarket salad bar. Again, you will pay a premium for the convenience.

Time Saving Rush Hour Ingredients

Instead of taking the time to:	I suggest purchasing the following for fast kitchen getaways:
Mince or grate fresh ginger	Minced or pureed ginger in a jar
Mince or press fresh garlic	Minced or pureed garlic in a jar
Slice fresh mango	Sliced mango in a jar
Slice fresh carrots	Baby carrots in a bag
Shred fresh carrots	Shredded carrots in a bag
Wash and cut lettuce	Washed ready-to-eat lettuce in a bag
Cut fresh broccoli and cauliflower	Washed ready-to-cook florets in a bag
Shred cabbage for coleslaw	Shredded cabbage in a bag
Clean a head of celery	Sliced celery in a bag
Shred cheese	Shredded cheese in a bag
Chop onions that will be cooked	Frozen, diced onions

A Few Notes About the Menus and Recipes

Consider how you use your electric indoor grill when you are making a meal. Like most people, you probably use it to cook your main dish and simultaneously use other appliances (stove, oven, or microwave, blender, food processor) to prepare your side dishes. Bearing that in mind, I designed this book in a menu format instead of offering just a volume of individual grill recipes. Each menu helps you orchestrate your culinary efforts around your electric indoor grill for maximum efficiency and minimum stress. Every time you make one of my menus, you'll learn more about coordinating a variety of appliances to put a hot, gourmet-style meal on the table within 45 to 60 minutes.

Before you try one of my menus, I suggest looking at the Basics chapter (page 38). It contains 5 basic grill recipes with very detailed preparation and grilling instructions that you can use as a reference for grilling everything to perfection. Whether you are a veteran or novice cook, I wrote the information and techniques in the chapter to help improve your grilling technique on electric indoor grills.

As you thumb through the menu section, you will notice that they all serve four. That's because four is the average size of American households. The recipes can easily be adjusted to serve more or fewer people, though. Cooking for five or up to twelve? Don't hesitate to double or triple the recipes. If you are only cooking for one or two, consider making a little more for leftovers. Singles can divide the recipes in half, while people cooking

for two can make the entire menu. In both cases, you will have enough leftovers to serve within one or two days or to freeze when appropriate.

Since most people use their indoor grills for cooking dinner or lunch I made the menus suitable for either. I have also included "Mix and Match" sections in many of the menus so you can reconfigure the individual recipes in the book to make entirely new meals.

Make Each Recipe in this Book Your Own

As you read the individual recipes and their ingredients please remember my motto, "A recipe is only a blueprint for creativity." If there is an ingredient that you are not fond of in one of my recipes, change it. If you have a better ingredient idea, try it. If you are lacking an ingredient and want to substitute another, do it. If you don't like the side dish I suggest in a particular menu, substitute something else. You are cooking in the privacy of your own kitchen and no one is looking over your shoulder, including me! What's the worst that could happen? If you don't like the results, you'll end up feeding your garbage disposal instead of yourself.

Serving Sizes

Don't want to overeat but want to feel satisfied? I designed the serving sizes in this book to help you eat healthy, yet filling, portions. Portions of the individual recipes may not be as large as you are used to eating. But when you put a variety of foods together in one meal the result is satisfying. Serving sizes follow American Heart Association, American Cancer Society and American Dietetic Association guidelines. Here is a breakdown of the portions that I used for this book:

- Meat, poultry, fish: 3 to 4 ounces cooked
- Vegetables: 1 cup raw leafy, 1/2 cup cooked or chopped raw vegetables
- Fruit: 1/2 cup chopped fresh, cooked, or canned fruit
- Cheese: 1 to 2 ounces low-fat or fat-free processed cheese
- Nuts: 1/4 cup
- Bread: 1 slice
- Cooked rice, pasta polenta, beans: 1/2 to 1 cup
- Tofu: 3 to 4 ounces

Nutritional Analysis

Always remember that nutritional analyses are only "exact approximations" of the true nutrients you are eating, and they are included to help you make educated food choices. For example, the type of turkey sausage you purchase may have slightly more filler than the type I used in creating my recipes. I calculated all nutritional analysis using ESHA Food Processor Plus Nutrition and Fitness Software.

Most of the recipes and menus that I created for this book are below 30% fat per serving. Some hover a few percentage points above 30% and a couple are above 40% fat. Every menu, though, is rich in complex carbohydrates (fruits, vegetables, grains and starches) and contains a moderate amount of protein (3 to 4 ounces cooked). For those of you who scrupulously watch your fat intake, please consider this: The nutritional guidelines suggested by the USDA and many other respected health organizations suggest a healthy person's total daily fat intake not exceed 30% of calories consumed. Notice the word "daily." The amount of fat you eat in one menu is part of a daily and weekly balancing act. Eating one of my

menus that is higher in fat won't bust your fat budget if you balance it with lower-fat meals before or after.

Herbs

I like to use fresh herbs whenever possible because the flavor is more pungent and pronounced. But if an herb I call for in the recipe is out of season, don't hesitate to use dried. Many of the recipes call for pressed garlic instead of chopped. That's because pressing garlic releases more of an enzyme called "allicin." If you want less garlic flavor, chop or dice it into larger pieces.

Oil and Oil Sprays

A spray of oil or fat-free cooking spray on food before placing on a tabletop grill encourages distinct grill marks. I suggest using canola and olive oil sprays in my recipes because these two oils are rich in monounsaturated fats. A diet that includes both monounsaturated and polyunsaturated fats can actually help protect against heart disease. It is believed that unsaturated fats reduce total cholesterol without lowering the HDL (the good cholesterol) which helps keep arteries plaque-free. If you don't want any excess fat in your diet, use fat-free cooking spray instead. If the fluorocarbons in a cooking spray can are a turnoff, purchase a pump spray bottle designed specifically for cooking oil, and fill it with your favorite brand.

Seasoning Solutions

Do you like your grilled food simple, flavored with just a hint of salt and pepper? Or do you like the robust flavor of a marinade or spicy barbecue sauce? Perhaps you like to grill your food without any seasoning at all and then give it a flavor boost with a splash of a finishing sauce or salsa. Whatever your fancy, each menu in this book offers a seasoning solution that will turn ordinary fare into something special.

If you are in a hurry and don't want to make my from-scratch seasonings, please feel free to substitute your favorite brand of premade marinade, dry

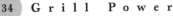

seasoning rub, salsa or sauce that fits with the ethnic character of the menu. My preference is making seasonings from scratch because they taste fresher, and I am in control of the ingredients. In order to make the most of the seasoning recipes in this book, it pays to understand how each of the different techniques work.

Marinades and Pastes

These will moisten, tenderize and flavor food using 1 or all 3 of the following types of ingredients: oil, acid, and seasonings. A marinade is made of mostly liquid (oil and/or acid based ingredients) with or without additional seasoning, while a paste is made of mostly seasonings (dry or fresh herbs, spices, pureed vegetables or fruit) with just enough liquid added to moisten them. Each of the three main ingredients used in making a marinade or paste serves a special purpose.

Tip: As a rule of thumb, for up to 1 1/4 pounds of meat, poultry or fish use 1/2 to 1 cup of liquid marinade or 1/4 cup of seasoning paste.

Acid ingredients in a marinade flavor and tenderize food by breaking down the protein in the cells. If you over marinate delicate foods in an acid-based marinade, you can make their texture mushy (pork tenderloin) or actually "cook" them (fish or shellfish). (See page 58 on Marinating Times.) You can use just about any ingredient that contains acid for a tenderizing effect in a marinade or paste. Here are some of my favorites: fruit juice, mustard, salsa, soy sauce, vinegar, liquor, wine, buttermilk, and yogurt.

Oil (vegetable or nut) adds flavor, moisturizes and lubricates the food, preventing it from drying out and/or sticking to the grill. It also helps seasonings suspended in the marinade (like dry or fresh herbs) adhere to the food. Oil also promotes grill marks. According to food scientist Shirley Corriher, oils that contain emulsifiers (mono- and diglycerides) help marinades penetrate deeper and faster. Extra virgin olive oil naturally contains monoglycerides. Taking Corriher's advice, I used

it in most of the marinades or pastes in this book that call for oil because I found it the best for infusing flavor quickly into food.

After trial and error, I discovered that you don't need a lot of oil in your marinades or rubs when using an electric tabletop grill. These grills cook food fast so it tends to stay juicy with or without oil. In addition, too much oil in your marinade will splatter and make a mess of your kitchen and raise the amount of fat you consume in the meal. Between 1 teaspoon and 2 tablespoons is all you need for moisturizing and quickly infusing marinades or pastes into food. If you are scrupulously counting fat grams, you can eliminate the oil in any marinade recipe in this book and still get a delicious result. If you leave the oil out, though, I suggest spraying the food with a nonfat cooking spray before putting it on the grill. Even though the surfaces of electric grills are nonstick, herbs or sugars in the marinade can sometimes make the food stick if there isn't any oil or fat-free spray on the food's surface.

Depending on what you are grilling, these recipes add oil to the food in 3 ways. First, oil may simply be mixed into the marinade or paste. This works well with moderately fatty or low-fat cuts of meat, poultry or fish. Second, oil can be rubbed or sprayed lightly onto the food before soaking it in the marinade. This is one of my favorite ways to keep extremely lean cuts of meat (pork tenderloin) or fish (tuna) moist on the grill. Third, oil can be sprayed lightly on the food immediately before grilling. I recommend doing this for fattier cuts of meat (pork chops), poultry (chicken thighs) or fish (catfish) and before putting any food on the grill that has been seasoned with a dry rub.

If I am adding fat to a marinade, I want it to be of nutritional benefit, so I select oils rich in monounsaturated fats which help raise the good-for-you HDL (high-density lipids) cholesterol and lower the bad-for-you LDL (low-density lipids) cholesterol. These include olive oil, canola oil, peanut oil, and sesame oil. The oil I use also depends on the character of the recipe. For example, if the recipe is

Asian and calls for strong flavors, I might choose roasted sesame oil in the marinade. But if I am using delicate herbs such as dill and scallions, I might choose a blander oil like canola.

Seasonings enhance the flavor of the oil and acid ingredients. Any of the following can be combined in a blender with oil and acid ingredients to make flavorful marinades or pastes: dry or fresh herbs and spices; vegetables (fresh or canned peppers, onion, garlic, etc.); fruit (citrus zest, fresh or canned apple, pear, peach, etc.) or condiments (chili sauce, chutney, horseradish, hot sauce, etc.).

Dry Rubs

These are used for flavor only and are an easy solution for quick grilled dinners. A combination of dry herbs, spices, salt and pepper as a dry rub can be applied to your food just before grilling. To prevent the herbs and spices from burning onto the food as it grills, I suggest a light spray of oil or fat-free cooking spray before placing on the grill.

Tip: Allow 1 to 3 tablespoons of dry rub per 1¼ pounds of meat, depending on how strong you want the flavors to be.

Glazes, Bastes and Barbecue Sauces

All these will put a flavorful outer coating on grilled food that also helps seal in moisture. These sauces are made by cooking the ingredients down (or reducing them) so they are thick enough to adhere to the food when brushed on. Since they usually contain some type of sugar (honey, maple syrup, corn syrup, white or brown sugar), they are brushed onto food during the last half of the grilling time to prevent them from burning.

Brining

You can also boost the flavor and add moisture to extra lean foods that tend to dry out easily on the grill with an extra step called brining. This is usually done before applying a rub or paste to the meat. To brine 1¼ pounds of pork tenderloin, turkey tenderloins or shrimp, in a 2-quart bowl dissolve 1 tablespoon salt and ½ cup sugar in 2 cups of hot water. Add 1 cup of cold water then immerse the food in the solution, cover the bowl with plastic wrap and let it sit in the refrigerator for 1 hour only. Do not brine shrimp over 45 minutes. Remove the food from the brine and dry it thoroughly with paper towels. Season the food liberally with a dry rub or paste from any recipe in the book and marinate in your refrigerator for 20 minutes or up to 2 hours. Grill according to the instructions in the recipe.

Season with a Little Salt

Although the international assortment of marinades, dry seasoning rubs and seasoning pastes that I created for this book were designed to make your mealtime exciting, the best way to season a spectacular cut of meat, fish or poultry before grilling is with the basics—salt and pepper.

I always believed that salting meat before cooking would make it dry and tough because the salt would leech the natural fluids out of the meat. I learned from my friend and meat guru Bruce Aidells, that this is an old wife's tale. Chef Aidells suggested that I conduct a personal taste test and grill two steaks simultaneously, one salted before grilling, the other salted afterward. Not only did I do his test with two fillet mignons, I included two boneless-skinless chicken breasts, and two pieces of swordfish. The result was the same. The food that I salted before grilling was the hands-down winner for overall flavor. Chef Aidells, also a biologist, explained why salting before grilling works. "When meat, poultry or fish is grilled over high heat, the surface becomes browned, crispy and caramelized due to a chemical reaction between the proteins, fats, and carbohydrates in the cells. When salt is applied before grilling, it combines with the surface juices to round out the full flavor potential of the browning meat."

Why, you may ask, is a professional healthy cooking and fitness instructor suggesting that you put salt on your meat? Because there has to be a balance between nutrition, health and tasty cooking.

In my classes I stress the importance of watching your sodium intake because high sodium diets have been linked to hypertension, stomach cancer, and osteoporosis. It is also true that although we require sodium in our diet for water and nervous system regulation, as well as for muscle contraction, most of us consume much more than we need. The recommended daily intake is 500 to 2,400 mg sodium per day for adults and less for children (from 225 to 1000 mg per day). Due to our heavy consumption of sodium laden processed foods, people in the United States are consuming a whopping 2,000 to 6,000 mg per day.

The simple fact is, though, that food tastes better when grilled with a little salt on it. Note the word "little." If you, like me, are mindful of your sodium intake, and are basing your diet on fresh foods instead of salty processed foods, a little salt goes a long way because your palate becomes more sensitive to sodium. As little as 1/2 teaspoon of salt sprinkled evenly over 1 1/4 pounds of meat can provide just the right amount of flavor for a sensitized palate. It also won't put you overboard on your daily sodium consumption if your diet is low in sodium to begin with. Throughout the book, I suggest using light salt, which gives all the flavor of its high-sodium table salt cousin, but about half the sodium. Another delicious alternative to table salt is sea salt. With slightly less sodium than table salt, but a more intense salty flavor, sea salt enables you to use less salt than you normally would. Top chefs worldwide season meat with sea salt before grilling because the chemical makeup of the salt enhances the flavor of meat in a way no other type of salt does.

Low-Sodium Ingredients

Just as I suggest using light salt to season your meat, fish and poultry to keep your sodium intake in check, I also suggest using other low-sodium ingredients in my marinades and side dishes, like low-sodium soy, and low-sodium canned beans and tomatoes. If you are not convinced, compare the differences below:

Seasoning	Amount	Sodium mg.
Table salt	1 teaspoon	2,325
Sea salt	1 teaspoon	2,301
Kosher salt	1 teaspoon	1,882
Light salt	1 teaspoon	1,100
Soy Sauce made from soy and wheat	1 tablespoon	914
Tamari Soy sauce made from soy	1 tablespoon	1,005
Low-sodium soy made from soy and wheat	1 tablespoon	533
Low-sodium tomato sauce, canned	1/4 cup	7
Tomato sauce, salted, canned	1/4 cup	280

Basic Recipes

When I first discovered electric indoor grills, the only instructions for using them were those that came in the use and care manuals of each grill. Most manuals simply give you grilling times for various foods plus a few recipes with very sparse instructions. I quickly learned that making perfectly grilled food on an indoor grill takes a little more finesse than throwing raw food on and pulling it off when it's done. At first, I applied what I knew about grilling on traditional charcoal grills, but found the technique for electric grills, especially depending on the type and model you are using, can be faster and is more controlled than grilling over fire. Once your food hits the preheated grill, how you handle it within the next 4 to 15 minutes makes all the difference between a so-so or a superb meal.

Whether you are using your electric grill for the first time or are a veteran griller, I created the following 5 recipes as references for grilling everything from meat, burgers, poultry, and fish to grilled cheese sandwiches. The preparation and grilling instructions are the most detailed and specific in the book for two reasons. First, to help newcomers become immediately successful and have the confidence to try the full menus in the book. And, second, to show experienced cooks some new techniques they may not have thought of.

Also for your reference, I designed each recipe in this chapter to represent a different method for seasoning grilled food. The grilled cheese sandwich is basted on the outside, the steaks get a dry rub, the fish a marinade, the chicken breast a seasoned crust, and the burgers have the seasonings mixed in. You will also notice that each recipe in this chapter includes a "Mix and Match" section of side-dish recipes found throughout the book. Take your pick from the list and you'll turn any of the following recipes into full meals.

Finally, these recipes are simply delicious! So, whatever your grilling skill, I hope you will try them all and make them part of your mealtime repertoire.

Grandma Jennie's Basic Burgers

When I crave a burger, I want to sink my teeth into one like my Grandma Jennie used to make, the big, succulent kind she whipped up from some meat plus whatever else she had on hand in the kitchen.

Grandma Jennie, a turn-of-the-century Middle Eastern immigrant and a survivor of the Great Depression, embraced hamburgers as her own gourmet solution to home economy. Starting with a pound or two of the best ground beef she could afford, Grandma added other ingredients to give the illusion of having more meat than she really did. Those extra ingredients helped her serve 6 to 10 people instead of half that many, and turned her burgers into an unparalleled culinary treat for her family and friends.

From the time I was tall enough to reach the counter (with the help of a stool), Grandma Jennie invited me to help her make burgers. With my hands at the ready in a large mixing bowl, Grandma taught me to fold breadcrumbs into ketchup, a bit of mustard and an egg. When the breadcrumbs were softened she had me work in finely chopped garlic, grated onion, and the meat, along with her "secret ingredients"–that is, any leftovers that struck her fancy to toss into the mix. "It's a shame to let any good food go to waste," she'd say. A sprinkle of the remaining fresh dill from her famous chicken soup, a spoon of leftover tomato paste which would have overpowered her delicately seasoned pot roast or a few yellow raisins that didn't make it into her crescent-shaped rugalach cookies, all found their way into Grandma's delicious burgers.

Grandma Jennie, one of the original healthy food enthusiasts, would have loved cooking her burgers on a tabletop electric grill. Since she never wanted to mess with charcoal, she cooked her burgers under the broiler to drain away as much fat as possible.

On the next page you'll find Grandma Jennie's Basic Burger recipe. I hope you enjoy every mouthwatering bite as much as I did when growing up. Make it once, then use it as your canvas for devising your own creative burger recipes. The Create Your Own Burger in Four Easy Steps on page 42 will help.

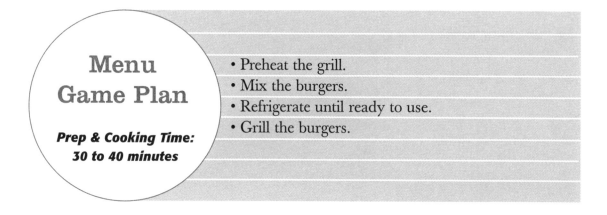

Menu Game Plan

**Prep & Cooking Time:
30 to 40 minutes**

• Preheat the grill.
• Mix the burgers.
• Refrigerate until ready to use.
• Grill the burgers.

Basic Burgers

Serves 4

¼ cup breadcrumbs

1 large egg or 2 egg whites or ¼ cup egg substitute

½ cup grated or finely chopped onion

3 tablespoons ketchup

1 teaspoon Dijon-style mustard

1 teaspoon pressed garlic

1 pound ground meat or vegetarian meat substitute

Nonfat or canola oil cooking spray

4 hamburger buns

1 medium ripe tomato, sliced into 4 equal rounds

4 romaine or curly leaf lettuce leaves

1 onion, sliced into thin rounds

4 pickles, sliced lengthwise or in rounds (optional)

Ketchup

Dijon-style or your favorite mustard

Nonfat or low-fat mayonnaise (optional)

1. Preheat the grill to the highest setting.

2. Mix the burgers. In a 2- or 3-quart mixing bowl, use a fork or spoon to evenly mix the breadcrumbs, egg, onion, ketchup, mustard and garlic. Using your hands, gently fold the meat into the wet mixture. When all ingredients are evenly distributed, divide the meat mixture into 4 equal portions. Wet hands and shape burgers, about 4 to 5 inches in diameter and no thicker than 3/4-inch. Set aside on a plate covered with plastic wrap in the refrigerator until ready to grill. Refrigeration helps the burgers set so they hold together better on the grill. Wash your hands thoroughly.

3. Grill the burgers. Spray each burger lightly on both sides with nonfat or canola oil cooking spray. Place the burgers on the grill and cook according to the Grill Times opposite until the burgers reach an internal temperature of 160°F on an instant-read thermometer.

4. To serve, on each plate, place a lettuce leaf, then top it with a burger, sliced tomato, and sliced onion. Place a bun on each plate, garnish with a pickle and serve, allowing diners to add their favorite condiments and assemble their own burgers.

Grill Times

Two-Sided Contact Grill: 6 to 7 minutes. Place the burgers on the pre-heated grill and put the upper grill plate down on top of it.

Immediately set your timer to the lowest number of the approximate grilling time above. In this case you would set your timer for 6 minutes. Do not lift the upper grill plate or disturb the food until the time is up or you will not get distinct grill marks.

If the burger has not reached 160°F internal temperature after the initial timing period, continue grilling and immediately reset your timer for additional 1 or 2 minute intervals until done.

Hibachi Grill, Combination Grill or Infusion Grill: 12 to 14 minutes. Place the burgers on the preheated grill and immediately set your timer to half of the lowest number of the approximate grilling time. In this case, you would set your timer for 6 minutes (half of 12 minutes). Do not disturb the burgers until the initial time is up or you will not get distinct grill marks.

Halfway through the grilling time, turn the burgers over and immediately reset the timer for the remaining grilling time (6 minutes).

If your grill has a lid, you may cover it halfway through the grilling time. Infusion grills may be covered for the entire grilling time.

If the burger has not reached 160°F internal temperature after the initial timing period, continue grilling and immediately reset your timer for additional 1 or 2 minute intervals until done.

Approximate Nutrients Per Serving of Entire Meal

Total Calories 346	Protein 30g / 35%	Carbohydrate 31g / 36%
Total Sugar 7g	Fat Total 11g / 30%	Saturated Fat 4 g / 11%
Cholesterol 41 mg	Sodium 494 mg	Fiber 4 g Calcium 58 mg

(Calculated with burger made with extra-lean ground beef, a bun, tomato, onion, and lettuce.)

Create Your Own Burger in Four Easy Steps

Start with Grandma Jennie's Basic Burger then substitute any of the following to create your own recipe. Follow the steps in the recipe for mixing and grilling. For consistent flavor, remember to thoroughly mix the filler, moisteners, and seasonings before adding the ground meat.

1. Start with the filler. Substitute 1/4 cup of one of the following ingredients for the 1/4 cup breadcrumbs: seasoned breadcrumbs, finely crushed stuffing mix, finely crushed nonfat or low-fat croutons, finely crushed corn flakes, finely crushed tortilla chips, finely crushed crackers, finely crushed melba toast, instant oatmeal, canned or freshly cooked beans, any kind, mashed.

2. Add the moisteners. Substitute a combination of any of the following to make a total of 1/2 cup for the egg, ketchup, or mustard: Milk, fruit or vegetable juice such as orange, lemon, or tomato, steak sauce, chili sauce, salsa, salad dressing, tomato sauce, canned fruit such as crushed pineapple or apple sauce, pureed baby food fruit such as peaches or cherries, fresh fruit such as grated fresh apple or pear, wine, flavored liqueurs such as Grand Marnier, brandy, rum or beer.

3. Stir in the seasonings. Use any combination of the following that strikes your fancy: Salt and pepper to taste, up to 1/2 cup chopped onions, any color, 1 to 2 teaspoons garlic puree (or 1 clove garlic, pressed), 1/4 to 2 teaspoons prepared dry seasoning mixes such as lemon pepper, Cajun or Creole blend, Jamaican Jerk blend, Chinese five-spice blend, herbes de Provence or bouquet garnis, chopped dried fruit such as apricots, apples, cranberries, raisins, currants, 2 tablespoons to 1/2 cup finely chopped fresh herbs such as basil, dill, oregano, thyme, or parsley, 1/4 to 1/2 cup low-fat shredded cheese such as cheddar, mozzarella, Monterey Jack or 1/4 cup higher-fat crumbled cheese such as blue, gorgonzola, or feta.

4. Mix in the ground meat. Mix 1 pound of any of the following into the wet filling mixture: beef, chicken, lamb, pork, turkey, veal, or vegetarian soy meat substitute.

Basic Gourmet Grilled Cheese Sandwich

Have you ever tasted a real "grilled" cheese sandwich? One that was actually made on a grill instead of in a fry pan or on a griddle? It wasn't until I started making grilled cheese sandwiches on my electric indoor grill that I realized what I was missing. The difference is those crispy grill marks that form as the grill toasts the bread and melts the cheese to oozy deliciousness inside. My basic recipe is the result of grilling more cheese sandwiches than I can count. Be warned, though. This is not a low-fat or low-sodium recipe, nor should it be. There are some recipes that are sacred, and a good grilled cheese sandwich is one that always tastes better with high fat and high sodium ingredients. Besides, most of the low-fat or non-fat cheeses do not melt well for a proper grilled cheese sandwich and there are not a large variety of low-fat cheeses to choose from. To show you how easy it is to use your grill to turn comfort food into a gourmet masterpiece, I have taken this recipe way beyond buttered white bread filled with processed orange cheese. My version starts with fresh slices of San Francisco-style sourdough bread filled with three complementary Italian cheeses—fontina, mozzarella, and Parmesan—and a sprinkling of green onions. Just before putting it on the grill, you'll baste the outside of the sandwich with a savory mixture of melted butter, garlic, and Dijon mustard. Once it's grilled to golden-brown perfection, it tastes better than your favorite garlic bread on the outside and like a cheese calzone on the inside (minus the pasta sauce)! Master this basic recipe, then try making the fun variations that follow.

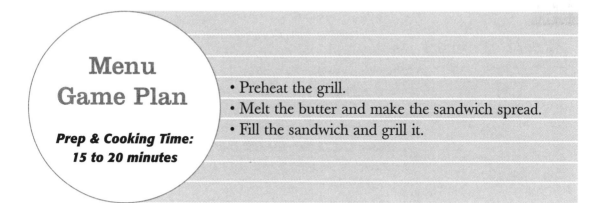

Menu Game Plan

Prep & Cooking Time: 15 to 20 minutes

- Preheat the grill.
- Melt the butter and make the sandwich spread.
- Fill the sandwich and grill it.

Mix & Match Serve the sandwich with any of the following side dishes: Waldorf Slaw, page 196; Salad with Lemon Herb Vinaigrette, page 253; Basil Parmesan Oven Fries, page 256.

Basic Grilled Cheese Sandwich

Makes 4 sandwiches

4 tablespoons salted butter

4 teaspoons Dijon-style mustard

4 teaspoons pressed garlic

8 slices extra-sour sourdough bread, ½-inch thick, about 3½ x 5½-inch or larger

6 ounces Fontina cheese

6 ounces mozzarella cheese

4 tablespoons shredded Parmesan, Asiago or Pecorino Romano cheese

4 tablespoons thinly sliced green onions

1. **Preheat the grill.** If you have a grill with a variable temperature control, set it to medium-high (one or two steps below high) or to about 350° to 400°F.

2. **Make the baste.** In a very small saucepan (1 quart or less), melt the butter over low heat. When the butter is melted, whisk in the mustard and garlic. Set aside.

3. **Assemble the sandwiches.** Put 4 slices of the bread on a large plate. Slice or grate the cheese and the green onions. Put 1 tablespoon of green onion on half of each sandwich. Top the onions with equal amounts of each of the cheeses. Top the cheese with a slice of bread. Using a basting brush, brush the top slice of bread evenly with the butter baste.

4. **Grill the sandwiches.** Carefully put each sandwich, basted side down, on the grill. Brush the top piece of bread on each sandwich evenly with the butter baste. Grill according to the Grill Times and techniques below.

5. **To serve,** remove from the grill and place on plate with a fresh tomato and basil salad sprinkled with red wine vinegar and extra virgin olive oil.

Grill Times

Two-Sided Contact Grill: 3 to 4 minutes. Place the sandwich on the preheated grill, and put the upper grill plate down on top of it. Immediately set your timer to the lowest number of the approximate grilling time above. In this case, you would set your timer for 3 minutes. Do not lift the upper grill plate or disturb the food until the time is up, or you will not get distinct grill marks. If the sandwich is not fully cooked after the initial timing period, continue grilling and immediately reset your timer for additional 1 or 2 minute intervals until it is done.

Hibachi Grill, Combination Grill or Infusion Grill: 6 to 8 minutes. Place the sandwich on the preheated grill and immediately set your timer to half of the lowest number of the approximate grilling time. In this case, you would set your timer for 3 minutes (half of 6 minutes). Do not disturb the food until the initial time is up, or you will not get distinct grill marks.

Halfway through the grilling time, turn the sandwich over and immediately reset the timer for the remaining grilling time (an additional 3 minutes).

If the cheese is not fully melted after the initial timing period, continue grilling and immediately reset your timer for additional 1- or 2-minute intervals until it is done. To prevent soggy bread, do not cover a combination grill or infusion grill during cooking.

Roasted Garlic Pizza Grilled Cheese: Make the baste in step 2. Spread 1 to 2 tablespoons of your favorite pizza sauce on half of each sandwich before sprinkling it with the green onions. On top of the green onions, add 1 to 2 teaspoons coarsely chopped roasted garlic cloves, then top with the fontina, mozzarella and Parmesan. Top with remaining slice of bread, then baste and grill according to the instructions in steps 3 and 4.

Southwest Express Grilled Cheese: Make the baste in step 2 but omit the Dijon-style mustard. Substitute equal amounts of jalapeño pepper-flavored Monterrey Jack cheese for the Fontina, and sharp cheddar for the mozzarella. Omit the Parmesan cheese. Spread 1 to 2 tablespoons of barbecue sauce on half of each sandwich before sprinkling it with the green onions and topping with the cheese. Top with remaining slice of bread, then baste and grill according to the instructions in steps 3 and 4.

Sundried Tomato Grilled Cheese Sandwich: Make the baste in step 2. Substitute Provolone cheese for the mozzarella cheese. Spread 1 to 2 tablespoons of finely chopped, oil-packed sundried tomatoes and 1 tablespoon chopped fresh basil or 1 teaspoon dried basil on half of each sandwich before sprinkling it with the green onions and topping with the Provolone, Fontina and Parmesan. Top with remaining slice of bread, then baste and grill according to the instructions in steps 3 and 4.

Apple-Cheddar Grilled Cheese: Make the baste in step 2 but substitute Dijon-style honey mustard for the Dijon-style mustard in the baste. Substitute equal amounts of Cheddar and Colby cheese for the Fontina and mozzarella. Use the Parmesan. Sprinkle half of the sandwich with the green onions. Arrange several slices of cored and peeled, very thinly sliced apple between the slices of cheese. Top with remaining slice of bread, then baste and grill according to the instructions in steps 3 and 4.

Prosciutto Grilled Cheese: Make the baste in step 2. Substitute Provolone cheese for the mozzarella cheese. Add 2 tablespoons thinly sliced Prosciutto on top of the green onion before topping with the Provolone, Fontina, Parmesan and the remaining slice of bread. Then baste and grill according to the instructions in steps 3 and 4.

Approximate Nutrients Per Serving of Entire Meal

Total Calories 565	Protein 30 g / 21%	Carbohydrate 30 g / 21%	
Total Sugar 3 g	Fat Total 36 g / 58%	Saturated Fat 22 g / 35%	
Cholesterol 108 mg	Sodium 1,194 mg	Fiber 2 g	Calcium 662 mg

How to Quickly Prepare Dry Fillers

A number of my recipes call for finely crushed croutons, tortilla chips or breadcrumbs. While you can usually find these in whatever form you need at your supermarket, it's just as easy to prepare them at home.

Food processor or blender method: Place torn pieces of bread, whole croutons, or broken tortilla chips or crackers in a food processor fitted with the metal chopping blade or in a blender. Process until no large pieces remain.

By hand: Place torn pieces of toasted bread, whole croutons, broken tortilla chips or crackers in a 1-quart freezer-weight zipper bag. Squeeze the air out and zip it closed. Put the filled bag on the counter, then place a dinner plate on top of the bag. Press the plate with your hands to evenly crush the contents into small crumbs. You can also use a rolling pin, heavy drinking glass, or jar instead of the plate.

Basic Power Grilled Steaks or Chops

I have three criteria for a perfectly grilled steak or chop. First, the aroma should stop you in your tracks with mouthwatering anticipation. Second, the outer appearance should entice you with heavily scored crusty grill marks while the first slice reveals a light pink center. Third, the flavor and texture should be crispy and well seasoned on the outside and succulent and juicy on the inside. This basic recipe is the culmination of my grilling pounds and pounds of steaks and chops on electric indoor grills in order to learn how to achieve these ideal results. You must start with good-quality meat, though, or my perfected grilling techniques won't help. (Check out page 99 to learn how to select meat for your electric indoor grill.) For this recipe, I chose to season the meat with a simple dry rub of salt, pepper, garlic powder, and onion powder to demonstrate that you don't really need any complicated flavors to produce delicious results. This recipe was written for beef, lamb, or veal steaks, chops or tenderloins because they all have similar grilling times and internal doneness temperatures. But if you would rather grill pork chops or tenderloins, please check the pork grilling chart on page 102 before putting the meat to the heat. Pork must be cooked to slightly higher internal temperatures than beef, veal, or lamb.

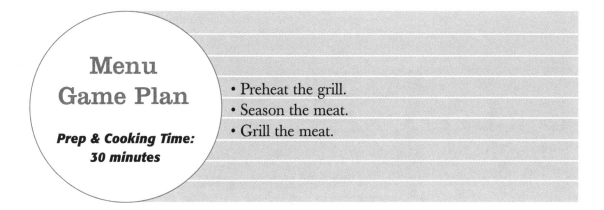

Menu Game Plan

Prep & Cooking Time:
30 minutes

- Preheat the grill.
- Season the meat.
- Grill the meat.

Mix & Match

Serve the steak or chops with any of the following sauces: Chimichurri Sauce, page 142; Maple-Balsamic Glaze, page 117; Buttermilk Gravy, page 105; Peach Salsa, page 126; Lemony Peanut Sauce, page 146; Easy Ridin' BBQ Sauce, page 150; Uncle Mannie's Secret BBQ Sauce, page 195.

Basic Steaks

Serves 4

1   to 2 teaspoons lemon pepper

½   to 1 teaspoon light salt or
    sea salt to taste

1   teaspoon garlic powder

1   teaspoon onion powder

1¼ pounds boneless beef or
    lamb tenderloin steaks such
    as New York, cut 1-inch thick
    into 4 equal pieces or 1½
    pounds bone-in beef or lamb
    steak or chops (4 steaks or
    chops)

Olive oil spray or nonfat cooking
    spray

1. Preheat the grill to the highest setting.

2. Make the seasoning rub. In a small bowl, mix the lemon pepper, salt, garlic powder and onion powder.

3. Rub the steaks with the dry seasoning. Wash the meat to remove any excess blood or impurities, then pat it dry with a paper towel. Put the meat in a 1-gallon zippered freezer-weight storage bag, a 1-quart airtight container or shallow square glass dish (8 x8 x 2). With your fingers, rub the seasoning evenly over all surfaces of the meat. Zip the bag closed or cover the container and set aside in the refrigerator for 20 minutes or up to 24 hours.

4. Grill the steaks. Lightly spray each steak with cooking spray to moisten the dry rub and help promote grill marks. Grill the steak according to the times and methods below until it reaches the doneness you desire.

5. To serve, remove the meat from the grill and let it rest 3 to 5 minutes on a covered plate to allow the juices to settle. Resting keeps meat moist and succulent because it allows juices to settle, preventing them from immediately running out of the food when you cut into it.

Grill Times

Two-Sided Contact Grill: (Note: all internal temperatures are Chef's Choice, page 101) Rare 4 to 5 minutes—125° to 130°F internal temperature. Medium 5 to 7 minutes—140° to 150°F internal temperature. Medium-well 6 to 8 minutes—150° to 165°F internal temperature. Place the meat on the preheated grill and put the upper grill plate down on top of it.

Set your timer to the lowest number of the approximate grilling time. For example, if you are grilling your steak to medium, you would set your timer for 5 minutes. Do not lift the upper grill plate or disturb the food until the time is up or you will not get distinct grill marks.

Check the meat's internal temperature: insert the probe of an instant-read thermometer ¾ to 1 inch into the side of the meat, parallel to the surface of the grill. Wait a full 10 seconds for the liquid crystal display to register. If the food is not fully cooked after the initial timing period, continue grilling and immediately reset your timer for additional 1 or 2 minute intervals until it is done.

Grill Times

Hibachi-Style, Combination, or Infusion Grills: *Rare 8 to 10 minutes—125° to 130°F internal temperature. Medium 10 to 14 minutes—140° to 150°F internal temperature. Medium-well 12 to 16 minutes—150° to 165°F internal temperature. Place the meat on the preheated grill, and immediately set your timer to half of the lowest number of the approximate grilling time. For example, if you are grilling your steak to medium, you would set your timer for 5 minutes (half of 10 minutes). Do not disturb the food until the initial time is up, or you will not get distinct grill marks.*

Halfway through the grilling time, turn the food over and immediately reset the timer for the remaining grilling time. In the case of medium, reset the timer for an additional 5 minutes.

When the time is up, check the meat's internal temperature. Insert the probe of an instant-read thermometer ¾ to 1 inch into the thickest side of the meat, parallel to the surface of the grill. Wait a full 10 seconds for the liquid crystal display to register. If the food is not fully cooked after the initial timing period, continue grilling and immediately reset your timer an additional 2 to 4 minutes until it is done. Grills with lids may be covered halfway through the grilling time to keep the food moist. Infusion grills with lids may be covered for the entire grilling time.

Approximate Nutrients Per Serving of Entire Meal

Total Calories 338	Protein 39 g / 47%	Carbohydrate 1 g / 1%
Total Sugar 0 g	Fat Total 19 g / 51%	Saturated Fat 7 g / 20%
Cholesterol 120 mg	Sodium 341 mg	Fiber 0.1 g Calcium 14 mg

(Calculated with boneless beef tenderloin steaks and ¹/₂ teaspoon light salt in the rub.)

Slicing Across the Grain

Meat is the muscle of the animal. Muscle fibers are known as the "grain of the meat." When you slice across the grain of the meat, you are slicing at a right angle to the way the muscle fibers run. You can make tougher cuts of cooked meat or poultry seem more tender by slicing them across the grain. That's because the length of the muscle fiber is very short and easier to chew. By the same token, the tenderest pieces of raw meat or poultry cut with the grain (or parallel to the muscle fibers) become extremely tough when grilled because the long muscle fibers shrink into a tough mass as they cook.

When slicing cooked or raw meat, it is sometimes hard to tell which way the muscle fiber runs. If in doubt after a close look, slicing off an extremely thin piece will usually give you the answer.

The muscle fibers in chicken and turkey breasts run lengthwise so always cut across the width of the meat. Fish have very short muscle fibers (which is why fish flakes) so you don't have to worry about which direction to slice fish.

Basic Cornmeal Crusted Chicken Breasts—
Cajun or Southwest Flavored

If you love chicken with a crust but you don't like the fat usually associated with deep-frying to get it crispy, this recipe will give you the technique for making a low-fat "grill-fried" facsimile. I chose it as my basic recipe for learning to cook chicken because it's easy to make, uses all the same techniques for grilling a chicken breast without a crust, and is something most people wouldn't necessarily think of making on their grill. The crust recipe is versatile. Just by changing the seasoning, you can change the character of your meal from Cajun to Southwestern. Whether you make your chicken breasts with or without a crust, it must be grilled to a minimum internal temperature of 160°F to be safe to eat. This can create a problem, though, when you grill boneless skinless chicken breasts because the meat tends to be teardrop shaped, thicker at the large round top of the breast and thinner at the opposite end. Unfortunately, if you put boneless skinless chicken breasts on the grill as is, the thinner ends tend to dry out as the thicker ends reach 160°F. To prevent this, I like to even out the breasts to a 1/4- or 1/2-inch thickness by pounding them with the bottom of a large heavy skillet, the flat side of a meat mallet, or a rolling pin. In addition to helping the meat cook evenly, it tenderizes it, making it easier for marinades and rubs to be absorbed. A more even surface also helps crispy coatings adhere to the chicken and ensures that they get evenly crisped as it grills.

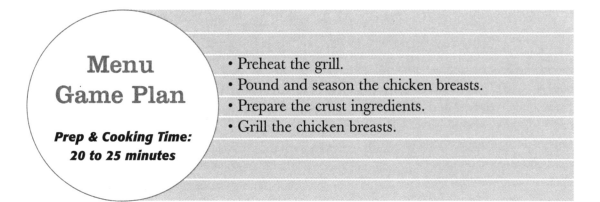

Menu Game Plan

Prep & Cooking Time: 20 to 25 minutes

- Preheat the grill.
- Pound and season the chicken breasts.
- Prepare the crust ingredients.
- Grill the chicken breasts.

Mix & Match

Serve the chicken breasts with any of the following side dishes: Stompin' Slaw, page 88; Muffaletta Pasta Salad, page 128; Rootin' Tootin' Texas Tabouli and Easy Ridin' BBQ Sauce, page 149; Uncle Mannie's Secret BBQ Sauce and Waldorf Slaw, page 195; Grilled Banana and Sweet Potatoes with Orange Pineapple Slaw, page 230; Avocado and Orange Salsa, page 269.

Cornmeal Crusted Chicken Breasts

Chicken

1¼ pounds boneless, skinless chicken breasts (4 pieces)

1 whole egg well beaten or ¼ cup fat-free egg substitute

3 tablespoons cornstarch

Light salt and freshly ground pepper to taste

Crust Mixture

½ cup yellow cornmeal

1 to 2 teaspoons Cajun seasoning or chili powder

1 teaspoon garlic powder

1 teaspoon onion powder

½ teaspoon light salt or to taste

Nonfat or canola oil cooking spray

Substitutions:
Instead of chicken, substitute an equal amount of flank steak or Abalone (if you can get it) and pound 1/4- to 1/2-inch thick using the technique described in step 2 above. Tuna and sword-fish steaks and catfish fillets also work well, and you don't have to pound them. Ask your fish vendor to cut the steaks 1/2-inch thick.
Instead of cornmeal, substitute equal amounts of finely ground cracker crumbs, corn flakes, garlic croutons, nuts or dry stuffing mix.

1. Preheat the grill. If you have a grill with a variable temperature control, set it to medium-high (one or two steps below high) or to about 350° to 400°F.

2. Flatten and marinate the chicken breasts. Arrange the chicken breasts in a single layer over a large piece of plastic wrap. Cover the chicken breasts with another large piece of plastic wrap. Pound the breasts with the bottom of a large heavy skillet, the flat side of a meat mallet or a rolling pin until flattened to about ¼- to ½-inch thick. Put the flattened breasts in a 2- or 3-cup shallow dish.

In a 1-cup bowl or measure, whisk the egg, cornstarch, salt and pepper to taste until the cornstarch is dissolved. Pour the mixture over the chicken. Turn the pieces so that all surfaces are coated with the egg mixture. Use immediately or cover tightly and refrigerate for up to 24 hours.

3. Mix the coating. In a shallow dish, use a fork to mix the cornmeal, Cajun seasoning or chili powder, garlic powder, onion powder and salt to taste, then place it near the grill.

4. Grill the chicken. Dip each chicken breast into the coating mixture so all sides are covered. As you finish coating each piece, put it on a large plate. Spray each coated piece of chicken lightly on both sides with the cooking spray before putting it on the grill. Grill the chicken according to the times and techniques listed on page 53 until the interior temperature reaches 160°F on an instant-read thermometer. The meat should not be pink in the center, and all of the juices should run clear when pricked with the tip of a knife.

5. To serve, remove the chicken from the grill, let it rest 2 or 3 minutes on a covered plate to allow the juices to settle. Resting keeps your food moist and succulent because it allows juices to settle, preventing them from immediately running out of the food when you cut into it.

Two-Sided Contact Grill: *5 to 6 minutes. Place the chicken on the preheated grill and put the upper grill plate down on top of it. Immediately set your timer to the lowest number of the approximate grilling time above. In this case, you would set your timer for 5 minutes. Do not lift the upper grill plate or disturb the food until the time is up or you will not get distinct grill marks.*

Check the chicken's internal temperature: insert the probe of an instant-read thermometer 3/4-inch to 1-inch into the side of the chicken, parallel to the surface of the grill.

Wait a full 10 seconds for the liquid crystal display to register. If the thermometer does not register 160°F, the chicken is not fully cooked. Continue grilling and immediately reset your timer for an additional one or two minutes until it is done.

Hibachi Grill, Combination Grill or Infusion Grill: *10 to 12 minutes. Place the chicken on the preheated grill and immediately set your timer to half of the lowest number of the approximate grilling time. In this case, you would set your timer for 5 minutes (half of 10 minutes). Do not disturb the food until the initial time is up, or you will not get distinct grill marks. Halfway through the grilling time, turn the food over and immediately reset the timer for the remaining grilling time (an additional 5 minutes).*

When the time is up, check the chicken's internal temperature: insert the probe of an instant-read thermometer 3/4- to 1-inch into the side of the chicken, parallel to the surface of the grill. Wait a full 10 seconds for the liquid crystal display to register. If the chicken has not reached 160°F internal temperature after the initial timing period, continue grilling and immediately reset your timer for additional 1 or 2 minute intervals until done. For a crispier crust, if you have a grill with a lid, do not cover it.

Approximate Nutrients Per Serving of Entire Meal

Total Calories 265	Protein 36 g / 57%	Carbohydrate 23 g / 37%
Total Sugar 0 g	Fat Total 2 g / 6%	Saturated Fat 0.5 g / 2%
Cholesterol 82 mg	Sodium 374 mg	Fiber 0.7 g Calcium 19 mg

Make Your Own Jerk or Cajun Seasoning Mixes

Want to make authentic Jamaican- or Cajun-style cuisine but can't find premixed spice blends in your area? Why not make homemade mixtures with one of the following recipes? Each blend makes 1/4 cup that will keep up to 6 months if you store in airtight containers in a cool, dry, dark place.

Homemade Dry Jerk Seasoning Blend

Mix 1 teaspoon of each of the following in a small bowl using a fork:

paprika

cinnamon

ground nutmeg

ground allspice

onion powder

garlic powder

ground ginger

finely ground black pepper

cayenne pepper

dried thyme

light salt

Homemade Cajun Seasoning Blend

In a small bowl using a fork, mix:

1 tablespoon sweet paprika

1 1/2 teaspoons table salt, light salt or 1 1/4 sea salt

1 teaspoon cayenne

1 teaspoon onion powder

1 teaspoon garlic powder

1/2 teaspoon white pepper

1/2 teaspoon black pepper

1/2 teaspoon ground cumin

1/2 teaspoon dried thyme

1/2 teaspoon dry mustard

1/4 teaspoon ground nutmeg

Basic Salmon Fillets with Simple Pineapple Soy Marinade

Once you master the techniques for grilling my pineapple and soy marinated salmon fillets, you will be able to tackle everything from tuna steaks to scallops on your grill. I created this basic recipe for you because marinating fish is trickier than just seasoning it with a simple dry rub or paste. If you let fish sit over one hour in a marinade, the acid ingredient can actually "cook" the flesh, turning it opaque and making it tough. For fillets, 20 minutes is the ideal marinating time. (See page 58 for more in-depth fish marinating information.) In addition, grilling fish fillets, especially with the skin on one side, and removing them from the grill intact takes more know-how than grilling any other cut of fish. When grilled at too high a temperature or for too long, fish will dry out, become tough and fall apart. If you have a variable temperature control, I suggest setting it no higher than medium high. For the tenderest results, I suggest grilling all fish to an internal temperature that does not exceed 130° to 140°F. Removing delicate fish fillets from the grill takes two spatulas so make sure you have both at the ready before you begin grilling.

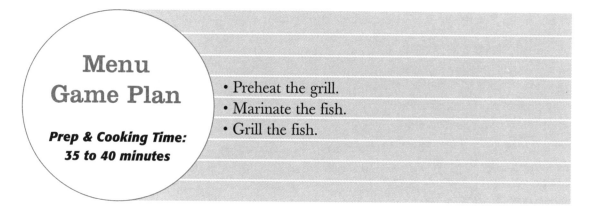

Menu Game Plan

Prep & Cooking Time: 35 to 40 minutes

- Preheat the grill.
- Marinate the fish.
- Grill the fish.

Mix & Match >

Serve the fish with any of the following side dishes: Quick Spinach Sauté, page 114; Coconut Rice, page 145; Petite Pea Salad, page 166; Pineapple Express Rice, page 277; Snow Pea Rice, page 174; Sticky Rice, page 199; Japanese Cucumber Salad, page 242; Lo Mein, page 182; Vermicelli Pilaf, page 169.

Salmon Fillet with Pineapple Soy Marinade

Marinade

¼ cup plus 2 tablespoons frozen pineapple juice concentrate, thawed

¼ cup plus 2 tablespoons low-sodium soy sauce

2 teaspoons finely minced fresh ginger

1 teaspoon pressed garlic

1 tablespoon sesame oil

Salmon

1¼ pounds salmon fillets, skin-on

Tip:
Many people won't eat fish fillets because of hidden bones. You can take care of this by making tweezers or needle-nose pliers one of your kitchen utensils. Just before marinating, run your fingertips back and forth along the spine of the fillets to find bones, then yank them out with the tweezers. If the fish is slipping out of your hand, use a piece of paper towel to improve your grip and hold it in place.

1. **Preheat the grill.** If you have a grill with a variable temperature control, set it to medium high (one or two steps below high) or to about 350° to 400°F.

2. **Make the marinade.** In a 2-cup bowl or measure, whisk the pineapple juice concentrate, soy sauce, ginger, garlic and sesame oil. Pour into a 1-gallon freezer-weight zipper bag or a 1-quart airtight container or shallow dish and set aside as you prepare the fish.

3. **Marinate the fish.** Check fish for bones by feeling along the spine with your fingers. If you find any sticking out, remove them with a tweezers or needle nose pliers. Wash fish and pat it dry with paper towels.

Cut the fish into four equal pieces then put it in the marinade filled bag or container. Turn the fish pieces so all the surfaces are coated with the marinade then let it rest with the skin side up and the flesh sitting in the marinade. Press out all the air before zipping the bag closed, or cover the container or dish. Marinate in the refrigerator for 20 minutes or up to 1 hour.

4. **Grill the fish.** Grill according to the times and techniques listed until the interior temperature reaches 135° to 140° F on an instant read thermometer. The fish should be opaque in the center and flaky when pricked with the tip of a knife.

5. **To serve,** remove the fish from the grill, using two spatulas to prevent it from falling apart. Place one on top of the fillet and slip the other underneath between the cooked flesh and the skin. As you lift the fish, the skin will remain on the grill. Remove it after the grill cools during cleaning. Place the fish on individual dinner plates skin-side down so the diner will see the grill marks.

Grill Times

Two-Sided Contact Grill: *6 to 7 minutes Place the fish on the preheated grill and put the upper grill plate down on top of it. Immediately set your timer to the lowest number of the approximate grilling time above. In this case, you would set your timer for 6 minutes. Do not lift the upper grill plate or disturb the food until the time is up, or you will not get distinct grilling marks.*

Check the fish's internal temperature: insert the probe of an instant-read thermometer 3/4- to 1-inch into the thickest side of the fish, parallel to the surface of the grill. Wait a full 10 seconds for the liquid crystal display to register. If the thermometer does not register between 135° to 140°F, the fish is not fully cooked. Continue grilling and immediately reset your timer for additional 1 or 2 minute intervals until it is done.

Hibachi Grill, Combination Grill or Infusion Grill: *12 to 14 minutes. Place the fish on the preheated grill skin-side-up, and immediately set your timer to half of the lowest number of the approximate grilling time. In this case you would set your timer for 6 minutes (half of 12 minutes). Do not disturb the food until the initial time is up, or you will not get distinct grill marks.*

Halfway through the grilling time, turn the food over and immediately reset the timer for the remaining grilling time (additional 6 minutes). Grills with lids may be covered halfway through the grilling time. Infusion grills with lids may be covered for the entire grilling time. When the time is up, check the meat's internal temperature: insert the probe of an instant-read thermometer 3/4- to 1-inch into the thickest side of the fish; parallel to the surface of the grill. Wait a full 10 seconds for the liquid crystal display to register. If the thermometer does not register 140°F, the fish is not fully cooked. Continue grilling and immediately reset your timer for an additional one or two minutes until it is done.

Infusion Grill Notes: *For a more intense flavor, pour 1/2 cup of leftover marinade into infusion cup before putting the fish on the grill. Do not baste with the marinade in the cup. Use it only for flavoring.*

Approximate Nutrients Per Serving of Entire Meal

Total Calories 204	Protein 29 g / 60%	Carbohydrate 5 g / 10%
Total Sugar 4 g	Fat Total 7 g / 30%	Saturated Fat 2 g / 6%
Cholesterol 105 mg	Sodium 374 mg	Fiber 0.1 g Calcium 22 mg

How Long to Marinate

Is your meat mushy and your fish tough after marinating? If you used a liquid marinade or a wet marinating paste containing an acid component like fruit juice, wine, vinegar, yogurt or mustard you might have marinated too long. Rubs made from dried herbs and spices are easier to use. They will flavor of meat, poultry or fish within a few minutes or can be left on the food for up to 48 hours if tightly covered in the refrigerator.

Each menu in this book gives a time range for marinating meat, poultry, fish, or vegetables. If you are in a hurry, use the shortest suggested marinating time. If time is not a problem, use the longer marinating times for maximum flavor absorption.

	Cut	Marinating Times *Longest suggested time is best for maximum flavor absorption. Always marinate in the refrigerator.*
MEAT		
Extremely tender	• Beef, lamb or pork tenderloin	No less than 20 minutes No longer than 2 hours
Tender	• Beef: sirloin, top loin, skirt steak or flank steak • Lamb: sirloin, leg of lamb, boneless • Pork: loin country ribs Boston butt or Boston blade steak, leg meat , lean	20 minutes to 48 hours
Somewhat tender	• Beef: tri-tip, top round, chuck roast (sometimes this cut can be tender, sometimes tough), rib steak	24 to 48 hours
POULTRY		
Chicken	• Boneless skinless breast • Boneless skinless thigh	Acid based marinade: 20 minutes to 24 hours
FISH		
Firm-fleshed fish	Sea bass, tuna, grouper, bluefish, whitefish, halibut, shark, or mahi-mahi	20 minutes or no longer than 1 hour
Shellfish	Fresh shrimp, scallops	No more than 30 minutes

Grill Power Menus

Better Burgers

How you prepare, cook, assemble and serve a burger makes all the difference between a great-tasting healthy meal and "the same old thing." This chapter promises to banish the boring burger from your table and replace it with an internationally inspired medley of mouthwatering, nutritious burger menus.

First, you'll learn how to mix up your own healthy burger creations by combining the most nutritious ground meats with the tastiest condiments, fillings, buns and breads. Then, each step-by-step menu ensures the side dishes, sauces and garnishes reach the table just as your burgers come off the grill.

Your electric indoor grill is a great tool, especially for cooking healthy burgers. These grills are designed so that fat drips away from meat during cooking, reducing fat in the finished burger. Also, burgers made from lower-fat meats stay more tender and juicy cooked on thermostatically controlled electric grills than on charcoal grills (fluctuating temperatures in charcoal grills can dry low-fat meats quickly). Combine your electric grill with my easy, healthy burger-making techniques and burgers will be on your menu more often than not.

Banish the Boring Burger

Prepare to give your taste buds an international culinary vacation. Since cooks use ground meat in just about every cuisine, I designed the burgers in this chapter to reflect the variety of ways it is seasoned and served throughout the world. You can make all my burgers with one pound of any type of low-fat ground meat that strikes your fancy (see the Ground Meat Calculator on page 62). Start by mastering my Grandma Jennie's Basic Burger (page 39), then design your own healthy burgers with Create Your Own Burger in Four Easy Steps on page 42. For vegetarian burgers, use substitute soy "meat" in any of the recipes.

What you put your burger in inspires variety as well. Why stop at buns? For a change, some of my burgers slip into pita pockets (Pita the Great Lamb Burgers, page 93), others are so substantial that you can serve them "nude" with potatoes (Bistro Burgers, page 82), rice (Bengal Turkey Burgers, page 90), or salad (Tortilla-Crusted Burgers, page 70) in place of bread.

As for burger accompaniments, all menu side dishes are vegetarian and perfectly compliment the flavor of the main burger. Feel free, of course, to mix and match them with any—or all—of the other grilled dishes in this book.

Build a Better Burger

Everyone loves an abundant burger that looks as good it tastes. But how do you make one?

Challenge: The Big Burger Dilemma

It's true! Traditional burgers are extremely high in calories and fat. How high? Take a juicy jumbo burger made from ground chuck. Top with a slice of cheddar cheese and two strips bacon, plop it on a bun slathered with a tablespoon of mayonnaise, and you've got a whopping 783 calories and more than 60 grams of fat. That's more than 1/3 of the calories and almost a full day's worth of fat and cholesterol in an average 2,000-calorie-per-day diet. Add potato salad, chips, fries, or cole slaw to round out the meal, and the calories and fat gram totals soar. So what's a burger lover to do?

Solution 1: Vary the Amount and Type of Meat

The American Dietetic Association, the American Heart Association, and the American Cancer Society all suggest:
- Limiting burgers to four ounces of lower fat meats. That means 1 pound of ground meat serves 4 people.
- Substituting lean or extra-lean ground beef, turkey or chicken breasts for higher fat meats (see the Ground Meat Calculator below).

Ground Meat Calculator

Listed Alphabetically

	Total calories	Protein grams & %	Total fat grams & %	Calories from fat	Saturated fat grams & %	Cholesterol
Beef, lean	191	23g (50%)	10g (50%)	92	4g (20%)	41 mg
Chicken breast, skinless	121	22g (79%)	3g (21%)	24	.7g (6%)	63 mg
Chicken thigh, skinless	134	22g (69%)	4g (31%)	40	1g (8%)	94 mg
Lamb	218	19g (36%)	15g (64%)	137	6g (26%)	75 mg
Pork	239	20g (35%	17g (65%)	151	6g (24%)	75mg
Turkey breast	133	30g (95%)	.7g (5%)	6	.2g (2%)	82 mg
Turkey dark meat	153	23g (64%)	6g (36%)	53	1g (12%)	69 mg
Turkey, mixed dark and light meat, lean	169	20g (48%)	9g (52%)	84	2g (14%)	89 mg
Veal	115	16g (59%)	5g (41%)	45	2g (17%)	69mg
Vegetarian ground meat substitute made from soy	139	18g (53%)	0g	0	0	0

Solution 2: Make More of Less

Once cooked, a healthy-sized, 4-ounce raw hamburger shrinks to a wimpy-looking 3-ounce burger. But more meat is not the answer—the extra calories and added fat cancel the nutritional benefits of using lower fat meat.

Instead, bulk up your burgers with healthy enhancements. Start with one pound of low-fat meat. Mix in a dry filler such as bread crumbs, couscous, cracker crumbs, crushed tortilla chips, and so on. Moisten the dry filling with wet condiments such as ketchup, mustard, or wine along with dry seasonings or chopped fresh herbs, fresh or dried fruit, or vegetables. Add an egg or egg white to hold it all together, and you'll transform one pound of low-fat ground meat into healthy burgers that taste even more delicious than their high-octane cousins do. I learned to make burgers like this at my grandmother's elbow. Her technique makes bigger burgers with a lighter, more succulent texture and fewer calories, fat and cholesterol. (See Grandma Jennie's Basic Burgers, page 39.)

Solution 3: Discover Meatless Burgers

Do you cringe at the thought of eating vegetarian burgers? Does soy seem a pale substitute for a juicy, real-meat burger? Think again. Vegetarian burgers can be delicious and good for you, too. The American Dietetic Association, American Heart Association, American Cancer Society, and American Diabetic Association all suggest we eat less animal protein and more complex carbohydrates such as fruits, vegetables, grains, and beans. Adding a couple of meatless meals, such as vegetarian burgers made from soybeans, to your weekly menus is one way to do that.

In addition to complex carbohydrates, soy provides a cornucopia of disease prevention benefits. Recent studies show that eating small amounts of soy protein daily may reduce your risk of breast and prostate cancer, help reduce annoying side effects of menopause and PMS, help lower your blood cholesterol, stabilize your blood sugar and even increase your bone density to help prevent osteoporosis.

Several manufacturers make soy-based products that mimic the texture and taste of hamburger meat without the calories, fat, or cholesterol. These products are a combination of textured soy protein concentrate, soy isolate and wheat gluten.

Nutritional Analysis for 3 Ounces Cooked

	Soy meat substitute	Lean ground beef
Calories	106	144
Fat (g)	0	8
Sat. Fat. (g)	0	3
Cholesterol (g)	0	31
Protein (g)	13	17

You can use soy products as a substitute for the ground meat in this chapter.

Challenge: The Burger Condiments Problem

Most people love the taste, but hate the fat and calories. Many spreads, including mayonnaise and some mustards, are loaded with fat and add 1 to 11 grams of fat to your burgers every time you smear a tablespoon on your bun. Cheese presents the same challenge: A 1-ounce slice of high-fat cheese contains more fat grams than most quarter-pound burgers made from low-fat meat.

Solution 4: Choose Condiments Wisely

Use spreads sparingly and choose those lower in fat and sodium. Instead of using a whole tablespoon of your favorite real mayonnaise on your burger bun, use 1 teaspoon. You'll get the flavor you want and ⅓ of the fat. Better yet, try some of the new low-fat and nonfat versions. But even if you use reduced-fat and fat-free condiments, don't go hog-wild with them either. When manufacturers reduce the fat, they often replace the flavor with sodium so that most people will like the taste. If you're sodium sensitive, be sure to read the label's nutritional information carefully.

If you're on a crusade to lower the fat in your diet, why not spread a nontraditional low-fat condiment on your bun? Try thick and chunky salsa, cranberry sauce, chili sauce, nonfat barbecue sauce, nonfat bean dip, hoisin sauce or plum sauce.

Burger Spread Calculator
(Comparison of 1-tablespoon portions)

CONDIMENT	Calories	Fat (g)	Fat %	Sodium (mg)
Barbecue sauce	12	.3	22	127
Barbecue sauce, fat-free hickory	20	0	0	200
Bean dip, nonfat	15	0	0	50
Chili sauce	18	.05	2	228
Chutney	26	.08	3	38
Cranberry-orange relish	30	0	0	5
Hoisin sauce	50	0	0	530
Ketchup	16	.06	3	181
Ketchup, low-sodium	16	.06	3	3
Mayonnaise, nonfat	10	0	0	105
Mayonnaise, light	50	5	92	110
Mayonnaise, regular	100	11	100	75
Mustard, brown	14	1	56	196
Mustard, Dijon	15	0	0	360
Mustard, honey	50	3	47	91
Mustard, yellow	12	1	45	195
Mustard, yellow with horseradish	12	1	48	196
Pickle relish, sweet	20	.07	3	124
Plum sauce, low-sodium	20	0	0	10
Salsa, thick and chunky, nonfat	5	0	0	110
Sour cream, nonfat	17	0	0	12

Cheese Topping Calculator
(Comparison of 1-ounce slices)

CHEESE	Calories	Fat (g)	Fat %	Sodium (mg)
American	106	9	75	405
American, reduced-fat	67	4	49	445
American, nonfat	33	0	0	270
Blue, crumbled	101	8	73	394
Brie	94	8	75	178
Cheddar, slice	114	9	74	176
Cheddar, reduced-fat	81	5	50	96
Cheddar, nonfat	40	0	35	222
Feta, crumbled	81	6	69	313
Monterey Jack, slice	111	9	65	192
Monterey Jack, reduced-fat	81	5	54	177
Monterey Jack, nonfat	40	0	35	223
Parmesan, shredded	113	9	63	510
Swiss	94	8	60	388
Swiss, reduced-fat	50	1	41	73
Swiss, nonfat	33	0	0	270

Solution 5: Don't Skip the Cheese—Just Use Less

A little goes a long way may be a cliché, but that's the right advice when you're deciding how much cheese to add to your burger. A half-ounce of crumbled feta or a 1-ounce slice of Swiss deliver the same flavor and mouth-feel you'd expect from a larger portion. To measurably lower the fat and calories, try some of the reduced-fat cheese varieties. Compare the cheeses in the chart to see how your favorites measure up.

Challenge: The Bun Misconception

Many people won't eat burger buns because they believe bread is too fattening. Of course, any food eaten to excess causes weight gain. But do you really need to worry about hamburger buns?

Solution 6: Don't Deprive Yourself

Realize that bread is a good source of carbohydrate, necessary for quick and long-lasting energy. Bread also contributes fiber to your diet, important for reducing the risk of chronic constipation, hemorrhoids, diverticulitis and colon cancer. Since your body burns fat inefficiently when it lacks carbohydrates, you don't want to shy away from bread. In fact, the USDA Food Guide Pyramid suggests 6 to 11 small servings from the bread, cereal, rice and pasta group each day. A hamburger bun is counted as 2 servings of bread: a larger bun such as a Kaiser roll adds up to 3 servings and has more calories. Still, you're hardly overindulging if you decide to enjoy a burger on a bun.

Broaden your burger horizons with some variations on the bun theme. Slide your burger into Middle Eastern pita bread. Wrap a chili-flavored burger into an extra-large tortilla with some salsa, lettuce and nonfat sour cream. A burger flavored with Italian seasonings and topped with a bit of Marinara and fresh basil leaves belongs between two slices of warmed foccacia bread. The chart below suggests more possibilities.

Bun, Bread, and Wrap Calculator

Buns	Calories	Fat (g)	Fat %	Fiber (g)
Hamburger bun	122	2	16	1
Hamburger bun, mixed-grain	113	2	20	2
Hamburger bun, low-calorie, high-fiber	84	1	8	3
Kaiser roll	190	3	14	2

Bread and Wraps	Calories	Fat (g)	Fat %	Fiber (g)
Challah bread (egg bread), 2 slices	229	5	19	2
Focaccia bread, 1 slice (4 x 4-inches)	300	2	13	4
French bread, 2 slices	113	1	5	1
Italian bread, 2 slices	162	2	12	2
Pita bread, whole wheat (5-inch diameter)	170	2	8	5
Pita bread, white (5-inch diameter)	165	1	4	1
Pumpernickel bread, 2 slices	130	2	11	3
Raisin bread, 2 slices	142	2	14	2
Rye bread, 2 slices	165	2	12	4
Sourdough bread, 2 slices	137	2	10	2
Tortilla, flour, 1 large (10 1/2-inch diameter)	184	4	20	2
Whole wheat bread, 2 slices	137	2	14	4
Wrap, white flour, 1 large	100	1	9	1

Grill Power Burger Making Tips

Mixing and forming the meat:

• If you're using a dry filling such as bread crumbs, don't mix in more liquid or moistener than it can absorb. If you do your burgers will become too soft and hard to handle.
• Mix the dry filler ingredients and herbs with the moisteners before adding the meat. The dry ingredients will hydrate faster and work their way throughout the ground meat more evenly.
• Don't overhandle your burger concoction when mixing. Your burgers will become dried out and tough during cooking.
• Wet your hands with cold water when forming your burgers. That way, the meat won't stick to your fingers.
• Form your burgers into patties no thicker than

1/2 to 3/4 inch. If they are too thick, they will burn on the outside before they are fully cooked on the inside.

- Wash your hands thoroughly after handling raw meat and use a nailbrush under your nails. Wash a good 20 seconds with hot water and plenty of soap, about the time it takes you to sing "Happy Birthday" twice through. If you touch any raw food such as lettuce and tomato with unwashed hands, you run a very high risk of making someone sick with *E. coli* or salmonella poisoning.

Grilling

- Spray the outside of the burgers lightly with oil spray or nonfat cooking spray. Not only does this prevent them from sticking to the grill, they'll develop nice grill marks as they cook. Even though most electric grills have nonstick coating on their racks, sticking can still happen, especially if your meat is extra lean and you're using sticky ingredients such as breadcrumbs.
- Don't press your burgers down with a spatula as they cook. Pressing makes the juices flow out of the burgers, drying them out, making them tough, and breaking them.
- Use two spatulas to turn your burgers. This gives you more control and prevents tender burgers from splitting when they are half cooked.
- Turn your burgers only once to prevent overcooking. The less you move burgers on the grill the better they hold together and stay tender and juicy. Grill one side thoroughly for about 4 to 5 minutes. Turn the burgers over and grill the other side until an instant-read thermometer registers 160°F.

Melting Cheese

- Hibachi, Combination or Infusion Grills: Top the cooked side of the burger with cheese (sliced, crumbled or shredded) 2 or 4 minutes until the cheese is melted but not running over the sides of the burger. If your grill has a lid, use it only during the last 2 minutes of the grilling time

because the heat buildup may make the cheese too runny.

- Two Sided Contact Grill: For grills that only open to 90°, lift the top grilling plate during the last 2 to 3 minutes of grilling time, put the cheese on the burgers (sliced, crumbled or shredded) and continue grilling with the top up. For grills with adjustable upper grilling plates, open the grill and top the burger with cheese during the last 2 or 3 minutes of grilling time. Adjust the upper grill plate to the warming position (see page 13) so that is is above but not touching the burger. Grill until cheese is melted but not running over the sides of the burger.
- In the Oven on the Buns or Bread: Position a rack in the middle of your oven and pre-heat to 425°F. Do this immediately after you turn your grill on. Place the buns cut side up, on a baking sheet. Put some cheese (sliced, crumbled, or shredded) on the upper half of each bun. Four or five minutes before the burgers are done, place the baking sheet on the middle rack of the oven and bake until cheese melts and buns are lightly toasted, about 3 or 4 minutes. Serve them immediately while still warm. Don't bake them too long or the buns will dry out and fall apart when you bite into your burger.

Toasting Burger Buns

If you have a large grill and want to toast your burger buns on it while the burgers are cooking, they'll toast best if they have a bit of fat spread or sprayed on the cut sides. Before grilling, lightly spray with nonstick cooking spray (try the garlic-flavored variety for zing), olive oil or canola oil spray or a light spread such as low-fat margarine or butter, prepared pesto or low-fat mayonnaise. Grill the buns cut side down for 2 to 4 minutes until toasted to your liking. Don't overtoast your buns—they'll dry out and fall apart when you eat your burger.

Freezing Burgers

- Raw meat: Use freshly ground meat that has not been frozen. Mix with remaining burger ingredients, form into patties and separate between layers of plastic wrap. Place in an airtight container or zipper freezer bag for up to 2 months. Squeeze out all air to prevent freezer burn.

• Cooked meat: Cook burgers to an interior temperature of 160°F. Cool the cooked burgers completely on a plate or wire rack. Separate between pieces of plastic wrap before putting them in an airtight container or zippered freezer bag. Squeeze out all air to prevent freezer burn. Freeze for up to 2 months.

• To avoid "mystery food," don't forget to label the package with the type of burger you created and the date you put it into the freezer. Masking tape is my favorite inexpensive label for airtight plastic containers. It stays put when frozen and is easy to write on with a ball-point pen.

Defrosting Burgers

Whatever you do, don't defrost your burgers on the kitchen counter at room temperature. Harmful bacteria may build up if you let meat defrost at room temperature.

• To defrost in the refrigerator, place freezer container or bag in the refrigerator immediately and thaw overnight.

• To defrost raw burgers in the microwave, place individual burgers on a dish and lightly cover with a plastic cover or plastic wrap. Microwave for 3 to 5 minutes at 10% power or until the center is defrosted. (Higher power tends to cook the meat around the edges.)

• To defrost cooked burgers in the microwave, separate and place burgers on a dish and lightly cover with a microwavable cover or plastic wrap. Microwave for 3 to 5 minutes at 30% power or until the center is defrosted. Reheat on a grill set to the highest temperature or in the microwave for 1 to 2 minutes on high (100% power) or until heated through.

• To grill frozen raw burgers after defrosting, follow cooking directions in each recipe. If the recipe calls for coating the burgers with ground croutons, bread crumbs, or chips before grilling, do so after defrosting the meat and just before putting on the hot grill.

Is Your Burger Safe to Eat?

Not unless it's cooked to an interior temperature of 160°F. In 1998, the U.S. Department of Agriculture determined that a reading of 160°F on an instant-read digital thermometer was the only reliable way to ensure ground meat had reached a temperature high enough to destroy harmful bacteria such as *E. coli*. At 160°F a safely cooked ground meat patty may look brown, pink, or some variation of both depending on a variety of factors (whether the meat was fresh or frozen, for instance, or how it was thawed). Some burgers actually turn brown at temperatures as low as 131°F, a temperature at which bacteria can thrive.

These harmful bacteria live on the outside surfaces of meat but are present throughout ground meat because the outside has been ground and mixed with the inside. If you want to play it safe and have perfectly cooked meat to boot, a digital instant-read thermometer is a good investment. Note that the large-dial food thermometers designed for testing whole poultry and roasts during cooking won't work accurately for burgers.

See page 24 to learn how to use an instant-read thermometer.

Tortilla-Crusted Burgers with Black Bean Salsa Salad

If you love tortilla chips and Mexican cuisine, you will love this burger. I mix the chips into the burger meat as filler and then coat the outside of each patty to give the burgers a crispy crust. Topped with salsa, low- or nonfat sour cream and thin slices of fresh avocado or a spoonful of guacamole, this burger requires no bun. Pair it with my Black Bean Salsa Salad for a lighter style Mexican menu.

Menu Game Plan

Prep & cooking time: 45 minutes

- Preheat the grill.
- Crush the tortilla chips.
- Mix and shape the burgers.
- Make the Black Bean Salsa Salad.
- Grill the burgers.
- Dress the plates while the burgers are grilling.

Cook's Notes

Guacamole is a Mexican avocado salad traditionally served with spicy entrees to cool down the heat. I use it as a condiment for Mexican- or Southwestern-flavored burgers, sandwiches and wraps. You can buy it ready-made in many grocery stores' freezer or deli sections, but I like to make it from scratch because it is so easy and good.

When selecting fresh avocados, color is not a good guide because the skin tone differs from one variety to another. Avocados are ready to use when they are heavy for their size, free of black spots or bruises, not too hard, and yield to the touch. Avocados that are too soft will be overripe.

If not serving the guacamole immediately after you make it, squeeze some lemon or lime juice over the surface, then press plastic wrap onto the surface and refrigerate. The lemon juice and plastic wrap will help keep the guacamole from turning brown. Stir the extra citrus juice into the guacamole just before serving.

Tortilla-Crusted Burgers

Serves 4

1   cup finely crushed low-fat tortilla chips

½   cup thick salsa, medium or hot

¼   cup finely chopped fresh cilantro

¼   cup thinly sliced green onions

1   teaspoon chili powder

1   teaspoon pressed garlic

¼   teaspoon ground cumin

¼   teaspoon ground cinnamon

¼   teaspoon light salt (optional)

¼   to ½ teaspoon finely chopped jalapeno pepper, fresh or canned (optional)

1   pound extra-lean ground beef, turkey, chicken breast or vegetarian meat substitute

Nonfat or canola oil cooking spray

8   Romaine lettuce leaves

2   medium tomatoes sliced into 8 rounds

1   medium avocado cut into 8 slices or guacamole

Thick salsa, hot or mild

Fresh cilantro sprigs

Nonfat or low-fat sour cream (optional)

1. **Preheat the grill** to the highest setting.

2. **Crush the tortilla chips.** In a food processor or blender process enough tortilla chips to make 1 cup. Use ⅓ cup to mix into the burgers. Reserve ⅔ cup to coat the outside of the burgers just before grilling.

3. **Mix and shape the burgers.** In a 2- or 3-quart mixing bowl using a fork or spoon, mix the crushed tortilla chips, salsa, cilantro, green onions, chili powder, garlic, cumin, cinnamon, and salt. Using your hands, gently fold the meat into the wet mixture.

When all ingredients are evenly distributed, divide the meat mixture into 4 equal portions. Wet hands and shape burgers, about 4 to 5 inches in diameter and no thicker than ¾-inch. Set aside on a plate covered with plastic wrap in the refrigerator until ready to grill, up to 24 hours.

3. **Grill the burgers.** Place the ⅔-cup of reserved tortilla chips on a dinner plate. Gently press all sides of each burger into the crushed chips so they are completely coated with chips.

Spray each burger lightly on both sides with cooking spray. Place the burgers on the preheated grill and cook according to the Grill Times opposite until the internal temperature reaches 160°F on an instant-read thermometer.

4. **Prepare the garnishes.** While the burgers are grilling, wash the lettuce, slice the tomatoes and avocado (or make the guacamole).

5. **To serve,** using a slotted spoon put even portions of the black bean salsa salad on four plates or into four small bowls (the salad is juicy, so you may want to serve it in separate bowls so it won't make your burgers soggy). On each plate, place 2 lettuce leaves next to the bean salsa or the small bowl. Top the lettuce with a cooked burger. Top the burger with some salsa and sour cream. Garnish with sliced tomato, avocado or guacamole, fresh cilantro and extra tortilla chips.

Grill Times

Two-Sided Contact Grill: *6 to 7 minutes.*

Hibachi Grill, Combination Grill or Fusion Grill: *12 to 14 minutes. Turn the burgers halfway through the grilling time. Grills with lids may be covered halfway through the grilling time. Infusion grills with lids may be covered for the entire grilling time.*

Black Bean Salsa Salad

Makes 4 (1 cup) servings

Salad

1   15-ounce can black beans, rinsed, well drained

1   cup petite frozen white or yellow corn kernels, thawed under cool running water

1   cup diced red bell pepper

1   cup diced jicama

1   medium orange, peeled, diced

¼   cup thinly sliced green onions

¼   cup finely chopped fresh cilantro

Dressing

¼   cup fresh lime juice

3   tablespoons canola or corn oil

2   teaspoons chili powder

1   teaspoon ground cumin

¼   teaspoon pressed garlic

¼   teaspoon ground cinnamon

1. Mix the salad in a 6- or 8-cup bowl. With a large rubber spatula mix the black beans, corn, bell pepper, jicama, orange, green onions and cilantro.

2. Make the dressing in a 1- or 2-cup bowl or glass measuring cup. With a fork mix the lime juice, oil, chili powder, cumin, garlic and cinnamon. Pour the dressing onto the salad, then fold in thoroughly with the spatula. Cover with plastic wrap and refrigerate until ready to serve or up to 24 hours.

Substitutions:
One of my recipe testers, Cheryl Branson, grilled zucchini and crookneck squash along with the burgers to add more veggies to the menu. Since she cooks for two (her husband and herself), Cheryl transformed the two leftover burgers into a completely different meal the next night. She crumbled the burgers, then heated it in the microwave and used it for taco filling.

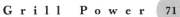

Guacamole

Makes about 12 (¹/₄ cup servings)

3   medium-sized ripe avocados, halved, pits removed and pulp scooped out with a spoon

1   tablespoon lemon or lime juice

½   cup thinly sliced green onions

½   cup seeded, chopped ripe tomato

1   teaspoon finely chopped fresh green chilies (serrano or jalapeño) or 1 teaspoon chili powder

½   teaspoon salt or to taste

½   teaspoon pressed garlic (optional)

2   tablespoons finely chopped cilantro (optional)

I like to make extra guacamole because everyone usually wants more. It also keeps well up to 3 days in an airtight container in the refrigerator if you drizzle the top with lemon juice to keep it from turning brown.

1. In a 4-cup bowl, thoroughly mash the avocados and lemon juice with a fork.
2. Mix in the green onions, chopped tomato, chilies, salt, garlic, and cilantro.
3. Serve immediately or store in the refrigerator as directed above.

Approximate Nutrients Per Serving of Entire Meal

Total Calories 547	Protein 36 g / 24%	Carbohydrate 54 g / 37%
Total Sugar 10 g	Fat Total 25 g / 39%	Saturated Fat 5 g / 8%
Cholesterol 41 mg	Sodium 627 mg	Fiber 7 g Calcium 108 mg

(Calculated with a burger made with extra-lean ground beef, avocado and tomato slices, lettuce and 1 cup of bean salsa)

Mighty Maui Burgers with Pele's Potato Poppers

*E*ach time I visit the Hawaiian Islands I renew my love affair with Hawaii's natural beauty, the Hawaiian culture and above all the local cuisine. So it is no surprise that two mythical Hawaiian gods were my inspiration for this menu filled with Hawaiian style ingredients. Maui is the mighty Paul Bunyan–like god who lives on Haleakala, the extinct volcano on the island of Maui. He made this mountain his home after he stood on its highest peaks and snared the sun from the sky in order to create longer days for the Hawaiian people. Madame Pele, the sensuous goddess of fire, resides in the active Kilauea volcano on the neighboring island of Hawaii. As I rhythmically mixed the meat into the seasonings for the pineapple-studded burgers, I had a humorous vision of the two deities meeting for a potluck luau, each offering something fiery on a dark night. Muscle-bound Maui ceremoniously presents his juicy, strength-building burgers, while Pele, her flaming hair illuminating her svelte figure, hulas over with a platter of spicy low-fat oven-"fried" potatoes.

Menu Game Plan

Prep & cooking time: 40 to 50 minutes

- Preheat the grill.
- Preheat the oven for the potatoes.
- Prepare Pele's Potato Poppers then bake them.
- Mix and shape the burgers.
- Grill the burgers.
- Assemble the garnishes while the burgers are grilling.
- Serve immediately when burgers come off the grill.

Cook's Notes

Sweet onions such as the Maui and Vidalia varieties are all light-colored, slightly flat in shape, juicy, and high in sugar content, which gives them a mild or even sweet flavor. Maui onions grown on the Hawaiian island of Maui in volcanic soil and under mild weather conditions are the sweetest. They are sold on the United States mainland from May to June. Vidalia onions, named after a town in Georgia, taste best when grown in the warmer climate of the Southeast and are also available May to June. Make sure the onions you buy were grown in their native area; cultivated elsewhere, they taste like common yellow onions.

Mighty Maui Burgers

Serves 4

1/3 cup finely crushed nonfat or low-fat garlic croutons

1 8-ounce can crushed pineapple, drained, pressed almost dry

1/3 cup finely chopped or grated onion

2 tablespoons ketchup

2 tablespoons finely chopped parsley

1½ teaspoons pressed garlic

1½ teaspoons grated gingerroot

1 tablespoon low-sodium soy sauce

½ to 1 teaspoon chili oil

1 pound ground extra-lean meat, poultry or vegetarian meat substitute

Nonfat or canola oil cooking spray

4 hamburger buns

4 curly leaf lettuce leaves

4 thin slices mild onion (Maui or Vidalia, if available)

Mustard and/or ketchup

1. Preheat the grill to the highest setting.

2. Mix and shape the burgers. In a 2- or 3-quart mixing bowl using a fork or spoon, evenly mix the croutons, pineapple, onion, ketchup, parsley, garlic, ginger, soy sauce and chili oil. Using your hands, gently fold the ground meat into the wet mixture.

When all ingredients are evenly distributed, divide the meat mixture into 4 equal portions. Wet hands and shape burgers, about 4 to 5 inches in diameter and no thicker than 3/4-inch. Set aside on a plate covered with plastic wrap in the refrigerator until ready to grill, up to 24 hours.

3. Grill the burgers. Spray each burger lightly on both sides with cooking spray. Put the burgers on the grill and cook according to the Grill Times below or until the internal temperature reaches 160°F on an instant-read thermometer.

4. To serve, spoon even portions of the potatoes on 4 plates. Place a lettuce leaf beside the potatoes and top it with a burger and sliced onion. Place a bun on each plate and serve, allowing diners to assemble their own burgers

Grill Times

Two-Sided Contact Grill: *6 to 7 minutes.*

Hibachi Grill, Combination Grill or Infusion Grill: *12 to 14 minutes. Turn the burgers halfway through the grilling time. Grills with lids may be covered halfway through the grilling time. Infusion grills with lids may be covered for the entire grilling time.*

Pele's Potato Poppers

Makes 4 (1½ cup) servings

⅓ cup finely crushed nonfat or low-fat garlic croutons

4 medium baking potatoes, scrubbed, skin left on

2 extra-large egg whites or ¼ cup egg substitute

½ to 1 teaspoon sweet paprika

½ to 1 teaspoon chili oil

½ teaspoon light salt or to taste

Nonfat or canola oil cooking spray

1. Preheat the oven to 450°F.
2. Leave the skin on the potatoes and slice into ½-inch wedges then place in a 3- or 4-quart mixing bowl.
3. In a 4-cup mixing bowl with a wire whisk or a fork, mix the egg whites, paprika, chili oil and salt to taste.
4. Whisk in the crushed crumbs. Pour mixture over potatoes then, using your hands, turn the potatoes to evenly coat.
5. Place the potatoes in a single layer on a nonstick-baking sheet. Spray lightly with cooking spray. Bake 20 to 25 minutes until potatoes are crisp and golden brown. Turn them halfway through the cooking time.

Mix & Match Serve Pele's Potato Poppers with the main dish from the following menu: Mac Nut Crab Cake Salad with Roasted Red Pepper and Pineapple Vinaigrette, page 223.

Approximate Nutrients Per Serving of Entire Meal

Total Calories 636	Protein 36 g / 22%	Carbohydrate 89 g / 56%
Total Sugar 10 g	Fat Total 16 g / 22%	Saturated Fat 5 g / 7%
Cholesterol 41 mg	Sodium 957 mg	Fiber 6 g	Calcium 103 mg

(Calculated with burger made with extra-lean ground beef, a bun, lettuce, tomato slice and 1 cup of potatoes.)

Double Whammy Texas BBQ Burger with Bunkhouse Beans

During the three years that I taught cooking classes and starred in a cooking segment on a local Saturday morning TV news magazine show in Austin, Texas, I learned that Austin residents have gourmet tastes. The city boasts some of the best restaurants in the United States, some of the most talented chefs anywhere, and grocery stores that stock an array of international cooking ingredients second only to their counterparts in New York City. Yet if you ask most Austinites to name their favorite food, they will say barbecue. By barbecue they mean grilled or slow-cooked barbecued meat slathered with their favorite barbecue sauce just before leaving the fire. Texans also pass around extra barbecue sauce at the table.

This burger recipe, which calls for barbecue sauce both inside and outside of the burgers for a double whammy of taste, is a salute to my friends in Texas. The beans are my mom Jean's addition to the menu. She lived in Austin for 7 years and says that she designed the flavors to satisfy a bunkhouse full of hungry cowboys.

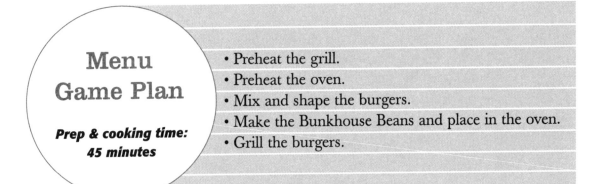

Menu Game Plan

Prep & cooking time: 45 minutes

- Preheat the grill.
- Preheat the oven.
- Mix and shape the burgers.
- Make the Bunkhouse Beans and place in the oven.
- Grill the burgers.

Cook's Notes

Barbecue, barbeque, Bar-B-Q, or however you spell it, became, over time, a blanket term to mean a variety of things having to do with meat that is slow cooked over a low steady heat for many hours. Barbecued meat is cooked with indirect heat. This type of cooking allows the heat to penetrate the meat slowly for even cooking and to prevent burned outsides or undercooked insides. BBQ sauce adds a finishing touch of flavor to both barbecued and grilled food. When using your tabletop grill, always add BBQ sauce at the very end of the cooking time to prevent the sugars in the sauce from burning onto the food.

Texas BBQ Burgers

¼ cup dried breadcrumbs

½ cup finely chopped or grated onion

¼ cup barbecue sauce

1 large egg white

1 teaspoon pressed garlic

¼ cup finely chopped fresh parsley (optional)

¼ to 1 teaspoon hot pepper sauce such as Tabasco (optional)

Light salt to taste (optional)

1 pound extra-lean ground beef, pork, poultry or vegetarian meat substitute

Nonfat or canola oil cooking spray

1 medium onion

4 hamburger buns

1 medium ripe tomato, sliced into 4 equal rounds

4 dill pickles, sliced lengthwise

4 curly leaf lettuce leaves

Extra barbecue sauce

1. Preheat the grill to the highest setting.

2. Mix and shape the burgers. In a 2- or 3-quart mixing bowl using a fork or spoon, evenly mix the breadcrumbs, onion, barbecue sauce, egg white, garlic, parsley, Tabasco, and salt. Using your hands, gently fold the ground meat into the wet mixture.

When all ingredients are evenly distributed, divide the meat mixture into 4 equal portions. Wet hands and shape burgers, about 4 to 5 inches in diameter and no thicker than ¾ inch. Set aside on a plate covered with plastic wrap in the refrigerator until ready to grill, up to 24 hours.

3. Slice the onions across the meridian into 4 rounds, each ½-inch wide.

4. Grill the burgers and onions. If you have a grill with a small cooking surface, grill the onions first, and then immediately grill the burgers. When the onions are done, keep them warm until serving time on a foil-covered plate.

Spray each burger and onion slice lightly on both sides with cooking spray. Grill the burgers and the onions according to the Grill Times below until grill marks appear on the onions, and the burgers reach an internal temperature of 160°F on an instant-read thermometer.

5. Prepare the garnishes. While the burgers are grilling, slice the tomatoes and pickles and wash the lettuce.

6. To serve, spoon even portions of the beans on 4 plates. Place a lettuce leaf beside the beans and top it with a burger, sliced tomato, and grilled onion. Place a bun on each plate, garnish with a pickle, and serve with extra barbecue sauce on the side, allowing diners to assemble their own burgers.

Grill Times

Two-Sided Contact Grill: Onions 7 to 10 minutes / burgers 6 to 7 minutes. Two minutes before the burgers are done, baste the top of each burger with 2 to 3 teaspoons barbecue sauce.

Hibachi Grill, Combination Grill or Infusion Grill: Onions 14 to 20 minutes / burgers 12 to 14 minutes. Turn the onions and burgers halfway through the grilling time then baste the burgers' cooked side with 2 to 3 teaspoons barbecue sauce. Grills with lids may be covered halfway through the grilling time. Infusion grills with lids may be covered for the entire grilling time.

Bunkhouse Beans

Makes 4 (1 cup) servings

- 1 cup nonfat or low-fat mayonnaise
- 1 teaspoon chili powder
- 1 teaspoon Worcestershire sauce
- ½ teaspoon garlic powder
- Dash hot pepper sauce such as Tabasco (optional)
- ½ teaspoon light salt (optional)
- 1 15-ounce can each black beans, kidney beans and black-eyed peas, rinsed, well drained
- 1 cup low-fat shredded Cheddar cheese
- 1 cup thinly sliced green onions
- ⅓ cup finely chopped dill pickle
- ½ cup crushed low-fat tortilla chips

1. Preheat oven to 450°F.

2. In a 2-quart bowl, thoroughly mix the mayonnaise, chili powder, Worcestershire sauce, garlic powder, hot pepper sauce and salt.

3. With a rubber spatula fold in the beans, cheese, green onions, and pickle.

4. Turn into a 1½-quart shallow glass casserole then sprinkle with the tortilla chips.

5. Bake uncovered for 10 to 15 minutes, or until beans are bubbling or in microwave covered, for 10 minutes on high (100% power). Stir halfway through the cooking time in microwave until beans are bubbling.

Approximate Nutrients Per Serving of Entire Meal

Total Calories 674	Protein 52 g / 30%	Carbohydrate 9 g / 51%
Total Sugar 16 g	Fat Total 15 g / 19%	Saturated Fat 5 g / 7%
Cholesterol 47 mg	Sodium 2,002 mg	Fiber 18 g Calcium 304 mg

(Calculated with a burger made with extra-lean ground beef, a bun, lettuce, tomato and 1 cup of beans.)

Memories of Manhattan Moroccan Burgers in Pita Bread with Tahini Sauce

I became enamored of Moroccan cuisine when I was studying for my graduate degree at the Manhattan School of Music in New York City. On Sunday afternoons, I traveled by subway to Greenwich Village with my boyfriend (now my husband) John to attend concerts or visit art galleries. We often finished the day with dinner at our favorite Moroccan restaurant. The restaurant is gone but the flavors we savored there live on in this menu.

Menu Game Plan

Prep & cooking time: 35 to 40 minutes

- Preheat the grill.
- Mix and shape the burgers.
- Make the Tahini Sauce.
- Slice and arrange the salad vegetables on the plates.
- Grill the burgers.

Cook's Notes

Mediterranean cured black olives are a delicacy dating from the time the first olive trees were cultivated on the sunny island of Crete somewhere between 3,000 and 5,000 B.C. Today Spanish olive processors first soak both young green and mature black olives in a lye solution to remove the fruit's natural bitterness. After a thorough rinsing, the olives are cured up to 12 months in a brine solution. Greek- and Italian-style olives, made from fully ripe dark purple or black fruit, are cured only in salt or a brine solution for up to six months. Meaty in texture yet fruity in taste, Greek- or Italian-style cured olives are my choice for providing the right amount of saltiness to balance Mediterranean-flavored burgers, sandwiches, or wraps.

Moroccan Burgers

Serves 4

1/3   cup finely crushed nonfat or low-fat garlic croutons

1/2   cup ketchup

1/4   cup finely chopped fresh parsley

1/4   cup finely chopped fresh cilantro

1/4   cup finely chopped or grated red onion

1   teaspoon pressed garlic

1   teaspoon paprika, hot or sweet

1/2   teaspoon ground cinnamon

1/2   teaspoon ground cumin

1/2   teaspoon light salt

1/4   teaspoon freshly ground pepper

1   pound extra-lean ground beef or ground lamb

Nonfat or olive oil cooking spray

16   Romaine lettuce leaves

1   cup thinly sliced cucumbers

2   large ripe tomatoes, cut in half then into half moons

1   small red bell pepper, sliced into thin strips

4   large pita bread rounds, white or whole wheat, cut in half

1   cup shredded carrots

Mediterranean-style cured black olives (optional)

1. **Preheat the grill** to the highest setting.

2. **Mix and shape the burgers.** In a 2- or 3-quart mixing bowl using a fork or spoon, evenly mix the croutons, ketchup, parsley, cilantro, onion, garlic, paprika, cinnamon, cumin, salt, and pepper. Using your hands, gently fold the meat into the wet mixture.

When all ingredients are evenly distributed, divide the meat mixture into 8 equal portions. Wet hands and shape burgers, about 2 to 3 inches in diameter and no thicker than 1/2-inch. Set aside on a plate covered with plastic wrap in the refrigerator until ready to grill, up to 24 hours.

3. **Make the fresh vegetable filling and prepare the garnish.** Wash and dry the lettuce and other vegetables. Slice the cucumber, tomatoes, bell peppers and pita bread. Artfully arrange equal amounts of each vegetable, pita and olives on 4 dinner plates, leaving space for the cooked burgers.

4. **Grill the burgers.** Spray each burger lightly on both sides with cooking spray. Place on the grill and cook according to the Grill Times opposite until the internal temperature reaches 160°F on an instant-read thermometer.

5. **To serve,** place 2 burgers on each plate and garnish with fresh cilantro or parsley. Place the tahini sauce on the table. Diners can stuff a burger and vegetables into each pita half, then drizzle each half with 1 to 2 tablespoons of the tahini sauce before eating. Extra tahini sauce can be drizzled over the remaining vegetables.

Grill Times

Two-Sided Contact Grill: *6 to 7 minutes.*

Hibachi Grill, Combination Grill or Infusion Grill: *12 to 14 minutes. Turn the burgers halfway through the grilling time. Grills with lids may be covered halfway through the grilling time. Infusion grills with lids may be covered for the entire grilling time.*

Tahini Sauce

Makes 12 (2 tablespoon) servings

½ cup tahini (sesame butter)

3 tablespoons fresh lemon juice

1 teaspoon pressed garlic

½ teaspoon light salt

Pinch sugar

¾ cup water

I suggest 2 tablespoons per serving, but this dressing is addictive. Since many people like a well-dressed salad, I designed this recipe for extra servings. Use leftover dressing on your grilled meat, poultry or fish, as a dip for veggies or pita bread triangles, or as a sauce for hot rice or cooked bulgur wheat. The dressing will keep up to 1 month in an airtight container in the refrigerator.

1. In a blender, process the tahini, lemon juice, garlic, salt, sugar and water until smooth.
3. Pour into a 2-cup pitcher or a sauceboat. Set aside until serving time. If not serving within the hour, store tightly covered in the refrigerator.

Approximate Nutrients Per Serving of Entire Meal

Total Calories 536	Protein 33 g / 25%	Carbohydrate 53 g / 40%
Total Sugar 8 g	Fat Total 21 g / 36%	Saturated Fat 5 g / 9%
Cholesterol 41 mg	Sodium 1,070 mg	Fiber 4 g Calcium 155 mg

(Calculated with 2 small burgers made with extra-lean ground beef, 1 pita bread round, 1 serving of salad fixings and 2 tablespoons tahini sauce.)

Bistro Burgers with Warm Tarragon Potato Salad

As an undergraduate student, I had the privilege of studying voice one summer in Florence, Italy. After 8 weeks of beautiful Italian opera, astounding art, and unforgettable cuisine, I was ready for a change. I needed Americana—I needed a burger! On the way home to New York I visited a friend in Paris. My quest for a burger led us to a romantic Parisian bistro, where we shared the menu I've re-created below. It's not very American, but it is delicious, and elegant enough to make for company. To round out the meal, follow with a light lemon sorbet surrounded by sliced seasonal fresh fruit and drizzled with warm chocolate sauce.

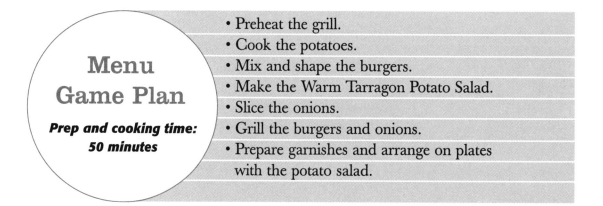

Menu Game Plan

Prep and cooking time: 50 minutes

- Preheat the grill.
- Cook the potatoes.
- Mix and shape the burgers.
- Make the Warm Tarragon Potato Salad.
- Slice the onions.
- Grill the burgers and onions.
- Prepare garnishes and arrange on plates with the potato salad.

Cook's Notes

Notes

Tarragon imparts a light, refreshing anise flavor when you crush or chop its spear-shaped leaves. A native of Central Asia and Siberia, tarragon was introduced to Europe by the crusaders who brought it back from the Near East. Adopted afterward as an important seasoning by a variety of international cuisines, it is especially prized by the French to season sauces and salads.

Whenever possible, I use fresh tarragon rather than dried because it imparts a more aromatic flavor to the recipe. Keep fresh tarragon in the refrigerator with the stems in a jar of water. Change the water every 2 days and it will keep for up to 5 days. If fresh tarragon is unavailable, by all means use dried. A jar of commercially dried tarragon will keep its pungency for over a year if stored in a cool, dry, dark place.

Bistro Burgers

Serves 4

1/3 cup finely crushed nonfat or low-fat garlic croutons

2 tablespoons Dijon-style mustard (honey or regular)

1/3 cup thinly sliced green onions

1 teaspoon pressed garlic

2 tablespoons chopped fresh tarragon or 2 teaspoons dried

1/4 teaspoon light salt

1/4 teaspoon freshly ground pepper

1 pound extra-lean ground beef, poultry or vegetarian meat substitute

1 medium onion

Nonfat or olive oil cooking spray

4 teaspoons Dijon-style mustard

4 leaves butter leaf lettuce

2 medium ripe tomatoes, thinly sliced

1 loaf fresh sourdough bread

Extra-virgin olive oil

Tarragon or white wine vinegar

1. **Preheat the grill** to the highest setting.

2. **Mix the burgers.** In a 2- or 3-quart mixing bowl using a fork or spoon, evenly mix the crushed croutons, mustard, green onions, garlic, tarragon, salt, and pepper. Using your hands, gently fold the wet mixture into the meat.

When all ingredients are evenly distributed, divide the meat mixture into 4 equal portions. Wet hands and shape burgers, about 4 to 5 inches in diameter and no thicker than 3/4-inch. Set aside on a plate covered with plastic wrap in the refrigerator until ready to grill, up to 24 hours.

3. **Slice the onion** across the meridian into 4 1/2-inch thick slices.

4. **Grill the burgers and onions.** Spray both sides of the onions and the burgers lightly with cooking spray. If you have a small capacity grill, grill the onions first then the burgers. When the onions are done keep warm until serving time on a foil-covered plate. Grill according to the Grill Times below or until the onions are tender and the burgers reach an internal temperature of 160°F on an instant-read thermometer.

5. **To serve,** spoon even portions of the potato salad onto 4 plates. Place a lettuce leaf beside it and top with the tomatoes arranged in a fan. Drizzle the tomatoes with a small amount of extra-virgin olive oil (or your favorite vegetable oil) and a bit of tarragon or white wine vinegar. Place a burger next to the lettuce and top with the grilled onions. Serve immediately with thick slices of crusty sourdough bread.

Grill Times

Two-Sided Contact Grill: Onions 7 to 10 minutes / burgers 7 to 8 minutes; Baste each burger halfway through the cooking time with 1 teaspoon mustard.

Hibachi Grill, Combination Grill or Infusion Grill: Onions 14 to 20 minutes / burgers 14 to 16 minutes. Turn the onions and burgers halfway through the grilling time and baste each burger with 1 teaspoon mustard. Grills with lids may be covered halfway through the grilling time. Infusion grills with lids may be covered for the entire grilling time.

Warm Tarragon Potato Salad

Makes about 4 (1 cup) servings

1½ pounds small, thin-skinned potatoes

2 tablespoons tarragon vinegar

½ teaspoon garlic powder

2 tablespoons extra-virgin olive oil

Light salt and freshly ground pepper to taste

½ cup thinly sliced green onions

2 tablespoons well drained capers

This recipe can be made up to 24 hours in advance of serving. To warm, microwave covered for 3 to 5 minutes on medium (50% power), stirring halfway through the cooking time. Or, after refrigeration, set on the counter 1 hour before serving and serve at room temperature.

1. Dice the potatoes into 1-inch pieces. Do not peel.
2. Place a steamer basket in a 4- or 5-quart pot, fill with 2 or 3 cups of water, and bring to a rapid boil over high heat. Add the potatoes and cover. Steam for 7 to 10 minutes, or until potatoes are tender but not falling apart. Pour the potatoes immediately into a strainer to drain. When well-drained put into a 2-quart mixing bowl and cover with plastic wrap or a lid to keep warm until ready to mix with other ingredients.
3. In a 1-cup bowl whisk together the vinegar, garlic powder, olive oil, salt and pepper. Slice the onions and drain the capers.
4. Use a large spatula or spoon to evenly mix the vinaigrette, capers and green onions into the warm potatoes.

   Cover with plastic wrap or aluminum foil and set aside until ready to serve. If you are preparing the salad more than 1 hour in advance, refrigerate. If the salad becomes too cold while the burgers cook, cover and microwave on medium (50% power) for 3 to 5 minutes to warm just before serving.

Approximate Nutrients Per Serving of Entire Meal

Total Calories 512	Protein 30 g / 24%	Carbohydrate 51 g / 40%
Total Sugar 2 g	Fat Total 20 g / 36%	Saturated Fat 5 g / 9%
Cholesterol 41 mg	Sodium 831 mg	Fiber 4 g Calcium 36 mg

Crazy Cajun Burgers with Stompin' Alligator Slaw

On a trip to New Orleans for a QVC Local Flavors Tour a few years ago, I met Chef Paul Prudhomme who encouraged me to savor the flavors of the bayou at his restaurant, K-Paul's. That night I experienced the secret to Chef Prudhomme's unique brand of Cajun cuisine . . . his magic mix of local herbs and spices. Back at home in my kitchen, I put together my own easy-to-make-seasoning blend to re-create the flavor. You'll find it on page 54 if you would like to make it from scratch. If you want to keep this menu extra simple, I suggest using a prepared Cajun spice blend (you'll find several brands in most major grocery stores).

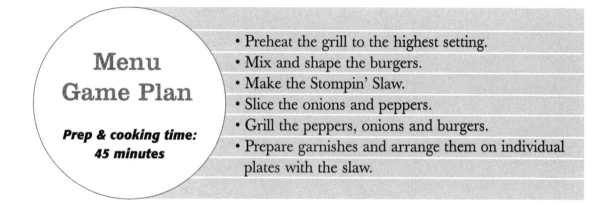

Menu Game Plan

Prep & cooking time: 45 minutes

• Preheat the grill to the highest setting.
• Mix and shape the burgers.
• Make the Stompin' Slaw.
• Slice the onions and peppers.
• Grill the peppers, onions and burgers.
• Prepare garnishes and arrange them on individual plates with the slaw.

Cook's Notes

Ketchup (or catsup) wasn't always that thick red tomato stuff that we love to slather on our burgers. Seventeenth-century European traders in Southeast Asia fell in love with a variety of spicy sauces based on fermented fish and brought the recipes back home. Using local ingredients, early English ketchup was made from a variety of ingredients—pickled oysters, mushrooms, cucumbers, tomatoes, berries or walnuts. American colonists brought ketchup with them from England where they made it at home until 1876 when Henry J. Heinz started producing it commercially at his factory in Pennsylvania. Today 97% of American homes keep bottled ketchup in their kitchen. If you are watching your weight, ketchup is one condiment you don't have to worry about. One tablespoon is only 15 calories, 0 g fat and 181 mg sodium.

Crazy Cajun Burgers

Serves 4

⅓ cup finely crushed corn flakes

3 tablespoons ketchup

⅓ cup thinly sliced green onions

1 teaspoon pressed garlic

¼ cup canned diced mild or hot chili peppers

¼ to 2 teaspoons Cajun seasoning

¼ to 1 teaspoon green or red hot pepper sauce such as Tabasco (optional)

¼ teaspoon light salt

1 pound ground chicken, meat or vegetarian meat substitute

1 medium red, yellow or orange bell pepper

1 medium red onion

Nonfat or canola oil cooking spray

4 burger buns

1 medium ripe tomato, thinly sliced

4 to 8 leaves romaine or curly leaf lettuce

1 bottle spicy ketchup

1. **Preheat the grill** to the highest setting.

2. **Mix and shape the burgers.** In a 2- or 3-quart mixing bowl using a fork or spoon, evenly mix the corn flakes, ketchup, green onions, garlic, chili peppers, Cajun seasoning, hot pepper sauce and salt. Using your hands, gently fold the ground meat into the wet mixture.

When all ingredients are evenly distributed, divide the meat mixture into 4 equal portions. Wet hands and shape into burgers about 4 to 5 inches in diameter and no thicker than 3/4-inch. Set aside on a plate covered with plastic wrap in the refrigerator until ready to grill, up to 24 hours.

3. **Slice the peppers and onions.** Slice the peppers lengthwise into 1/2-inch strips. Slice the onions across the meridian into 4 1/2-inch thick slices.

4. **Grill the peppers, onions and burgers.** On small surface grills, grill the peppers and onions first, and then immediately grill the burgers. As the vegetables come off of the grill, keep them warm until serving time on a foil-covered serving platter.

On large surface grills, start with the food that takes the longest to grill, which in this recipe are the onions. Add the peppers and burgers a few minutes later so everything will be done simultaneously for a perfectly timed meal.

To grill, put the vegetables into a 3- to 4-cup bowl. As you toss them, spray all surfaces lightly with cooking spray. Grill according to the Grill Times opposite or until peppers are cooked through, yet tender-crisp and the onions are tender.

Spray each burger lightly on both sides with cooking spray and cook according to the Grill Times opposite until the meat reaches an internal temperature of 160°F on an instant-read thermometer.

5. **To serve,** use a slotted spoon to place even portions of the slaw on 4 plates or into 4 small bowls (the slaw is juicy, so you may want to use separate bowls to keep the burgers and buns from getting soggy). On each plate, place 2 lettuce leaves next to the slaw. Top the lettuce with a cooked burger. Top the burger with some grilled onions and a few strips of grilled pepper. Place a bun on each plate and serve, allowing diners to assemble their own burgers.

Grill Times

Two-Sided Contact Grill: Onions 7 to 10 minutes / peppers 6 to 8 minutes / burgers 6 to 7 minutes.

Hibachi Grill, Combination Grill or Infusion Grill: Onions 14 to 20 minutes / peppers 12 to 15 minutes / burgers 12 to 14 minutes. Turn vegetables and burgers halfway through the grilling time. Grills with lids may be covered halfway through the grilling time. Infusion grills with lids may be covered for the entire grilling time.

Substitutions:
If red, yellow or orange bell peppers aren't available, use green bell peppers. They won't be as sweet, because they are not as mature as their red or yellow cousins. Or drain a jar of roasted red or yellow bell peppers. Slice them, if necessary, before using as burger toppers.

Mix & Match

Serve the Stompin' Slaw on the next page with the main dishes from the following menus: Mardi Gras Wrap, page 215; How's Bayou? Louisiana Shrimp and Orange Brochettes, page 235.

Stompin' Slaw

Makes 4 (1 cup) servings

Slaw

1   bag preshredded slaw mix (about 3 cups)

⅓   cup shredded carrot

1   cup thinly sliced green bell pepper

¼   cup thinly sliced green onions

2   tablespoons canned diced mild or hot chili peppers

⅓   cup frozen petite white or yellow corn

Dressing

½   cup nonfat or light sour cream

½   cup nonfat or light mayonnaise

2   tablespoons apple cider vinegar

2   tablespoons all-fruit peach jam

¼   to 1 teaspoon Cajun seasoning

1. In a 6- or 8-cup bowl with a large spatula mix the slaw mix, grated carrot, bell pepper, green onion, canned chili peppers. Thaw the corn in a strainer under cool running water and drain well. Add it to the slaw mixture.

2. Mix the dressing in a 1- or 2-cup bowl, using a fork to mix the sour cream, mayonnaise, vinegar, jam and Cajun seasoning.

3. Using a rubber spatula, scrape the dressing onto the slaw, then mix thoroughly. Cover with plastic wrap and refrigerate until ready to serve or up to 24 hours.

Approximate Nutrients Per Serving of Entire Meal

Total Calories 364	Protein 34 g / 38%	Carbohydrate 51 g / 56%
Total Sugar 9 g	Fat Total 3 g / 7%	Saturated Fat 0.5 g / 1%
Cholesterol 65 mg	Sodium 831 mg	Fiber 7 g Calcium 156 mg

(Calculated with burger made with ground skinless chicken breast, a bun, romaine lettuce and 1 cup of slaw.)

Bengal Turkey Burgers with Grilled Apples, Chutney and Basmati Rice

When I first created this menu, the combined aroma of the burgers and Basmati rice transported me back to my grad school days when I cooked with my girlfriend, Malabika, in her New York City kitchen. A native of Calcutta, India, who was studying dance in the Big Apple, Malabika loved to show me the intricacies of regional Indian cooking. I have taken some liberties with Malabika's traditional techniques in this menu and used a prepared curry powder instead of taking time to make curry seasoning from scratch. To enhance the curry, I mixed in some ground cardamom, cinnamon, fresh ginger, and garlic. Applesauce and yogurt round out the flavors, and make normally dry ground turkey quite juicy. I serve this burger with Basmati rice, but it also tastes great in a bun or flatbread wrap, slathered with prepared chutney and topped with grilled apples.

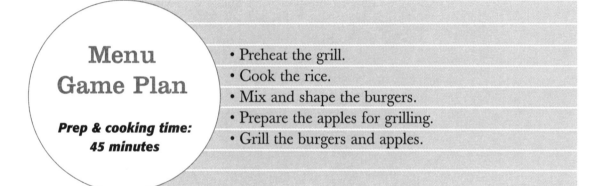

Menu Game Plan

Prep & cooking time: 45 minutes

- Preheat the grill.
- Cook the rice.
- Mix and shape the burgers.
- Prepare the apples for grilling.
- Grill the burgers and apples.

Cook's Notes

Curry powder is the commercial version of Garam Masala, a mixture of aromatic spices unique to Indian cooking. Recipes vary, but the predominant spices include black peppercorns, cumin seeds, cardamom, coriander seeds, cloves, nutmeg and cinnamon. When made at home, the curry spices are usually slow roasted to release their flavors, ground in a blender and stored for up to six months. Many Indian cooks have different Garam Masala mixtures for specific recipes.

Bengal Burgers

Serves 4

1/3 cup finely crushed nonfat or low-fat garlic croutons

2 tablespoons applesauce

2 tablespoons plain nonfat yogurt

3 tablespoons ketchup

2 teaspoons finely minced gingerroot

2 teaspoons pressed garlic

2 teaspoons curry powder, mild or hot

1/2 teaspoon light salt

1/2 teaspoon ground cinnamon

1/2 teaspoon ground cardamom (optional)

1 pound lean ground turkey

1/2 cup thinly sliced green onions

2 medium apples, skin left on

Nonfat or canola oil cooking spray

4 to 8 leaves romaine or curly leaf lettuce

Chutney (any flavor)

Lime wedges

1. **Preheat the grill** to the highest setting.

2. **Mix the burgers.** In a 2- or 3-quart mixing bowl, evenly mix the garlic croutons, applesauce, yogurt, ketchup, ginger, garlic, curry powder, salt, cinnamon and cardamom. Using your hands, gently fold the ground meat and green onions into the wet mixture. When all ingredients are evenly distributed, divide the meat mixture into 4 equal portions. Wet hands and shape burgers, about 4 to 5 inches in diameter and no thicker than 3/4-inch. Set aside on a plate covered with plastic wrap in the refrigerator until ready to grill, up to 24 hours.

3. **Prepare the apples.** Cut each apple in half. Remove the seeds with a melon baller and trim the stem ends with a sharp knife. Slice the halves into 1/2-inch-thick half moons.

4. **Grill the burgers and apples.** Spray each burger and apple slice lightly on both sides with cooking spray. If you have a small surface grill, grill the apples first and then the burgers. Keep the apples warm on a foil-covered plate.

On a larger surface grill, grill apples and burgers simultaneously. Grill according to the times below or until the apples are tender and the meat reaches an internal temperature of 160°F on an instant-read thermometer.

5. **To serve,** arrange equal portions of the rice on the side of 4 plates. Place 1 or 2 lettuce leaves next to the rice and top with a burger. Arrange grilled apple slices and 1 to 2 tablespoons of chutney near each burger and serve.

Grill Times

Two-Sided Contact Grill: Burgers 6 to 7 minutes / apples 3 minutes.

Hibachi Grill, Combination Grill or Infusion Grill: Burgers 12 to 14 minutes / apples 6 minutes. Turn the burgers and apples halfway through the grilling time. Grills with lids may be covered halfway through the grilling time. infusion grills with lids may be covered for the entire grilling time.

Basmati Rice

1½ cups white Basmati rice

1 tablespoon canola, corn or safflower oil

2¼ cups canned nonfat chicken broth

¼ cup yellow raisins

You can make the rice up to 2 days in advance; it freezes well in zippered freezer bags for up to 2 months.

1. In a fine-mesh colander under cool running water, rinse the rice until the water runs clear. Drain well.
2. In a 2-quart pot over medium heat, bring the oil to a slow sizzle.
3. Add the rinsed rice. Cook stirring constantly about 2 to 3 minutes until rice is coated with the oil and is slightly translucent.
4. Stir in the chicken broth and the raisins. Turn the heat to high then bring to a boil.
5. When the broth comes to a boil, turn the heat down immediately to a low simmer, cover, and cook for 15 to 20 minutes. Remove the pot from the heat. Do not lift lid and stir rice; let stand covered for 10 minutes before fluffing with a fork.

Variation:

Bengal Burger Wrap: Instead of serving this burger with rice, fold it in a warmed chapati (Indian flat bread sold in the refrigerator section of health food grocery stores) or a large warmed flour tortilla. Spread tortilla or chapati with prepared chutney and top with a lettuce leaf, a burger, grilled apples, and a dollop of nonfat sour cream or yogurt before folding up like a burrito. This burger also tastes great served on traditional hamburger buns.

Approximate Nutrients Per Serving of Entire Meal

Total Calories 623	Protein 41 g / 27%	Carbohydrate 100 g / 64%
Total Sugar 29 g	Fat Total 6 g / 9%	Saturated Fat .6 g / 1%
Cholesterol 82 mg	Sodium 548 mg	Fiber 6 g Calcium 87 mg

Pita the Great Lamb Burgers with Apricot Yogurt Sauce and Cucumber Feta Salad

I named this burger after Alexander the Great who, legend has it, introduced apricots to the Western world. Actually, Arab traders brought apricots to the Mediterranean from China where they were first cultivated, but why quibble? Stuffed into pita halves, these petite lamb burgers tantalize your taste buds with juxtaposing flavors of chopped sweet apricots and savory cumin, mint, and cayenne pepper. Couscous gives these burgers a tender, juicy texture that complements the crunchy cucumber feta salad. Whether you stuff the salad into the pitas along with the burgers or serve it on the side, I hope this "great" menu will please you as much as it does my family and friends.

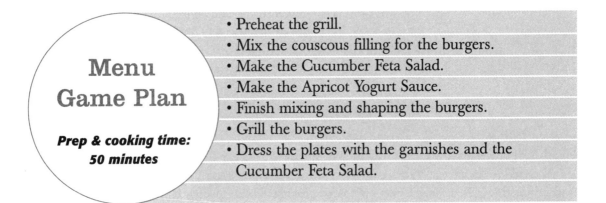

Menu Game Plan

Prep & cooking time: 50 minutes

- Preheat the grill.
- Mix the couscous filling for the burgers.
- Make the Cucumber Feta Salad.
- Make the Apricot Yogurt Sauce.
- Finish mixing and shaping the burgers.
- Grill the burgers.
- Dress the plates with the garnishes and the Cucumber Feta Salad.

Cook's Notes

Couscous is my favorite side dish to make when time is short but I still want to cook an exciting meal. Ready in 5 minutes, these delicious tiny grains of North African–style pasta taste similar to Italian pasta because both are made from semolina wheat. For a side dish, measure 1^1/$_3$ cups couscous into a bowl, add 2^1/$_4$ cups boiling water, cover, and let rest for 5 minutes until all of the liquid is absorbed.

One day when I ran out of breadcrumbs, my favorite extender for ground meat, I discovered that couscous is a terrific substitute. I use ^{1}/$_2$-cup couscous per pound of meat plus, ^{3}/$_4$ cup of liquid to help hydrate it. In this recipe, I combined ketchup and eggs to make up the liquid.

Pita the Great Burgers

Serves 4

½ cup couscous

½ cup finely chopped onion

¼ cup finely chopped
dried apricots

¼ cup ketchup

¼ cup finely chopped fresh
mint or 2 tablespoons dried

2 large eggs, beaten or ½ cup
egg substitute

1 teaspoon pressed garlic

1 teaspoon ground cumin

¼ teaspoon light salt

⅛ to ½ teaspoon cayenne
pepper

1 pound lean ground lamb

4 pita bread rounds, cut in half

2 medium tomatoes

8 Romaine lettuce or curly leaf
lettuce leaves

Fresh mint leaves (optional)

Nonfat or canola oil cooking
spray

1. Preheat the grill to the highest setting.

2. Mix and shape the burgers. In a 2- or 3-quart mixing bowl using a fork or spoon, evenly mix the couscous, onion, apricots, ketchup, mint, eggs, garlic, cumin, salt and cayenne pepper. Let mixture stand 10 minutes. Using your hands, gently fold the meat into the wet mixture.

When all ingredients are evenly distributed, divide the meat mixture into 8 equal portions. Wet hands and shape burgers, about 2 to 3 inches in diameter and no thicker than ½-inch. Set aside on a plate covered with plastic wrap in the refrigerator until ready to grill, up to 24 hours.

3. Prepare the optional garnishes. Slice the pita breads in half, and the tomatoes into ¼-inch-thick half moons. Wash and dry the lettuce and herbs.

4. Grill the burgers. Spray each burger lightly on both sides with cooking spray. Grill according to the times below until the internal temperature reaches 160°F on an instant-read thermometer.

5. To serve, use a slotted spoon to put even portions of the cucumber salad on 4 plates or into 4 small bowls (the salad is juicy, so you may want to serve it in separate bowls so your burgers and pita don't get soggy). Place two lettuce leaves next to the salad or the small bowl. Top each lettuce leaf with two cooked burgers; garnish with some fresh mint leaves and surround with two pita bread halves. Place the apricot-yogurt sauce on the table with a serving spoon. Diners can stuff each pita half with a burger and some lettuce and tomatoes then drizzle with one to two tablespoons of the apricot-yogurt sauce.

Grill Times

Two-Sided Contact Grill: 6 to 7 minutes.

Hibachi Grill, Combination Grill or Infusion Grill: 12 to 14 minutes. Turn the burgers halfway through the grilling time. Grills with lids may be covered halfway through the grilling time. Infusion grills with lids may be covered for the entire grilling time.

Apricot Yogurt Sauce

Makes 8 (2 tablespoon) servings

½ cup plain yogurt

½ cup thinly sliced green
    onions

¼ cup ketchup

¼ cup apricot jam

½ teaspoon garlic powder

Pinch to ⅛ teaspoon cayenne
    pepper (optional)

Fresh mint leaves (optional)

This yogurt sauce keeps well in an airtight container in your refrigerator for up to 1 week. Use any leftover sauce as a marinade or condiment for grilled lamb chops, chicken or pork.

1. In a 2-cup bowl, mix the yogurt, green onions, ketchup, jam, garlic powder and cayenne thoroughly with a fork.
2. Using a rubber spatula, scrape the sauce into a decorative bowl, garnish with fresh mint leaves (if using), cover with plastic wrap and set aside in the refrigerator until ready to serve.

Cucumber Feta Salad

Makes 4 (¾ cup) servings

Salad

2   cups diced cucumber (preferably hothouse)

1   cup cherry tomatoes, sliced in half (or 2 medium ripe tomatoes, diced)

¼   cup thinly sliced green onions

¼   cup crumbled feta cheese

Dressing

¼   cup plain nonfat or low-fat yogurt

2   tablespoons lemon juice

2   tablespoons finely chopped fresh mint or 2 teaspoons dried

1   tablespoon extra-virgin olive oil

½   teaspoon pressed garlic

½   teaspoon light salt

Freshly ground pepper, to taste

1. Slice the cucumbers, tomatoes, and green onion and put them in a 4- to 6-cup bowl. With a spatula, fold the feta cheese into the vegetables.

2. In a 1-cup measure or bowl, thoroughly mix the yogurt, lemon juice, mint, olive oil, garlic, salt and pepper with a fork.

3. Pour the dressing over the salad and using a rubber spatula gently fold it into the salad until all ingredients are evenly coated. Cover the bowl with plastic wrap and set aside in the refrigerator until ready to serve or up to 24 hours.

Approximate Nutrients Per Serving of Entire Meal

Total Calories 584	Protein 33 g / 23%	Carbohydrate 61 g / 43%
Total Sugar 15 g	Fat Total 21 g / 34%	Saturated Fat 8 g / 13%
Cholesterol 84 mg	Sodium 835 mg	Fiber 4 g Calcium 215 mg

(Calculated with 2 small burgers made with ground lamb, 1 pita bread round, 2 tablespoons of yogurt sauce and 1 cup of cucumber salad.)

Calypso Chicken Burgers with Jerked Cranberry Sauce and Sweet Potato Oven Fries

Jerk cooking is Jamaican grilling at its finest although Jamaicans don't quite agree about the exact meaning of "jerk". Some say it comes from the way the meat is turned over and over (or jerked) on the grill. Others say the word describes how the cook pulls a portion of meat off the grill to serve. My taste buds define the term as divine. For this menu I've re-created the authentic hot-sweet spiciness of Jamaican jerk flavorings the easy way—with prepared jerk paste or dry jerk seasoning. Look for both in the specialty condiment section of your grocery store or create your own version with my easy jerk seasoning recipe (see page 54). In a pinch, you can substitute your favorite hot sauce. The Jerked Cranberry Sauce doubles as a burger condiment and a dip for the sweet potato oven fries. Leftover sauce will keep in an airtight container in your refrigerator for up to 2 months. It is also delicious as a marinade and baste for meat, poultry, or fish.

Menu Game Plan

Prep & cooking time: 50 to 55 minutes

- Preheat the grill.
- Preheat the oven.
- Prepare and bake the Sweet Potato Oven Fries.
- Mix and shape the burgers.
- Grill the burgers.
- Make the Cranberry Jerk Sauce.
- Lay out plates and place the garnishes on them.

Cook's Notes

Notes

Ginger is one of my favorite ingredients for burgers, grill marinades, and seasoning pastes. Its natural oils perfume the food with a pungent aroma and add sharp, spicy-hot flavor. Ginger also contains a natural enzyme that tenderizes. A native of Southeast Asia, ginger was brought to Jamaica by the Spanish in about 1525 and soon became an important cash crop. Jamaicans use it to flavor everything from Jerk sauces, marinades, soups, stews, baked goods and fruit salads to ginger beer. Mature ginger, which is what we usually find in the produce section of the grocery store, has a thick skin that must be peeled away before using.

Calypso Burgers

Serves 4

⅓ cup finely crushed low-fat or nonfat garlic croutons

1 large egg white

½ cup thinly sliced green onions

¼ cup chili sauce

1½ teaspoons pressed garlic

1½ teaspoons freshly grated gingerroot

⅛ to ½ teaspoon jerk paste or dry jerk seasoning

⅓ cup dried cranberries

1 pound ground chicken or turkey

Nonfat or canola oil cooking spray

4 hamburger buns

4 romaine lettuce leaves

2 medium ripe tomatoes, sliced

½ red onion, thinly sliced

4 dill pickles, thinly sliced

1. Preheat the grill to the highest setting.

2. Mix and shape the burgers. In a 2- or 3-quart mixing bowl, using a fork or spoon, evenly mix the crushed croutons, egg white, green onions, chili sauce, garlic, ginger, jerk paste and cranberries.

Using your hands, gently fold the ground meat or poultry into the wet mixture.

When all ingredients are evenly distributed, divide the meat mixture into 4 equal portions. Wet hands and shape burgers, about 4 to 5 inches in diameter and no thicker than ¾-inch. Set aside on a plate covered with plastic wrap in the refrigerator until ready to grill, up to 24 hours.

3. Grill the burgers. Spray each burger lightly on both sides with cooking spray. Put the burgers on the grill and cook according to the times below until the internal temperature reaches 160°F on an instant-read thermometer.

4. To serve, spoon even portions of the potatoes onto 4 plates. Place a lettuce leaf beside the potatoes and top with a burger, tomato and onion. Spoon 2 tablespoons of the cranberry jerk sauce next to the burger (use as a burger condiment and a dip for the potatoes). Artfully arrange the pickle slices in a fan near the sauce. Offer buns on a separate platter and serve, allowing diners to assemble their own burgers.

Grill Times

Two-Sided Contact Grill: *6 to 7 minutes.*

Hibachi Grill, Combination Grill or Infusion Grill: *12 to 14 minutes. Turn the burgers halfway through the grilling time. Grills with lids may be covered halfway through the grilling time. Infusion grills with lids may be covered for the entire grilling time.*

Sweet Potato Oven Fries

Makes 4 (1¼ cup) servings

2 to 3 medium-sized sweet potatoes

2 large egg whites or ¼ cup egg substitute

⅛ to ½ teaspoon jerk paste or dry jerk seasoning, to taste*

⅓ cup finely crushed nonfat or low-fat garlic croutons

Dash ground nutmeg (optional)

½ teaspoon light salt to taste

Nonfat or canola oil cooking spray

1. Preheat oven to 450°F.
2. Prepare the sweet potatoes. Leave the skins on and slice the potatoes into ½-inch-thick wedges and put into a large 2- to 3-quart mixing bowl.
3. In a 4-cup mixing bowl whisk the egg whites, jerk paste or seasoning, crushed croutons, nutmeg and salt. Pour the mixture over potatoes and toss, using your hands to evenly coat them.
4. Arrange the potatoes in a single layer on a nonstick baking sheet. Spray potatoes lightly with cooking spray. Bake 20 to 25 minutes until potatoes are crisp and golden brown. Using a spatula or tongs, turn potatoes halfway through the cooking time.

Cranberry Jerk Sauce

Makes 16 (1 tablespoon) servings

½ cup chili sauce

½ cup canned cranberry sauce made from whole cranberries

⅛ to ½ teaspoon jerk paste or dry jerk seasoning*

1. While the burgers are grilling and the potatoes baking, in a 2-cup bowl mix the chili sauce, cranberry sauce and jerk seasoning thoroughly with a fork. Set aside until serving time. If not using within an hour, store in refrigerator in an airtight container for up to 2 months.

* If jerk seasoning is unavailable, see page 54 for homemade recipe.

Approximate Nutrients Per Serving of Entire Meal

Total Calories 611	Protein 35 g / 23%	Carbohydrate 113 g / 72%
Total Sugar 53 g	Fat Total 4 g / 5%	Saturated Fat .61 g / 1%
Cholesterol 66 mg	Sodium 2,115 mg	Fiber 10 g / Calcium 117 mg

(Calculated with burger made from ground chicken breast, a bun, 2 tablespoons jerked cranberry relish and 1¼ cups sweet potato fries.)

Super Steaks, Chops, and Tenderloins

Do you long to grill a steak or chop the way the chef does at your favorite restaurant . . . succulent, juicy and, in a word, perfect? In this chapter, you'll find solutions for making professional-style grilled beef, lamb and pork the centerpiece of a wide variety of easy-to-make meals. Does your mouth water at the mention of down-home Farmhouse Steak with Savory Buttermilk Gravy, page 103? Or, are you are tempted by more exotic fare like Malaysian-Style Beef and Pear Satays with Lemony Peanut Sauce over Coconut Rice, page 143? Whatever your pleasure, I suggest reading the following carefully, then start by making Basic Power Grilled Steak or Chops, page 47. Once you master the easy grilling techniques in this introductory recipe, your steaks and chops will be perfect every time.

How to Grill a Perfect Steak or Chop—Beef, Pork or Lamb

Solution 1: Choose the Kindest Cuts

The single most important factor in orchestrating a fast and successful steak dinner is selecting the tenderest meat you can afford. That's because tender meat grills faster and begins absorbing the flavors of a marinade or spice rub in as little as 20 minutes. You can marinate longer if you wish (check marinating chart for exact times on page 58), but if you are in a hurry, 20 minutes will give you a flavorful result.

The tenderest cuts of beef, lamb and pork come from the back of each animal where it does the least amount of work. These cuts include the sirloin, top loin (New York strip steak), and tenderloin. Skirt steak and flank steak, which come from the belly (another underexercised part of the animal), though not quite as tender as the loin cuts, also make great steaks. Whether you purchase your meat from an old-fashioned meat market or an upscale supermarket, consult a knowledgeable butcher when in doubt about the right cut of meat for particular recipes. Since the butcher cuts each piece of meat, he will have the most accurate information about what is in the case or under the plastic.

Solution 2: Choose Choice Grade Meat

The U.S. Department of Agriculture classifies meat into 3 grades of eating quality: Prime, Choice, and Select. The age, color, texture and the amount of marbling (veins of fat) running through the meat determines its grade. The more marbling, the tastier the meat, the higher the grade. Prime, the highest quality grade with the most fat marbling, is usually reserved for specialty butcher shops and restaurants. Most grocery stores offer Choice and Select. I always use Choice cuts because they have a moderate amount of marbling, which keeps them juicy and tender after grilling. Select contains the least amount of marbling and makes a drier and tougher grilled steak or chop.

Best Cuts for Steak and Chops – Choice Grade (1-inch-thick)		Nutritional Analysis *In 3-ounce serving cooked/ 4 ounces raw boneless, fat trimmed to 1/4-inch or less before cooking.*			
BEEF		Cal.	Fat	Sat. Fat	Protein
Extremely Tender	Tenderloin (boneless) market names: fillet mignon, fillet de boeuf, fillet steak, Chateaubriand	178	8 g/ 43%	4g	24g
Tender	Sirloin (with bone) market names: flat bone, pin bone, round-bone, wedge bone	161	6 g/ 35%	2g	25g
	Top Loin (boneless) market names: New York strip steak, strip steak, boneless club steak, Kansas City steak, Veiny steak, hotel-style steak	163	6 g/ 35%	2g	25g
	Top Loin (with bone) market names: Club Steak, Country Club Steak, Delmonico, Shell Steak, Sirloin Strip, Strip	102	4 g/ 35%	1 g	16 g
	Skirt Steak or Flank Steak	180	9g/ 46%	4g	24g
	Porterhouse or T-bone, lean	181	9g/ 48%	3g	23g
	Rib Steak	172	8g/ 45%	3g	23g
	Rib Eye market names: Delmonico, Spencer	188	10g/ 48%	4g	24g
Somewhat Tender	Top Sirloin (boneless) market names: Sirloin Butt, London Broil	163	6g/ 35%	2g	26g
LAMB					
Most Tender	Loin, lean	194	9g/ 42%	3g	26g
	Rib chop	214	16g/ 75%	7g	13g
	Shoulder arm chop (boneless), lean	170	8g/ 42%	11g	19g
	Sirloin, leg of lamb (boneless), lean	143	6g/ 42%	2g	19g
PORK					
Most Tender	Tenderloin	139	4g/ 28%	1g	24g
	Pork Loin, lean	144	6g/ 38%	2g	21g
	Pork Loin chop (with bone)	175	11g/ 59%	4g	17g
	Sirloin pork chops	232	15g/ 61%	5g	22g
	Rib chop (with bone)	237	15g/ 60%	5g	23g
Tender	Blade chop (with bone)	167	13g/ 71%	5g	12g

Solution 3: Choose the Best Thickness and Weight

For even and fast grilling, I recommend 4- to 10-ounce steaks and chops no thinner than 1/2 inch, no thicker than 1 inch. It is easy to overcook steaks and chops on the grill that are thinner than 1/2 inch and weigh 3 ounces or less. Steaks and chops thicker than 1 inch and over 10 ounces may take longer than 20 minutes to grill and can easily burn and get tough on the outside while the inside remains uncooked.

Cooking smaller pieces of meat not only is a good rule of thumb for getting out of your kitchen faster, but it is also healthier. The American Dietetic Association, American Heart Association, and the American College of Sports Medicine, among others, all suggest that a healthy portion of meat is 3 to 4 ounces cooked (4 to 5 ounces raw). Can't resist those large juicy steaks but would like to keep your waistline within reason? Balance the fat and calories in the steak by cutting down on the amount of fat and calories for several meals before and after you indulge.

Solution 4: Grill the Meat to the Right Internal Temperature

As we discussed at the beginning of the book, the best way to get perfect results every time, is to check the internal temperature of the meat as it grills using an instant-read thermometer. (See page 48 for instructions.)

The following chart gives 2 options for gauging the approximate internal temperature of your meats. Chef's Choice gives the temperatures for doneness frequently used by professional chefs. The USDA's internal temperature recommendations, 10° to 15° higher than those used by professional chefs, are more conservative because of their concern for public safety. I leave it to your discretion to decide which one to use.

Beef, Veal or Lamb

Meat	Raw serving size Note: 4 to 5 ounces raw becomes 3 to 4 ounces when cooked	Degree of doneness (interior color)	Approximate grilling time refrigerator temperature, grilled on highest setting; for Two-sided Contact Grill, divide time in half	Chef's Choice temperature	USDA Temperature recommendation
Steak or chops of any kind	4 to 5 ounces 1/2- to 1-inch thick	Very Rare (red) Rare (red) Medium rare (pink) Medium (lt. pink) Medium well (brown)	7 to 8 minutes 8 to 10 minutes 9 to 12 minutes 10 to 14 minutes 12 to 16 minutes	115° to 120°F 125° to 130°F 130° to 140°F 140° to 150°F 150° to 165°F	No recommendation 140°F 150°F 160°F 170°F
Ground meat patties	4 to 5 ounces, 3/4-inch thick	Medium well (brown)	10 to 12 minutes	160°F	160°F
Kebabs	1-inch cubes	Rare (red) Medium rare (pink) Medium (light pink) Medium well (brown)	8 to 10 minutes 9 to 12 minutes 10 to 14 minutes 12 to 16 minutes	125° to 130°F 130° to 140°F 140° to 150°F 150° to 165°F	140°F 150°F 160°F 170°F

Pork

Do you overcook your pork because you want to kill trichinosis parasites? Overcook no more! To kill those bad bugs, you only have to cook pork to 137°F or to medium rare. This may be a bit too pink for most people, though. To prevent overcooking lean pork chops or pork tenderloin yet have them tender, juicy, and still pink in the center, don't cook them over 145° to 150°F, or medium. At this internal temperature, the meat will be slightly pink in the center. For those who like extremely dry pork, I have included the medium-well and well cooking times and temperatures. But please be warned: if you cook lean pork cuts such as tenderloin or loin to 160°F or above, your meat will be dried out because high internal temperatures make the connective tissue become harder and less elastic, and the high heat tends to push the moisture out of the meat.

Meat	Raw serving/ Serving size Note: 4 to 5 ounces raw becomes 3 to 4 ounces when cooked	Degree of doneness (interior color)	Approximate grilling time refrigerator temperature, grilled on highest setting; for Two-sided Contact Grill, divide time in half	Chef's choice temperature recommendation	USDA temperature recommendation
Chops, bone in or boneless	4 to 5 ounces, 1- to 1½-inches-thick	Medium (light pink)	10 to 14 minutes	145° to 150°F	160°F
		Medium Well (brown)	11 to 15 minutes	155° to 160°F	160°F
		Well (brown)	12 to 16 minutes	160° to 170°F	170°F
Tenderloin, butterflied, or loin scallops	¼ to ½ pound, ¾-to 1½-inches thick	Medium	10 to 14 minutes	145° to 150°F	160°F
		Medium Well (brown)	11 to 15 minutes	155° to 160°F	160°F
Ground meat patties	4 to 5 ounces, ¾-inch-thick	Medium well (brown)	10 to 12 minutes	160°F	160°F

Solution 5: Season with a little salt

As I discussed in "Seasoning Solutions" at the beginning of the book, salting meat before grilling really does enhance the flavor in a big way and does not dry the meat out (see page 36). If you use a very small amount of salt to improve the flavor, especially light salt, you won't be adding a huge amount of sodium per serving. I like to use anywhere between ½ teaspoon to 1 teaspoon for 1¼ pounds of meat, depending on what the other seasonings are in the recipe.

Farmhouse Steaks with Savory Buttermilk Gravy and Garlicky Smashed Potatoes

Do a juicy farmhouse style steak and mashed potatoes smothered in milky pan gravy tickle your taste buds but torture your calorie conscience? No problem! This menu delivers enough flavor to satisfy your comfort food cravings without the fat of traditional down-home recipes. Instead of pan-frying your steak in grease, you'll season it in a full-bodied Buttermilk Marinade Paste before grilling it fat-free. My Savory Buttermilk Gravy is made with just a tablespoon of fat instead of a pan full and my easy-to-make Garlicky Smashed Potatoes get their flavor from light garlic cheese spread that you can find at the cheese counter of your supermarket.

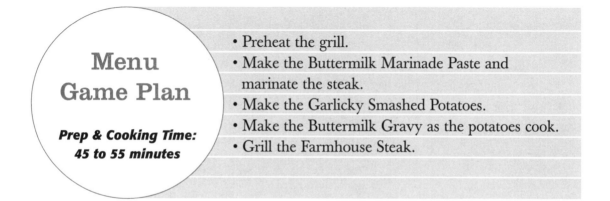

Menu Game Plan

Prep & Cooking Time: 45 to 55 minutes

- Preheat the grill.
- Make the Buttermilk Marinade Paste and marinate the steak.
- Make the Garlicky Smashed Potatoes.
- Make the Buttermilk Gravy as the potatoes cook.
- Grill the Farmhouse Steak.

Cook's Notes

Buttermilk was once an American staple. Savvy cooks made the most of buttermilk's high acidity to tenderize baked goods. They also used it as a tenderizing ingredient in marinades such as in this menu. Its thick, sticky texture makes it a good "glue" for holding coatings onto fish, meat and poultry when deep frying. Prior to the 1940's and 1950's, the era of commercial dairies, buttermilk was the liquid squeezed out when cultured cream was churned into butter. Today, the only thing rich about buttermilk is its name. In the United States, commercial buttermilk is no longer made from cream. Instead, nonfat or low-fat milk is cultured with special bacteria to produce the tangy flavor and thick consistency. Buttermilk contains about 2 grams of fat and 91 calories per 8-ounce serving, so don't be afraid to use it.

Farmhouse Steaks

Serves 4

Buttermilk Marinade Paste

½ to 1 teaspoon light salt

½ to 1 teaspoon freshly ground pepper

3 teaspoons dried thyme

1 tablespoon pressed garlic

1 tablespoon Worcestershire sauce

1 tablespoon buttermilk

Steak

1 1¼ pound lean boneless top loin steak*

Finely chopped parsley

Ripe tomatoes or cherry tomatoes, sliced

1. Preheat the grill to the highest setting.

2. Make the Buttermilk Marinade Paste and marinate the meat. In a small bowl use a fork to mix the salt, pepper, thyme, garlic, Worcestershire sauce and buttermilk.

Place the meat in a 1-gallon zippered freezer-weight storage bag, a 1-quart airtight container, or a shallow square glass dish (8 x 8 x 2-inch).

Scrape the marinade paste onto the meat, then, with your fingertips, smear the marinade paste onto all sides of the meat. Squeeze the air out of the bag and zip it closed, or cover the container or dish and marinate in the refrigerator for 20 minutes or up to 24 hours.

3. Grill the meat. Grill the steaks according to the Grill Times opposite or until the internal temperature reaches the doneness you desire on an instant read thermometer. Consult the grilling chart on page 101 for exact internal temperatures: 140° to 150°F for medium.

4. To serve, put 1-cup of the Garlicky Mashed Potatoes on one side of 4 dinner plates. Put ¼ cup of the gravy on the other half of the plate and put a grilled steak on top of the gravy. Sprinkle with finely chopped parsley, garnish with fresh tomato slices or cherry tomatoes and serve with steamed green beans and fresh biscuits.

Substitutions:
Instead of beef for the farmhouse steak, substitute pork loin medallions or turkey breast medallions.

* Top loin steak is also known as strip, Kansas City and New York. Have your butcher cut the steak into 4 equal pieces ½- to 1-inch thick.

Two-Sided Contact Grill: *5 to 7 minutes for medium.*

Hibachi Grill, Combination Grill or Infusion Grill: *10 to 14 minutes for medium. Turn the steaks halfway through the grilling time. Grills with lids may be covered halfway through the grilling time. Infusion grills with lids may be covered for the entire grilling time.*

Buttermilk Gravy

Makes 6 (¼ cup) servings

½   cup buttermilk

1   cup nonfat canned chicken or beef broth

¼   teaspoon dried thyme

½   teaspoon Worcestershire sauce

1   tablespoon canola oil

1   cup diced white or yellow onion

1   teaspoon minced garlic

1½ tablespoons flour

Light salt and pepper to taste

Dash hot pepper sauce such as Tabasco (optional)

You can make this delicious gravy 2 ways. For a lighter flavor, use fat-free chicken broth. For a richer, more complex flavor, use fat-free beef broth. This recipe can be made up to 48 hours in advance of serving if refrigerated in an airtight container. It can also be frozen up to 3 months. To reheat refrigerated sauce, whisk constantly over medium heat, or reheat covered in the microwave for 2 to 3 minutes on high (100% power). If the sauce is too thick, whisk in a couple of tablespoons of buttermilk or broth. To reheat frozen sauce, defrost in the microwave and reheat in the microwave according to the instructions above.

1. In a 2-cup measure, whisk the buttermilk, broth, thyme, and Worcestershire sauce. Set aside near the stove.
2. In a 1-quart pot, heat the oil over medium heat until sizzling. Add the onions and garlic and stir with a spoon to coat evenly with the oil. Cover the pot and cook, lifting the cover to stir every 2 minutes until the onions are tender, about 5 to 7 minutes.
3. Whisk in the flour and cook, whisking constantly, for about 30 seconds.
4. Whisk in the buttermilk mixture, bring the heat to medium-high and bring to a boil, whisking constantly, about 3 to 5 minutes or until thickened. Be careful not to turn the heat too high or the buttermilk will burn onto the bottom of the pot.
5. Remove from the heat and season to taste with salt, pepper and hot pepper sauce. Cover until ready to serve.

Garlicky Smashed Potatoes

Makes 4 (1 cup) servings

2   pounds thin skinned
     potatoes

¾   cup light garlic and herb
     flavored cheese spread
     (1 6.5-ounce container)

¾   cup nonfat canned chicken
     or beef broth

Light salt and freshly ground
     pepper to taste

You can refrigerate this recipe for up to 48 hours in advance of serving or freeze it in an airtight container for up to 3 months.

1. Do not peel the potatoes, but dice them into about 1-inch square pieces. The skins are part of the dish and get mashed in with everything else.
2. Put a steamer basket into a 3- to 4-quart pot with a tight fitting lid. Fill it with water to cover the bottom of the pot but not rising above the bottom of the basket. Cover and bring to a boil over high heat. Add the potatoes, cover and steam about 15 to 20 minutes, until the potatoes are tender but not falling apart. Drain the potatoes well then put them into a 2 or 3 quart casserole.
3. Using a potato masher or large fork, mash the potatoes, gradually adding the cheese spread and the broth. Mash in salt and pepper to taste. Cover to keep warm in a 325°F oven until ready to serve.

Variations:

Onion Mashed Potatoes: Sauté 1 cup chopped onion in 1-tablespoon olive or canola oil until tender. Mash into the hot potatoes along with other ingredients above. Or mash in ½ cup thinly sliced greed onions with the rest of the ingredients above.

Pesto Potatoes: Substitute ¾ cup pesto sauce for the garlic and herb spreadable cheese.

Mix & Match ▷ Serve the Garlicky Smashed New Potatoes with the main dishes from the following menus: Smart and Saucy Rosemary-Cherry Lamb Chops, page 119; Not-So-French Dijon Pepper Steaks, page 107; Cowboy Kebabs with Easy Ridin' BBQ Sauce, page 147; Chicken Romagna, page 159; A Turkey for All Seasons, page 163.

Approximate Nutrients Per Serving of Entire Meal

Total Calories 627	Protein 53 g / 34%	Carbohydrate 57 g / 36%
Total Sugar 6 g	Fat Total 21 g / 30%	Saturated Fat 4 g / 6%
Cholesterol 133 mg	Sodium 719 mg	Fiber 5 g Calcium 121 mg

Not-So-French Dijon Pepper Steaks and Grilled New Potatoes

The French traditionally make pepper steak or "steak au poivre" by coating the meat with freshly crushed peppercorns then frying it in fat. Sometimes the pepper steak is grilled or broiled and served with a peppercorn sauce. In my version, lemon pepper accents a flavorful marinade of Dijon-style mustard, Worcestershire sauce and vinegar. Instead of a heavy butter-based sauce, my rich tasting mushroom sauté balances the full-bodied marinade without adding much fat to the overall menu.

Menu Game Plan

Prep & Cooking Time: 45 to 50 minutes

- Preheat the grill.
- Marinate the steaks.
- Steam the potatoes.
- Make the Mixed Mushroom Sauté.
- Grill the potatoes and the steaks.

Cook's Notes

Shallots are small garlic-shaped brown bulbs that taste like a combination of onion and garlic. Prized for the subtle flavor they impart, shallots can be substituted for equal amounts of onion in any recipe

Don't want to take the time to slice mushrooms? Many grocery store produce sections sell presliced, fresh mushrooms in boxes. I have found both button mushrooms and Cremini mushrooms presliced.

You can use any variety of mushroom for my Mixed Mushroom Sauté. My favorites are cremini—flavorful brown mushrooms that look like button mushrooms, but have a more robust flavor—and Porcini—wild mushrooms with a meaty, earthy flavor. Porcini mushrooms are usually sold dried and must be reconstituted before using. To hydrate, put them in a microwavable pot, pour boiling water over them to cover, microwave covered on high (100% power) for about 4 to 5 minutes. Remove from the oven and let stand oin the hot water 10 to 15 minutes, or until tender. Three ounces of dried mushrooms makes 1 pound reconstituted.

Dijon Pepper Steaks and Grilled New Potatoes

Serves 4

2 tablespoons grainy Dijon-style mustard

2 tablespoons Worcestershire Sauce

1 teaspoon cider vinegar

1 teaspoon pressed garlic

1 to 2 teaspoons lemon pepper

1 teaspoon light salt

4 tenderloin steaks, such as New York (1¼ pounds total)

2 pounds small, thin-skinned potatoes

Nonfat or olive oil cooking spray

Light salt and freshly ground pepper to taste

1. Preheat the grill to the highest setting.

2. Make the Marinade. In a small bowl, mix the mustard, Worcestershire sauce, vinegar, garlic, lemon pepper, and salt with a fork. Set aside until ready to use.

3. Marinate the steaks. Place meat in a 1-gallon zippered freezer-weight storage bag, a 1-quart airtight container or a shallow square glass dish (8 x 8 x 2 inch).

Scrape the marinade paste onto the meat, then, with your fingertips, smear the marinade paste onto all sides of the meat. Squeeze the air out of the bag and zip it closed, or cover the container or dish and marinate in the refrigerator for 20 minutes. Do not marinate for longer than 2 hours. This marinade is strong and can overpower the flavor of the meat.

4. Steam the potatoes. Slice the potatoes in half. Put a steamer basket into a 3- to 4-quart pot with a tight fitting lid. Fill it with water to cover the bottom of the pot but not rising above the bottom of the basket. Cover and bring the water to a boil over high heat. Add the potatoes, cover and steam about 12 to 15 minutes, until the potatoes are tender enough to be pierced with a fork but still slightly resistant. Drain well.

Put the potatoes in a bowl and spray with the cooking spray then season with salt and pepper to taste as you lightly toss them.

5. Grill the potatoes and steaks. If you have a smaller grill, grill the potatoes first, then the steaks. If your grill is larger, grill everything simultaneously.

Grill the potatoes cut side down until golden brown grill marks appear according to the Grill Times opposite. Since the potatoes are pre-cooked, you don't have to turn them over when using a Hibachi-style, Combination or Infusion Grill. Transfer grilled potatoes to a platter covered with aluminum foil to keep them warm until serving time.

Remove each steak from the marinade and lightly spray both sides with cooking spray before placing on the grill. Grill the steaks according to the Grill Times below or until the internal temperature reaches the doneness you desire on an instant read thermometer. Consult the grilling chart on page 101 for exact internal temperatures: 140° to 150°F for medium.

6. To serve, put equal amounts of the grilled potatoes and one steak on 4 dinner plates. Top each steak with ½ cup of the mushrooms. Serve immediately with Quick Spinach Sauté, page 114, a steamed vegetable like broccoli or a side salad of mixed field greens.

Grill Times

Two-Sided Contact Grill: *Potatoes 4 to 5 minutes / steaks 3 to 5 minutes for medium.*

Hibachi Grill, Combination Grill or Infusion Grill: *Potatoes 8 to 10 minutes / steaks 10 to 14 minutes for medium. Turn the steaks halfway through the grilling time. Grills with lids may be covered halfway through the grilling time. Infusion grills with lids may be covered for the entire grilling time.*

Mixed Mushroom Sauté

Makes 4 (½ cup) servings

- ⅓ cup canned double strength beef broth or consommé
- 1 tablespoon Worcestershire sauce
- ½ teaspoon light salt
- ¼ teaspoon freshly ground pepper
- 1 tablespoon olive oil
- ½ cup diced shallots or white onions
- 1 teaspoon pressed garlic
- 1 pound fresh mushrooms, any type, sliced

Make this steak topping with a combination of your favorite mushrooms . . . button, Cremini, Portobello, Porcini, etc. This can be made 24 hours in advance of serving and reheated in the microwave. See reheating instructions below.

1. In a 1-cup bowl or measure, mix the beef broth, Worcestershire, salt and pepper with a fork. Set aside.
2. In a large nonstick skillet, heat the oil over medium-high heat.
3. With a large spoon or spatula, stir in the shallots and garlic, sautéing for 1 minute.
4. Stir in the mushrooms to coat evenly with the oil. Pour in the beef broth mixture. Cover the skillet with a cover or large piece of aluminum foil and cook for 3 minutes.
5. Uncover and stir. Cook uncovered 10 minutes longer, stirring occasionally, boiling the liquids rapidly until they have evaporated.
6. Serve immediately or cover immediately to keep warm.
7. If making ahead, cover and refrigerate. To reheat, transfer the mushroom sauté to a microwavable casserole and reheat by microwaving covered 2 to 3 minutes on high (100% power).

Approximate Nutrients Per Serving of Entire Meal

Total Calories 535	Protein 40 g / 30%	Carbohydrate 58 g / 44%
Total Sugar 4 g	Fat Total 15 g / 26%	Saturated Fat 5 g / 8%
Cholesterol 96 mg	Sodium 1191 mg	Fiber 5 g Calcium 62 mg

Provencal Kissed Veal Chops with Easy Mushroom Risotto and Quick Spinach Sauté

When I want to brighten my cooking with the flavors of Southern France, I reach for my mixture of Herbes de Provence. I call it my sun-in-a-jar because it combines many of the fragrant herbs that grow in wild profusion under the nurturing Provencal sun: savory, rosemary, marjoram, oregano, basil, thyme and lavender. If I can't find Herbes de Province at my local gourmet store, I make my own concoction from dry herbs. (See recipe on page 112.) For a quick main dish, I like to rub a generous sprinkle directly on meat or poultry just before grilling. Even more delicious is a wine-based marinade perfumed with Herbes de Provence such as the one for veal chops in this menu. When matched with Easy Mushroom Risotto and Quick Spinach Sauté, these veal chops become a delicacy that reflects the vivid sun kissed spirit of Provencal cuisine.

Menu Game Plan

**Prep & Cooking Time:
50 to 60 minutes**

- Preheat the grill.
- Marinate the veal.
- Make the Easy Mushroom Risotto.
- Make the Quick Spinach Sauté.
- Grill the veal.

Cook's Notes

Contrary to popular belief, alcohol does not evaporate completely when cooked. A 1992 study done by the Department of Food, Science, and Human Nutrition at Washington State University in Pullman, Washington, revealed that between 5 to 85% of the alcohol was retained in 6 popular recipes after cooking. Included in these were a pot roast cooked in red wine for over 2 hours which retained 5% alcohol; Cherries Jubilee, flamed for 48 seconds, retained 75% alcohol; and Grand Marnier Dessert Sauce where the Grand Marnier was added to hot sauce just before serving, retained 85% alcohol.

If you don't drink alcohol, simply substitute sparkling grape or apple juice.

Veal Chops

Serves 4

½ cup dry white wine or dry vermouth

½ cup lemon juice

1 tablespoon extra-virgin olive oil

2 teaspoons grated lemon zest

2 teaspoons pressed garlic

2 tablespoons Herbes de Provence*

1 teaspoon black pepper

½ teaspoon light salt

1½ pounds bone-in veal chops, ½- to 1-inch thick

Nonfat or olive oil cooking spray

Fresh herb sprigs like rosemary, sage or thyme (optional)

* If you don't have a commercial Herbes de Provence blend, substitute the following: 2 teaspoons dry rosemary, crushed, 1 teaspoon each dry marjoram, thyme, basil, sage and lavender if available.

1. Preheat the grill to the highest setting.

2. Make the marinade. In a blender, mix the wine, lemon juice, oil, lemon zest, garlic, herbs, pepper and salt. Set aside until ready to use.

3. Marinate the veal chops. Place the meat in a 1-gallon zippered freezer-weight storage bag, a 1-quart airtight container, or a shallow square glass dish (8 x 8 x 2 inch).

Zip the bag closed, or cover the container or dish and marinate in the refrigerator for 20 minutes or up to 1 hour. This is a strongly flavored marinade that will mascerate the veal if left on too long.

4. Grill the veal chops. Remove each chop from the marinade and spray both sides with cooking spray before placing on the grill. Grill the chops according to the Grill Times below or until the internal temperature reaches the doneness you desire on an instant read thermometer. Consult the grilling chart on page 101 for exact internal temperatures: 140° to 150°F for medium.

5. To serve, place a veal chop and equal amounts of risotto and spinach on each of 4 dinner plates. Put a sprig of fresh herbs on top of the chop and serve immediately.

Grill Times

Two-Sided Contact Grill: *5 to 7 minutes for medium.*

Hibachi Grill, Combination Grill or Infusion Grill: *10 to 14 minutes for medium. Turn the veal chops halfway through the grilling time. Grills with lids may be covered halfway through the grilling time. Infusion grills with lids may be covered for the entire grilling time.*

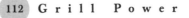

Easy Mushroom Risotto

Makes 4 (1¼ cup) servings

3 cups nonfat canned chicken broth

1 tablespoon extra-virgin olive oil

⅓ cup finely chopped white onion

1 teaspoon pressed garlic

1 cup sliced mushrooms such as button, Cremini, porcini

1⅓ cups Arborio rice (Italian short grain rice) or medium grain rice like pearl rice

½ cup grated Parmesan cheese

Light salt and freshly ground pepper to taste

Substitutions:
If fresh mushrooms are not available, use 1 8-ounce can drained.

1. Put broth in a 1-quart pot and heat to almost boiling. Remove from heat until ready to use.
2. While broth is heating, mix onions, garlic, mushrooms, and olive oil in a covered 2- to 3-quart covered pot. Cook covered over high heat until you hear the onions sizzle. Then immediately turn the heat down to extra low and sweat the onions and mushrooms until tender, about 4 to 5 minutes.
3. Stir in the rice and stir to coat with oil. Cover and cook over low heat for 2 minutes, or until rice starts becoming transparent.
4. Stir broth into rice mixture, cover and bring to a rapid boil. When broth starts to boil, immediately turn the heat down to extra low. Surface of broth should barely bubble. Keep covered and cook 20 to 25 minutes.
5. When time is up, remove the pot from the heat, and then stir in the Parmesan cheese, salt and pepper to taste. Cover immediately and let stand 5 minutes away from the heat in order for the risotto to absorb any excess moisture. Sprinkle with chopped parsley before serving. Risotto can be refrigerated in an airtight container for up to 2 days and frozen for up to 2 months.

Mix & Match

Serve the Easy Mushroom Risotto with any of the main dishes in the following menus: Farmhouse Steaks, page 103; Not-So-French Dijon Pepper Steaks, page 107; Chicken Romagna, page 159; Pick-Me-Up Poultry Piccata, page 175.

Quick Spinach Sauté

Makes 4 (¹/₄ cup) servings

1 tablespoon olive oil

1 teaspoon finely chopped garlic

1 10-ounce package washed, trimmed fresh spinach leaves

¼ cup canned nonfat chicken broth

Light salt and freshly ground pepper to taste

Lemon juice to taste

Substitutions:
Instead of spinach, substitute Swiss chard.

1. In a 4- or 5-quart pot, heat the oil over medium-high heat.

2. When the oil is sizzling, stir in the garlic and sauté for 30 seconds. Put the spinach in the pot, add the broth and cover to steam about 2 to 3 minutes.

4. Lift the lid, and stir the spinach until completely wilted. Season with salt, pepper and lemon juice to taste. Serve immediately.

Approximate Nutrients Per Serving of Entire Meal

Total Calories 608	Protein 39 g / 26%	Carbohydrate 66 g / 44%
Total Sugar 1 g	Fat Total 18 g / 28%	Saturated Fat 5 g / 8%
Cholesterol 86 mg	Sodium 424 mg	Fiber 4 g Calcium 261 mg

Amazing Maple Glazed Pork Chops with Cranberry Mashed Sweet Potatoes

*D*id you ever wonder how the chefs at fancy bistro-style restaurants made the light sauces that flavor their grilled steaks and chops? You'll learn their secret when you make my easy Maple-Balsamic Glaze: a technique called reduction. To create a reduction, the sauce boils for several minutes to evaporate, or reduce some of the liquid. This thickens the sauce while concentrating the flavors, making it perfect as a baste or finishing sauce. Since the flavors in my Maple-Balsamic Glaze are intense, just baste lightly with it. Then drizzle a couple of teaspoons over your grilled pork chops to transform them into restaurant quality fare.

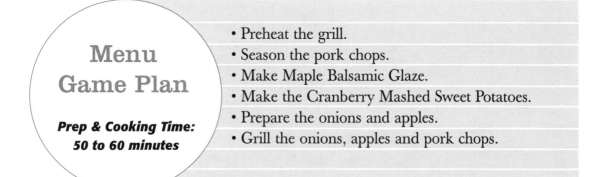

Menu Game Plan

Prep & Cooking Time: 50 to 60 minutes

- Preheat the grill.
- Season the pork chops.
- Make Maple Balsamic Glaze.
- Make the Cranberry Mashed Sweet Potatoes.
- Prepare the onions and apples.
- Grill the onions, apples and pork chops.

Cook's Notes

Maple syrup is a North American original. At factories in New England and Canada, sap is sent in tubes directly from the tree to a sap house where it is boiled down. It takes approximately 35 gallons of sap to make 1 gallon of maple syrup, so this labor-intensive product is expensive. You do get a lot for your money, though, because a little maple syrup goes a long way. Pure maple syrup is twice as sweet as cane or beet sugar, so you need half as much when baking or cooking. In addition, high concentrations of calcium, iron, phosphorus and potassium make pure maple syrup one of the most nutritious sweeteners available. Read the label carefully when buying it though. There are government regulations both in the United States and Canada to prevent maple syrup substitutes from being sold as "pure." If the product is labeled "maple flavored syrup," it probably contains only a small amount of pure maple syrup and/or maple flavoring.

Maple-Balsamic Glazed Pork Chops

1¼ to 1½ pounds* center cut
pork chops about ½- to
1-inch thick

Light salt and freshly ground
pepper to taste

2   medium-size firm apples
such as Granny Smith, Fuji or
Braeburn

1   medium onion, white or
yellow

Nonfat or canola oil cooking
spray

Maple-Balsamic Glaze (see recipe
on page 117)

* 1¼ pounds if boneless, up to 1½
pounds if the chop contains a bone

Substitutions:
*Instead of pork chops, substitute lamb chops, steak or
boneless-skinless chicken
breasts.*

1. **Preheat the grill** to the highest setting.
2. **Season the pork chops** with salt and freshly ground pepper to taste. Set aside covered in the refrigerator until ready to grill.
3. **Prepare the apples and onions.** Leave the peel on the apples. Cut each one in half then remove the stem ends by cutting small V's around them with a sharp pairing knife. Remove the core with a melon baller. Slice each half into 1-inch thick half moons. Put the apples into a medium bowl.

Slice the onions into 1-inch thick rings. Put them in the bowl with the apples.

With your fingers, toss the onions and apples with 2 tablespoons of the Maple-Balsamic Glaze to cover all cut surfaces. Then, toss and spray lightly with cooking spray. Cover and set aside on the counter 10 minutes or up to 1 hour.

4. **Grill the apples, onions and pork chops.** If you have a grill with a small grilling surface, grill the onions first then the apples, followed by the pork chops. On a medium-size grill, grill the onions first then the apples and pork chops together. If you own a large capacity grill, grill everything simultaneously.

Transfer grilled food to a platter covered with aluminum foil to keep it warm until serving time.

Grill the onions according to the Grill Times opposite until they are tender. Grill the apples until grill marks appear distinctly on both sides and they are tender.

Spray each pork chop lightly with the cooking spray. Brush with 1 tablespoon Maple-Balsamic Glaze then place immediately on the grill. Grill the chops according to the times opposite or until the internal temperature reaches the doneness you desire on an instant read thermometer. Consult the grilling chart on page 102 for exact internal temperatures: 145° to 150°F for medium.

5. **To serve,** heat the reserved ¼-cup of Maple-Balsamic Glaze on the stove over low heat until warmed through. Do not bring to a boil, or the sauce will become too thick. Put equal amounts of Cranberry Mashed Sweet Potatoes on 4 dinner plates. Put a pork chop beside the sweet potatoes and garnish it with grilled onions and apples. Drizzle each pork chop with 1 tablespoon of the Maple-Balsamic Glaze. Serve immediately.

Two-Sided Contact Grill: *Onions 7 to 10 minutes / apples 5 to 6 minutes / pork 5 to 7 minutes for medium. Baste with the Maple Balsamic Glaze halfway through the cooking time.*

Hibachi Grill, Combination Grill or Infusion Grill: *Onions 14 to 20 minutes / apples 10 to 12 minutes / pork 10 to 14 minutes for medium. Turn the onions and apples halfway through the grilling time. Turn the pork chops halfway through the grilling time and baste the grilled side with the Maple Balsamic Glaze. Grills with lids may be covered halfway through the grilling time. Infusion grills with lids may be covered for the entire grilling time.*

Maple-Balsamic Glaze

Makes 4 (1 tablespoon) servings plus ¼ cup for basting

¼   cup frozen apple juice concentrate

¼   cup real maple syrup

¼   cup balsamic vinegar

1   teaspoon pressed garlic

⅛   teaspoon white pepper

1   teaspoon brown sugar

This glaze is delicious used as a baste or finishing sauce for grilled pork, beef, lamb or chicken. You can also make it up to 5 days in advance of serving if refrigerated in an airtight container. A little of this goes a long way. But if you would like extra sauce, simply double the recipe.

1. In a 1-quart saucepan, whisk juice concentrate, maple syrup, balsamic vinegar, garlic, pepper and sugar.
2. Bring to a boil over high heat, whisking constantly and cook for 5 to 6 minutes until sauce is reduced to ½ cup. Remove from the heat and reserve ¼-cup of the sauce to finish the chops just before serving. Use the remaining ¼ cup as a marinade for the onions, apples and as a baste for the pork chops.

Cranberry Mashed Sweet Potatoes

Make 4 (1 cup) servings

2   pounds sweet potatoes or yams

1   cup canned whole cranberry sauce

½   teaspoon cinnamon

1   tablespoon brown sugar

1   tablespoon real maple syrup

2   tablespoons butter

½   teaspoon light salt or to taste

1. Peel the potatoes, then dice them into about 1-inch square pieces.
2. Put a steamer basket into a 3- to 4-quart pot with a tight fitting lid. Fill it with water to cover the bottom of the pot but not rising above the bottom of the basket. Cover and bring to a boil over high heat. Add the potatoes, cover and steam about 12 to 15 minutes, until the potatoes are tender but not falling apart. Drain the potatoes well in a strainer then put them into a 2- or 3-quart casserole.
3. Using a potato masher or large fork, mash the potatoes, gradually adding the cranberry sauce, cinnamon, brown sugar, maple syrup and salt. Cover and keep warm in a 325°F oven until serving time.

Mix & Match

Serve the Cranberry Mashed Sweet Potatoes with any of the main dishes in the following menus: A Turkey for All Seasons, page 163; Armenian Apricot Sauced Poultry, page 167; Chicken Romagna, page 159.

Approximate Nutrients Per Serving of Entire Meal

Total Calories 678	Protein 38 g / 22%	Carbohydrate 112 g / 65%
Total Sugar 84 g	Fat Total 9 g / 12%	Saturated Fat 3g / 4%
Cholesterol 98 mg	Sodium 607 mg	Fiber 10 g Calcium 116 mg

Smart and Saucy
Rosemary-Cherry Lamb Chops

Rosemary was the answer to forgetfulness for the ancient Greeks and Romans who believed that winding sprigs in their hair would improve their memory. Ancient herbalists believed that rosemary was the quintessential cure-all, and used it to treat everything from depression and rheumatism to the Black Plague. In the Middle Ages, people put rosemary under their pillows before they went to bed because they believed it to be instant protection from evil spirits and bad dreams. No one has ever proven that rosemary makes you smart, is a universal cure-all or keeps demons at bay. I do know that I feel pretty smart when I mix rosemary and cherry jam into a sauce, drizzle it over a succulent grilled lamb chop and serve it up with my pecan and brussels sprouts couscous. One taste of this unforgettably delicious menu will make you feel so good that no demon would ever want to bother with you.

Menu Game Plan

Prep & Cooking Time: 50 minutes

- Preheat the grill.
- Preheat the oven to toast the pecans.
- Season the lamb chops.
- Make the Rosemary Cherry Sauce.
- Make the Toasted Pecan Couscous with brussels sprouts.
- Grill the lamb chops.

Cook's Notes

Brussels sprouts, those petite members of the cabbage family, are not only tasty, but are a good defense against cancer and diabetes. An excellent source of vitamin C, folic acid and potassium, brussels sprouts also contain substances called indoles, which affect the metabolism of estrogen. Indoles prompt the body to make benign forms of the hormone that help prevent breast cancer. In addition, brussels sprouts are high in fiber, which is an important nutrient in preventing colon cancer and diabetes.

Lamb Chops

Serves 4

1	teaspoon light salt
½	teaspoon white pepper
1	tablespoon pressed garlic
2	teaspoons grated gingerroot
1¼	pounds loin lamb chops

Nonfat or olive oil cooking spray

1. **Preheat the grill** to the highest setting.
2. **Season the lamb chops**. In a small bowl mix the salt, pepper, garlic and ginger thoroughly with a fork.

   Smear the paste on all surfaces of the lamb chops and put them on a plate or dish. Cover tightly and refrigerate 20 minutes to 24 hours.
3. **Grill the lamb chops.** Spray each piece of meat lightly with the cooking spray before placing on the grill. Grill the chops according to the Grill Times below until the internal temperature reaches the doneness you desire on an instant-read thermometer Consult the grilling chart on page 101 for exact temperatures: 140° to 150° F for medium.
4. **To serve,** spoon equal amounts of the couscous on 4 dinner plates. Put a lamb chop beside the couscous and drizzle 2 to 3 tablespoons of hot cherry sauce over the lamb chop before serving.

Grill Times

Two-Sided Contact Grill: 5 to 7 minutes for medium.

Hibachi Grill, Combination Grill or Infusion Grill: 10 to 14 minutes for medium. Turn the chops halfway through the grilling time. Grills with lids may be covered halfway through the grilling time. Infusion grills with lids may be covered for the entire grilling time.

Substitutions:
Instead of lamb chops, substitute pork chops, steak or boneless skinless chicken breasts.

Variation:
For Vegetarians: Substitute extra firm tofu sliced into ½-inch thick steaks for the lamb chops. Add ¼-cup balsamic vinegar to the marinade ingredients and marinate in the refrigerator 20 minutes or up to 24 hours.

Rosemary-Cherry Sauce

Makes 8 (2 tablespoon) servings

1   teaspoon olive oil

¼   cup finely chopped white or
      yellow onion, or shallots

1   teaspoon pressed garlic

½   teaspoon grated gingerroot

2   teaspoons finely chopped
      fresh rosemary or 1 tea-
      spoon dried, crushed

½   cup canned nonfat
      chicken broth

½   cup all-fruit cherry jam

1   tablespoon balsamic vinegar

2   teaspoons cornstarch

Light salt and freshly ground
      pepper to taste

Substitutions:
For the cherry jam, substitute
seedless raspberry or black-
berry jam.

This delicious sauce can be made up to 48 hours in advance of serving if refrigerated in an airtight container. You can also freeze it for up to 2 months. Defrost and reheat it in the microwave.

1. In a 1-quart pot, heat the olive oil over medium-low heat. Stir in the onions, garlic, ginger and rosemary. Cover, turn down the heat to low and cook 10 minutes, stirring occasionally until the onions are translucent and tender.
2. Whisk the chicken broth and cherry jam into the onions. Turn the heat up and bring to a boil.
3. Meanwhile, in a 1-cup measure or small bowl, whisk the balsamic vinegar and the cornstarch. When the broth comes to a boil, whisk in the cornstarch mixture. Continue whisking until the sauce is thickened, 1 to 2 minutes.
4. Remove from the heat, cover and set aside until serving time. If the sauce becomes too cool before serving, reheat, covered, over low heat on the stove. If it gets too thick while reheating, whisk in a few teaspoons of chicken broth.

Variation:
Spirited Sauce: Substitute 1 to 2 tablespoons brandy or dry Sherry for the balsamic vinegar.

Toasted Pecan Couscous with Brussels Sprouts

Makes 4 (1¼ cup) servings

⅓ cup chopped pecans

2 cups fresh or frozen Brussels sprouts

1 tablespoon olive oil

1 teaspoon pressed garlic

2¼ cups nonfat chicken broth

½ teaspoon light salt or to taste

1 10 ounce box couscous

Substitutions:
For the brussels sprouts, substitute an equal amount of green beans, sliced carrots or broccoli.

1. Preheat the oven to 325°F and position a rack in the center of the oven.

2. Put the pecans on a nonstick baking sheet or piece of aluminum foil and toast in the preheated oven for 5 to 10 minutes or until light and fragrant. Remove from the oven and set aside to cool.

3. While the nuts are toasting, cut the stems off of the brussels sprouts and slice them in half.

4. In a 2-quart pot, heat the olive oil to sizzling over medium-high heat. Stir in the garlic and cook 30 seconds to 1 minute until fragrant. Stir in the brussels sprouts and sauté for 1 to 2 minutes to coat with the oil and garlic.

5. Pour in the chicken broth, turn the heat to high, cover and bring to a rolling boil about 5 minutes

6. Stir in the couscous, cover the pot and remove it from the heat. Allow to stand covered a minimum of 5 minutes to hydrate the couscous and finish steaming the brussels sprouts. Stir in the toasted chopped pecans. Cover immediately until ready to serve. If the couscous becomes too cool before serving time, transfer it to a microwavable casserole and reheat covered 2 to 4 minutes on high (100% power).

Mix & Match

Serve the Toasted Pecan Couscous with any of the main dishes in the following menus: Amazing Maple Glazed Pork Chops, page 115; Not-So-French Dijon Pepper Steaks, page 107; Provencal Kissed Veal Chops, page 111; Chicken Romagna, page 159; Rockin' Moroccan Lamb Kebabs, page 151; A Turkey for All Seasons, page 163.

Approximate Nutrients Per Serving of Entire Meal

Total Calories 599	Protein 41 g / 27%	Carbohydrate 65 g / 44%
Total Sugar 5 g	Fat Total 19 g / 29%	Saturated Fat 4 g / 6%
Cholesterol 81 mg	Sodium 672 mg	Fiber 7 g Calcium 76 mg

(Calculated with 5 ounce lamb chop, 2 tablespoons sauce and 1¼ cups couscous.)

Pride of Texas Chili Lime Pork with Grilled Zucchini and Corny Cheddar Cheese Grits

Several years ago I was about to teach a series of healthy cooking classes in Austin, Texas and was perplexed. How could I make healthy food palatable to Texans used to heavy meat dishes and deep-fried foods? Once in Austin, I realized that the only thing dearer to a meat-loving Texan's heart than a slow cooking BBQ is a lickety-split grill. Bingo! Grilling is one of the lowest fat and fastest ways to cook meat. So, I developed this and many other grill menus that feature light versions of Lone Star favorites delicious enough to be the pride of any Texas table.

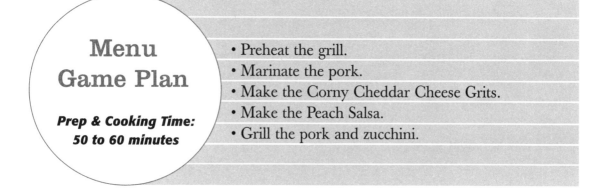

Menu Game Plan

Prep & Cooking Time:
50 to 60 minutes

- Preheat the grill.
- Marinate the pork.
- Make the Corny Cheddar Cheese Grits.
- Make the Peach Salsa.
- Grill the pork and zucchini.

Cook's Notes

Notes

A prime ingredient in Tex-Mex cooking, chili peppers originated in South America and have been cultivated there for over 7000 years. In tropical regions they grow as a perennial and in temperate zones as an annual. Chilies are really a fleshy berry containing seeds and are members of the nightshade family, which includes eggplant, potato and tomato. Hot peppers vary greatly in size, shape, color and flavor. When choosing fresh hot peppers look for brightly colored glossy skin. Avoid peppers with soft areas or black spots. Don't wash fresh hot peppers when you get them home because they will spoil quickly. Fresh chilies will keep for up to 2 weeks in a dry bag in the vegetable drawer of your refrigerator.

It's hard to know how hot a fresh chili is until you cut into it. Some are so hot the essential oils will burn your eyes just by slicing them. As fresh hot peppers cook, their heat intensifies, so use them sparingly. Whether fresh or dried, the seeds are the hottest part of the chili and should be removed before cooking.

Pride of Texas Chili Lime Pork and Grilled Zucchini

Serves 4

¼ cup lime juice

2 teaspoons finely grated lime zest

1 tablespoon chili powder or more to taste

1 teaspoon light salt

2 teaspoons pressed garlic

1¼ to 1½ pounds* lean center cut pork chops, about ½- to 1-inch thick

2 medium zucchini, sliced in half lengthwise

Nonfat or olive oil cooking spray

* 1¼ pounds if boneless, up to 1½ pounds if the chop contains a bone

1. Preheat the grill to the highest setting.

2. Make the marinade. In a 1-cup bowl or measure, mix the lime juice, lime zest, chili powder, salt and garlic with a fork. Set aside until ready to use.

3. Marinate the pork chops. Place meat in a 1-gallon zippered freezer-weight storage bag, a 1-quart airtight container or a shallow square glass dish (8 x 8 x 2 inch).

Scrape the marinade paste onto the meat, then, with your fingertips, smear the marinade paste onto all sides of the meat. Zip the bag closed, or cover the container or dish and marinate in the refrigerator for 20 minutes or up to 24 hours.

4. Grill the zucchini and pork chops. On a small grilling surface, grill the zucchini first, then the pork chops. On a larger capacity grill, grill everything simultaneously. Transfer grilled food to a platter covered with aluminum foil to keep it warm until serving time.

Spray each zucchini and pork chop lightly with the cooking spray before placing the meat on the grill. Grill the zuchini until tender but not translucent or limp. Grill the chops according to the Grill Times below or until the internal temperature reaches the doneness you desire on an instant read thermometer. Consult the grilling chart on page 102 for exact internal temperatures: 145° to 150°F for medium.

5. To serve, put equal amounts of Corny Cheddar Cheese Grits on each of 4 dinner plates. Place a pork chop and zucchini beside the grits, and spoon 2 to 3 tablespoons of Peach Salsa over the pork chops. Serve immediately.

Grill Times

Two-Sided Contact Grill: *Zucchini 5 to 6 minutes / pork 5 to 7 minutes for medium.*

Hibachi Grill, Combination Grill or Infusion Grill: *Zucchini 10 to 12 minutes / pork 10 to 14 minutes for medium. Turn the zucchini and pork chops halfway through the grilling time. Grills with lids may be covered halfway through the grilling time. Infusion grills with lids may be covered for the entire grilling time.*

Corny Cheddar Cheese Grits

Makes 4 (1 cup) servings

3¾ cups canned nonfat
   chicken broth

⅛ teaspoon white pepper

½ teaspoon light salt or to taste

1 cup yellow grits, coarse
   polenta style grind
   (not instant)

1 cup frozen petite sweet corn,
   white or yellow

½ cup thinly sliced green onion

¾ cup shredded sharp
   Cheddar cheese

My Corny Cheddar Cheese Grits are not mushy and slushy. They have body like a stiff polenta. That's because instead of making them with instant grits, I use a polenta grind cornmeal. You can make this recipe up to 48 hours in advance of serving if you refrigerate it in an airtight container. Reheat in the microwave (see step 4 below). It also freezes well up to 2 months. Defrost and reheat in microwave.

1. In a 2- or 3-quart pot, bring the broth, white pepper and salt to a boil over high heat.
2. Stir in the grits and bring back to a boil. As soon as the grits come to a boil, turn the heat down to a low simmer, stir and cover. Continue to simmer for 20 to 25 minutes lifting the lid occasionally to stir the grits. Cook until the grains become tender and thickened to your liking. If grits become too thick, stir in 1 or more tablespoons of boiling broth.
3. While the grits are cooking, defrost the corn in a strainer under cool running water and drain well; slice the green onion, and if not using preshredded cheese, shred it on a medium hand grater.
4. Remove the pot from the heat and stir in the corn, green onion and Cheddar cheese. Allow to stand covered until serving time. (Note: If you are not serving the grits within 10 minutes, scrape them into an ovenproof casserole; cover and keep warm in a 325°F oven. If the grits become too thick, stir in ¼ cup boiling chicken broth.)

Or, reheat by scraping the grits into a microwavable casserole and microwave covered 4 to 5 minutes on high (100% power). Microwave uncovered if you want a thicker consistency.

Mix & Match

Serve the Corny Cheddar Cheese Grits and/or the Peach Salsa with any of the main dishes in the following menus: Tortilla-Crusted Burgers with Black Bean Salsa Salad, page 69; Cowboy Kebabs with Easy Ridin' BBQ Sauce, page 147; Adobo Tofu Steaks, page 267.

Peach Salsa

Makes 8 (¹⁄₄ cup) servings

1 cucumber (preferably hothouse)

1 to 2 fresh serrano chili peppers, chopped

¹⁄₃ cup chopped green onions,

¹⁄₄ cup packed cilantro

¹⁄₂ cup red bell pepper

1¹⁄₂ cup diced fresh peaches or canned peaches, well drained

2 tablespoons lime juice

1. Cut the cucumber in half lengthwise and use a teaspoon to scoop out the seeds. Coarsely chop the cucumber and measure ¹⁄₂ cup. Set aside.

2. Seed the serrano chili wearing kitchen gloves to protect your hands from the oils. Using a small sharp knife, slice off the stem end, then slice the pepper in half lengthwise. Using the tip of the knife, remove the seeds then cut the pepper into chunks.

3. Put the serrano pepper slices in a blender or food processor fitted with the metal chopping blade along with the onions and cilantro. Blend or process until the mixture is finely chopped.

4. Add the bell pepper, cucumber and the peaches. Pulse to combine. To prevent the mixture becoming like baby food, do not over-blend or process. You want a mixture of large and small chunks in the salsa for a variety of textures and shapes.

5. Using a spatula, scrape the salsa into a medium dish or airtight container. Mix in the lime juice, cover and refrigerate for 20 minutes or up to 48 hours.

Substitutions:
Instead of peaches, substitute fresh nectarines or fresh apricots.

Approximate Nutrients Per Serving of Entire Meal

Total Calories 609	Protein 50 g / 34%	Carbohydrate 61 g / 42%	
Total Sugar 15 g	Fat Total 16 g / 24%	Saturated Fat 7 g / 11%	
Cholesterol 120 mg	Sodium 668 mg	Fiber 7 g	Calcium 228 mg

Big Easy Grilled Andouille Sausage with Muffaletta Pasta Salad

A famous New Orleans sandwich called "muffaletta" inspired me to create this menu. Named after "muffuliette", which are soft saffron and anise flavored rolls traditionally served at teatime in Sicily, this Frisbee-sized sandwich is hardly dainty enough to be considered a tea goodie. That's because when Lupo Salvadore, a Sicilian immigrant, created it in 1906 at his Central Grocery Store on Decatur Street, he intended to satisfy the hearty appetites of the Sicilian stevedores who worked the nearby wharves and produce stalls of the French Market. The secret of the muffaletta's success is not the generous combination of cold cuts and cheeses that fill the large round sesame seed studded loaf. It's the Mediterranean style olive sauce slathered on each half of the bread that defines this chin-dribbling delight. Made from a savory mixture of olives, artichokes, anchovies and capers, it occurred to me that this same sauce would also be delicious on pasta. The perfect solution for this "Big" and "Easy" menu, was grilled Andouille sausage–a spicy Cajun smoked pork sausage.

FYI: The Central Grocery store is now run by Lupo's grandchildren and has been reported to serve up to 500 muffaletta a day during Mardi Gras season.

Menu Game Plan

Prep & Cooking Time: 40 minutes

- Preheat the grill.
- Boil the pasta.
- Prepare the vegetables.
- Make the olive sauce and finishing dressing.
- Grill the sausages.
- Mix the pasta with the sauce and dressing.

Cook's Notes

The recipe for Andouille sausage, which originated in France, came to Louisiana with the first wave of French-Acadian immigrants in around 1766. These exiles from the Canadian Maritime Provinces are also known as Cajuns. Traditionally Andouille sausages are made with pork, garlic and liberal amounts of pepper, then slowly smoked over pecan wood and sugar cane. Some manufacturers sell Andouille sausages made from a combination of pork, beef and turkey. This variety is lower in fat and in sodium than traditional Andouille sausage.

Muffaletta Pasta Salad

Serves 4

Grilled Sausage

1¼ pounds Andouille sausage, about 4 links

Pasta and vegetables

½ pound dried medium-size pasta, such as fusilli, radiatore, elbow macaroni, shells or orechiette

2 tablespoons shredded Parmesan cheese

¼ cup shredded provolone or mozzarella

½ cup shredded carrot

½ cup petite frozen corn

½ cup diced red, yellow, orange or green bell peppers

¼ cup finely chopped parsley

¼ cup thinly sliced green onion

Olive Sauce

1 4-ounce can water packed artichoke hearts (5 whole), drained

¼ cup canned sliced black olives, drained

¼ cup pimento-stuffed green olives

¼ cup pitted Kalamata olives

2 teaspoons drained capers

If you are serving hearty eaters, this pasta salad is easily doubled.

1. Preheat the grill. If you have a grill with a variable temperature control, set it to medium-high (one or two steps below high) or to about 350° to 400°F.

2. Cook the pasta following instructions on the package or on page 226. When the pasta is "al dente," rinse in a strainer under cool running water to stop the cooking and drain well.

3. Prepare the cheese and vegetables while the pasta is cooking. Put the Parmesan, provolone and carrot in a 3-quart mixing bowl. (If you are not using preshredded cheese or carrots from a bag, grate the provolone or mozzarella and carrots using a medium size hand grater, or use your food processor fitted with the medium size grating disk.)

Thaw the corn in a strainer under cool running water. Drain well and add it to the bowl.

Prepare the bell pepper, parsley, and onion and mix them into the other ingredients using a spatula. Set the bowl aside until ready to mix in the Olive Sauce and Finishing Dressing into the pasta.

4. Make the olive sauce. In a food processor fitted with the metal chopping blade or in a blender, pulse to coarsely chop artichoke hearts, olives and capers. Scrape the salad into the bowl containing the prepared cheese and vegetables. Do not clean your food processor or blender. Use it to make the dressing.

5. Make the finishing dressing. In your food processor or blender, blend the olive oil, vinegar, anchovy paste, garlic, oregano, cayenne and black pepper. Pour into the bowl containing the cheese, vegetables and olive salad, then fold the ingredients together with a rubber spatula until well mixed.

Finishing dressing

2 tablespoons extra-virgin olive oil

3 tablespoons red wine vinegar

½ to 1 teaspoon anchovy paste

½ teaspoon pressed garlic

¾ teaspoon dried oregano, crushed

⅛ to ¼ teaspoon cayenne pepper

Freshly ground black pepper to taste

6. Mix the pasta salad. Put the drained and cooled pasta on top of the vegetable and olive mixture. Using a rubber spatula, fold the ingredients from the bottom of the bowl evenly into the pasta. Set aside until ready to serve.

7. Grill the Andouille sausage according to the Grill Times below. For sausage grilling techniques, see page 130.

8. To serve, put equal amounts of the Muffaletta Pasta Salad on 4 dinner plates. Serve 1 or 2 of the grilled sausages beside it. Accompany this meal with slices of warm foccacia bread, or crusty French or Italian baguette.

Grill Times

Two-Sided Contact Grill: 5 minutes.

Hibachi Grill, Combination Grill or Infusion Grill: 10 minutes. Turn the sausage halfway through the grilling time. Grills with lids may be covered halfway through the grilling time. Infusion grills with lids may be covered for the entire grilling time.

Variation:

For vegetarians: Instead of grilled sausage, grill a variety of vegetables. See page 244 for vegetable grilling instructions.

Mix & Match

The main dishes from the following menus also taste great with this pasta salad: How's Bayou Louisiana Shrimp and Orange Brochettes, page 235; Crazy Cajun Burgers, page 85; Pride of Texas Chili Lime Pork, page 123.

Approximate Nutrients Per Serving of Entire Meal

Total Calories 576	Protein 30 g / 21%	Carbohydrate 66 g / 47%
Total Sugar 13 g	Fat Total 21 g / 33%	Saturated Fat 4 g / 7%
Cholesterol 59 mg	Sodium 1,987 mg	Fiber 5 g Calcium 212 mg

(Calculated with 1½ cups of pasta salad and 5 ounces sausage made from a turkey, pork and beef combination.)

Tips for Grilling Sausages on Tabletop Grills:

Sausage is one of my favorite grilled fast foods because each link is a neat, completely seasoned meal that you don't have to take time to marinate. Even though sausages are easy to grill, there are a few things you should know for perfect results:

- Don't pierce sausages before cooking them. This causes the juices to run out, which results in dry sausages.
- To prevent exploding sausages, don't grill or cook them on the highest temperature setting. Even if you do use a lower heat, they may burst. You can't always prevent it.
- Don't peel the casing off of a precooked sausage. All the casings are edible, and the sausage will hold together better and be juicier with the casing intact.

Is it Creole or Cajun?

Creole was the term for the European-born aristocrats who settled in New Orleans in the 1690s. These second-born sons could not inherit any land or titles in their homelands. But in New Orleans, where they could retain their titles and own land, they were treated as nobility. The classically trained chefs who came from Europe with these aristocrats created the foundation for Creole cuisine purely out of necessity. A formal meal of several courses might have included foods introduced to them by the native Indians like corn, wild game, bay leaves and sassafras leaves (used to season and thicken gumbo soup).

Cajuns are descendents of the French Catholic refugees who began arriving in Southern Louisiana around 1766 just as Spain assumed control of the colony from France. In contrast to the Creole chefs with their elegant armory of cooking equipment and techniques, the Cajuns used one rustic cooking utensil, a large black iron pot. Cajun cooks used the bounty of their land to create their legendary one-pot recipes that we continue to make today—Jambalaya, stews, fricassees, soups and gumbos.

As the population in Southern Louisiana grew with immigrants from France, Spain, Germany, Italy, Africa and the West Indies, Creole and Cajun cuisine continued to evolve. Roux, the base for sauces came from France. Spanish paella is the great-grandfather of jambalaya. The Germans who arrived in 1725 with pigs, cattle and chicken perfected Louisiana style sausages, among them the Andouille. From the West Indies and Haiti came such exotic vegetables as tomatoes and hot peppers, as well as the technique of slow cooking used for making gumbos. Slaves from Africa introduced okra which is a main ingredient in gumbo. At the beginning of the twentieth century, Italians introduced pasta dishes and the muffaletta sandwich.

Ai, Chihuahua!
That's a Powerful Salad!

I have always believed that one delicious salad could be a more powerful wellness weapon than a cabinet full of supplements. To prove my point, I created this Mexican flavored salad several years ago for one of my corporate cooking classes and it was a hit. After tasting the colorful combination of vegetables, fruit, grilled beef and salsa dressing, one participant enthusiastically summed up my intent: "It looks great, tastes better than pills and protein powders, and all those vegetables and fruit make you feel full but not overstuffed." The class later learned that the salad is also packed with a powerhouse of nutrients that can increase your mental and physical energy and boost your immune system. Grilled beef is a rich source of protein and iron, both important nutrients for alertness and improved mental function. But protein alone won't make you a clearer thinker or give you stamina. You need a good supply of carbohydrate, the major fuel for your muscles and brain. So, I chose spinach, broccoli, orange, jicama, and kidney beans. This powerful carbo combo is also rich in potassium, a nutrient your body needs for regulating water balance and releasing energy within the muscles. In addition these veggies and fruits also pack a healthy dose of folate, beta-carotene, and vitamin C, all nutrients that recent research indicates may help prevent cancer. The olive oil in the dressing provides monounsaturated fat which helps lower your risk of heart disease by lowering total and LDL (bad) cholesterol without lowering HDL (good) cholesterol.

Menu Game Plan

Prep & Cooking time: 40 minutes

- Preheat the grill.
- Marinate the meat.
- Blanch the broccoli.
- Make the salad dressing.
- Prepare the salad vegetables.
- Grill the meat.
- Assemble the salad.

Cook's Notes

Notes

Mixed into salsa, pureed in a salad dressing, made into pesto, mixed with hot peppers in a stir-fry, cilantro's bold sage-citrus flavor makes some people go crazy with delight whenever they taste it. Cilantro leaves are extremely perishable, so when you get them home, don't wash them. If the leaves are already moist, wrap them in a dry paper towel; if they are dry, wrap them in a damp paper towel. Store the paper wrapped leaves in a closed plastic bag in your refrigerator for 3 to 4 days.

Steak Salad

Serves 4

Steak

1¼ pounds flank steak or skirt steak trimmed of fat, cut into 4 equal square pieces

½ cup mild or hot chunky salsa

2 teaspoons chili powder

2 teaspoons pressed garlic

¼ cup dry red wine, non-alcoholic red wine or 2 tablespoons red wine vinegar

Nonfat or canola oil cooking spray

Spinach Salad

2 cups broccoli fleurettes cut into bite sized pieces

1 cup thinly sliced bell pepper

1 cup jicama root

2 navel oranges

2 green onions

3 cups pre-washed ready-to-eat baby spinach leaves

1 8¾-ounce can kidney beans, well drained

Fresh cilantro for garnish

Low-fat corn chips

1. **Preheat the grill** to the highest setting.
2. **Flatten the meat**. Spread a large piece of plastic wrap on a flat work surface. Arrange the meat in a single layer over the plastic wrap. Cover the meat with another large piece of plastic wrap. Pound the meat with the bottom of a large heavy skillet, flat side of a meat mallet, or rolling pin until flattened to about ¼- to ½-inch thick.

Place the meat in a 1-gallon zippered freezer bag, a 1-quart airtight container or a shallow square glass dish (8 x 8 x 2-inch).
3. **Make the marinade and marinate the meat.** Measure the salsa, chili powder, garlic and wine into a 1-cup bowl or measure and mix thoroughly with a fork. Pour the marinade over the meat and then, with your hands, turn the meat so that the marinade has contact with all surfaces. Zip the bag closed or cover the container or dish and marinate in the refrigerator for 20 minutes or up to 24 hours.
4. **Blanch the broccoli.** Place freshly washed vegetables in a microwavable casserole. Microwave 2 to 3 minutes, or until bright and still crisp. Immediately place vegetables in a strainer and run under cold tap water, or immerse in ice water to stop the cooking. When vegetables are cooler than room temperature, drain thoroughly, use right away, or chill in an airtight container.
5. **Cut up the vegetables for the salad.** As you finish preparing each salad ingredient, place it into a large 8-cup bowl. Slice the bell pepper. Peel the jicama with a vegetable peeler or a knife and then slice or dice it into bite-size pieces before measuring 1 cup. Peel the oranges, then slice them in half and then slice each half into thin half-moons. Thinly slice the green onions. Add the spinach, cooled broccoli and kidney beans to the salad and lightly toss. Set aside until the meat is done.
6. **Grill the steak.** Remove the meat from the marinade and spray each piece lightly with the canola oil spray before placing on the grill. Discard the marinade unless using an infusion grill. Grill the steaks according to the Grill Times opposite or until the interior temperature reaches the doneness you desire on an instant read thermometer. Consult the grilling chart on page 101 for exact internal temperatures: 140° to 150° F for medium.

7. To serve, put equal amounts of the tossed salad on 4 plates. Thinly slice the meat across the grain and place equal amounts artfully on top of each salad. Drizzle each salad with 2 tablespoons of the dressing, garnish with fresh cilantro leaves and corn chips. Serve immediately.

Grill Times

Two-Sided Contact Grill: *5 to 7 minutes for medium.*

Hibachi Grill, Combination Grill or Infusion Grill: *10 to 14 minutes for medium. Turn halfway through the grilling time. Grills with lids may be covered halfway through the grilling time. Infusion grills with lids may be covered for the entire grilling time.*

Infusion Grill Notes: *For a more intense flavor, pour the leftover marinade mixture into infusion cup just before preheating grill. If there is not much leftover marinade, combine it with some extra wine or salsa to make ½ cup. If putting extra marinade in infusion cup, grill covered for the entire grilling time if the grill is equipped with a cover. Grill either covered or uncovered if infusion cup contains no marinade. To prevent salmonella contamination, do not baste with leftover marinade mixture in the infusion cup. Use only for steamed flavor.*

Salsa Salad Dressing

Makes 16 (1 tablespoon servings)

Super-Easy Version

½   cup bottled vinaigrette

½   cup mild chunky salsa

¼   cup fresh cilantro (optional)

Easy 10-Minute Version

¼   cup red wine vinegar

¼   cup olive oil

½   cup mild or hot chunky salsa

¼   cup fresh cilantro

⅛   teaspoon pressed garlic

Light salt and freshly ground
    pepper to taste

Choose either the Super-Easy Version ingredients or the Ten-Minute Version ingredients from the two salad dressing versions. Place all dressing ingredients in the blender and puree until smooth. Pour the dressing into an airtight container and set aside in the refrigerator until ready to serve the salad. This recipe will keep in an airtight container in your refrigerator for up to 2 weeks.

Approximate Nutrients Per Serving of Entire Meal

Calories 463	Protein 38 g / 32%	Carbohydrate 36 g / 31%	
Total sugar 13 g	Fat Total 18 g / 35%	Saturated Fat 6 g	
Cholesterol 73 mg	Sodium 460 mg	Fiber 12 g	Calcium 104 mg

(Calculated with 2 tablespoons of Salsa Salad Dressing.)

Cow Puncher's Favorite Fajitas with South Texas Smashed Beans

Hankering for a taste of the old west? Why not rustle up some gen-U-ine Tex-Mex cowboy food—grilled fajitas. Chuck wagon cooks along the Rio Grande River on the Texas-Mexico border created this tortilla and beef fast food for busy cattle wranglers. "Cookie" always took special care of the head cowboy by reserving the best cuts of meat for him. These were usually thin slices of skirt steak, known as "fajitas," or literally "sashes" in Spanish. The original fajitas were served straight up, as seasoned meat in tortillas with refried beans cooked in lard. My easy-to-make South Texas Smashed Beans give all the flavor of traditional refried beans without the fat. Through the years, savvy restaurateurs added all the other goodies that are now offered to fill our fajitas such as salsa, guacamole and shredded cheese, turning working man's food into a work of culinary art.

Menu Game Plan

Prep & Cooking Time: 50 to 60 minutes

- Preheat the grill.
- Preheat the oven for the tortillas.
- Prepare and season the meat.
- Make the South Texas Smashed Beans.
- Put the garnishes into serving bowls.
- Grill the vegetables and arrange them on a platter.
- Grill the meat then slice.
- Warm the tortillas while the meat is grilling.

Cook's Notes

Notes

The best way to serve flank or skirt steak is sliced across the grain because it keeps the meat tender and juicy. Here's why: Meat is the muscle of the animal. Muscle fibers are known as the "grain of the meat." When you slice across the grain of the meat, you are slicing at a right angle to the muscle fibers. You can make tougher cuts of cooked meat seem more tender by slicing them across the grain because the length of the muscle fiber is very short and easier to chew. The tenderest pieces of raw meat or poultry cut with the grain (or parallel to the muscle fibers) become extremely tough when grilled because the long muscle fibers shrink into a tough mass as they cook.

Cow Puncher's Fajitas

Tequila Seasoning Paste

2 tablespoons lime juice

2 tablespoons tequila or orange juice

2 teaspoons pressed garlic

2 tablespoons chili powder

½ to 1 teaspoon ground cinnamon (optional)

1 teaspoon canola or corn oil

Fajitas

1¼ pounds flank steak or skirt steak

2 medium bell peppers, red, yellow or green

1 medium red onion

Canola or fat-free cooking oil spray

8 (6- to 10-inch) low-fat flour or corn tortillas

1 large or 2 small avocados, sliced

Prepared salsa or one of my salsa recipes

Nonfat sour cream

Nonfat or low-fat shredded Cheddar cheese

Fresh cilantro

1. Preheat the grill to the highest setting.

2. Preheat the oven to 350°F for warming the fajitas.

3. Make the Tequila Seasoning Paste and marinate the meat. Measure all paste ingredients into a 1-cup bowl or glass measure and mix thoroughly with a fork. Set aside until ready to use.

4. Flatten the meat. Trim the excess fat from the meat and cut it into 4 equal square pieces.

Spread a large piece of plastic wrap on a flat work surface. Arrange the meat in a single layer over the plastic wrap then cover it with another large piece of plastic wrap. Pound the meat with the bottom of a large heavy skillet, flat side of a meat mallet, or rolling pin until flattened to about ¼- to ½-inch thick.

Place meat in a 1-gallon zippered freezer-weight storage bag, a 1-quart airtight container, or a shallow square glass dish (8 x 8 x 2-inch).

With your fingertips, smear the marinade paste onto all sides of the flattened meat. Squeeze the air out of the bag and zip it closed, or cover the container or dish and marinate in the refrigerator for 20 minutes or up to 24 hours.

5. Prepare and grill the bell peppers and the onion. Slice each bell pepper in half lengthwise and remove the stem and seeds. Cut each half lengthwise into ½-inch strips. Slice onion across the meridian into ½-inch rings. Put the vegetables into a 3- to 4-cup bowl and spray all surfaces lightly with cooking spray. Start grilling the vegetables as soon as the grill has reached the set temperature. Grill according to the Grill Times opposite until the peppers are cooked through yet tender-crisp, and the onion slices are tender. When the vegetables are done, keep them warm until serving time on a platter covered with aluminum foil.

6. Grill the steak. Remove the meat from the marinating dish and discard any paste not adhering to the meat. Spray the meat lightly with the cooking spray before placing it on the grill. Grill the steaks according to the Grill Times or until the internal temperature reaches the doneness you desire on an instant read thermometer. Consult the grilling chart on page 101 for exact internal temperatures: 140° to 150°F for medium.

Instead of beef substitute equal amounts of boneless-skinless chicken breasts, pork tenderloin, a firm fleshed fish like tuna or swordfish, shellfish such as shrimp or scallops, or extra firm tofu.
If you want a smoky flavor, add a couple of drops of liquid smoke to the marinade.

7. Warm the tortillas while the meat is grilling. Place the tortillas on a nonstick baking sheet and cover with a damp color-free paper towel. Cover with aluminum foil then place in a preheated 350°F oven for 4 to 5 minutes until tortillas are warmed.

(Microwave Method: Place the tortillas on a dinner plate and cover with a color-free paper towel. Sprinkle the towel with about 2 teaspoons water. The towel should be damp, not wet. Microwave 20 to 30 seconds on high (100% power).)

8. Put garnishes into decorative serving bowls while the meat is grilling (guacamole, sour cream, salsa and shredded cheese).

9. To serve, transfer the meat to a cutting board and let stand covered with aluminum foil 2 to 3 minutes to let the juices settle. Thinly slice each piece of meat across the grain into 1/4- to 1/2-inch strips. Arrange the meat on the serving platter with the grilled peppers and onions.

Put the warmed tortillas on a plate. Set out the optional garnishes. Let diners assemble their own fajitas by putting a tortilla in the middle of their plate then topping with a couple of strips of meat, grilled onions and peppers, a couple of avocado slices or a spoonful of guacamole, a spoon full of nonfat sour cream, salsa and top with a sprinkling of cheese. Fold two sides of the tortilla over one another to make a long tube. Then, before eating, fold up the bottom end so the food doesn't slip out when you pick up the filled tortilla. Serve the South Texas Smashed Beans on the side.

Grill Times

Two-Sided Contact Grill: Peppers and onions 7 to 10 minutes / meat 5 to 7 minutes for medium.

Hibachi Grill, Combination Grill or Infusion Grill: Peppers and onions 14 to 20 minutes / meat 10 to 14 minutes for medium. Turn the peppers, onions and meat halfway through the grilling time. Grills with lids may be covered halfway through the grilling time. Infusion grills with lids may be covered for the entire grilling time.

Infusion Grill Notes: For a more intense flavor, mix 1 tablespoon pressed garlic with 1/4 cup orange juice and 1/4 cup tequila or lime juice in a 1-cup measure or bowl. Pour mixture into infusion cup before preheating grill.

South Texas Smashed Beans

Makes 4 (½ cup) servings

1   tablespoon canola or corn oil

½   cup chopped onion

1   teaspoon pressed garlic

1   tablespoon chili powder

3   tablespoons diced canned chilies, mild or hot

2   16-ounce cans pinto or pink beans

½   cup nonfat beef broth

½   teaspoon light salt

These beans can be refrigerated up to 3 days in advance or frozen in an airtight container for up to 2 months. The flavors mature after 24 hours.

1. In a 1- or 2-quart nonstick pot, heat the canola oil over a low flame. Add the onion, garlic, chili powder and canned chilies.
2. Cook onion mixture covered over a low flame, 10 to 15 minutes, lifting the lid to stir occasionally, until the onions are tender.
3. Rinse the beans in a colander under cool running water and drain well.
4. In a food processor fitted with the metal chopping blade or a blender, puree the beans, beef broth and salt.
5. When the onions are done, scrape the bean mixture into the pot using a rubber spatula. Mix the beans thoroughly with the onions using a heatproof spoon. Heat covered over a low flame until hot, about 5 to 6 minutes, stirring every 2 minutes to prevent burning. Take off of the flame and set aside. Keep covered until serving.

Reheat over a low flame stirring constantly. Or, transfer the beans to a microwavable casserole and microwave covered for 3 to 4 minutes on high (100% power), stirring halfway through the cooking time. If the mixture becomes too thick as it reheats, stir in a tablespoon or two of beef broth.

V a r i a t i o n :

For vegetarians: Substitute thick strips of extra firm tofu for the beef. Marinate according to the directions above and spray lightly with the cooking spray before grilling. See page 247 for tofu grilling instructions.

Approximate Nutrients Per Serving of Entire Meal

Total Calories 797	Protein 53 g / 27%	Carbohydrate 106 g / 53%
Total Sugar 12 g	Fat Total 19 g / 20%	Saturated Fat 6 g / 7%
Cholesterol 73 mg	Sodium 1756 mg	Fiber 34 g Calcium 189 mg

(Calcuated with 2 flank steak fajitas per serving, each containing 2.5 ounces raw meat, 1 fat-free flour tortilla, bell peppers, onions, 1 tablespoon nonfat sour cream, 1 tablespoon salsa, and ½ cup smashed beans.)

Chimichurri Pork Burritos

Chimichurri is the ketchup of South America. Whether you dine in a private home, at an outdoor barbecue stall, or in a posh restaurant, chimichurri is available whenever meat is on the menu. Served throughout South America, from Nicaragua to Chile, each version of this pungent sauce is as unique as the cook who created it. The basic recipe, a puree of four basic ingredients—olive oil, salt, garlic and parsley—may be enlivened with any combination of the following: hot peppers, carrots, celery, vinegar, bell peppers, thyme and capers. Although this sauce is served as a raw puree like Italian pesto, there are some recipes that require cooking. My chimichurri is raw and serves both as a marinade for the pork and a seasoning sauce for the rice and beans.

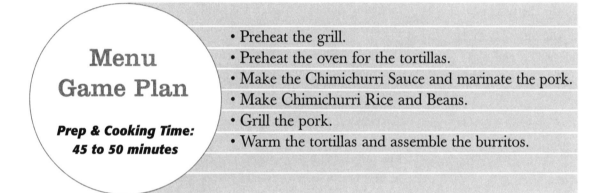

Menu Game Plan

*Prep & Cooking Time:
45 to 50 minutes*

- Preheat the grill.
- Preheat the oven for the tortillas.
- Make the Chimichurri Sauce and marinate the pork.
- Make Chimichurri Rice and Beans.
- Grill the pork.
- Warm the tortillas and assemble the burritos.

Cook's Notes

Pork tenderloin has become a favorite of waist-watchers because it is low in fat (about 7 grams of fat in 4 ounces cooked). That's because it lacks a marbling of fat throughout the muscles. Fat adds flavor and moisture as it melts during cooking, so without that extra fat, pork tenderloin can dry out on the grill and become bland. Since pork tenderloin is an extremely tender cut of meat, you can replace the flavor and juiciness of the missing fat with a highly seasoned rub, paste or marinade in just 20 minutes to 2 hours. Another way to prevent your pork tenderloin from drying out on the grill is to cook it to medium, or an internal temperature of 145°F, leaving it slightly pink in the center and extremely tender and juicy. (See page 102 about pork grilling temperatures.) You can also boost the flavor and add moisture to the cut with an extra step called brining. This is usually done before applying a rub or paste to the meat. (See page 36 for brining instructions.)

Pork Burritos

Serves 4

1   1¼ pound pork tenderloin

½   cup Chimichurri Sauce (see recipe page 42)

3   cups Chimichurri Rice and Beans (see recipe page 141)

4   10- to 11-inch flour tortillas

4   butter or leaf lettuce leaves

1   cup cherry tomatoes

1   cup cucumber slices

Low-fat or nonfat sour cream

Parsley sprigs

1. Preheat the grill to the highest setting.

2. Prepare the Chimichurri Sauce according to the directions on page 134, then pour ½ cup into a 1-quart zippered freezer bag, or airtight container or shallow glass dish (8 x 8 x 2-inch).

3. Prepare and marinate the pork tenderloins. Remove the silver skin from the tenderloin by slipping a sharp knife under the skin then angling it slightly upward as you use a gentle sawing motion to cut it away. Cut the pork tenderloin across the grain into 3-inch lengths.

Butterfly the meat by placing the pieces on your cutting board so that the length is perpendicular to your body. Holding your free hand on top of the pork, slice ¾ of the way through, leaving it "hinged" along one side so that it can open up to twice its original size like a book. Be sure that you cut evenly through the middle of the meat. With the palms of your hands, press the "hinge" down to flatten evenly.

Put the pork in the zippered bag, container or dish containing the marinade then turn it so all the surfaces are coated with the marinade. Squeeze the air out of the bag and zip it closed or cover the container or dish and refrigerate for 20 minutes or up to 2 hours.

4. Grill the pork tenderloins. (There is plenty of oil in the marinade, so you don't have to spray the meat with cooking spray.) Grill the meat according to the Grill Times opposite or until the internal temperature reaches the doneness you desire on an instant read thermometer. Consult the grilling chart on page 102 for exact internal temperatures: 145 to 150°F for medium.

5. Warm the tortillas while the meat is grilling. Place the tortillas on a non-stick baking sheet and cover with a damp color-free paper towel. Cover with aluminum foil then place in a pre-heated 350°F oven for 4 to 5 minutes until tortillas are warmed.

(Microwave Method: Place the tortillas on a dinner plate and cover with a color-free paper towel. Sprinkle the towel with about 2 teaspoons water. The towel should be damp, not wet. Microwave 20 to 30 seconds on high (100% power).)

6. To serve, garnish 4 dinner plates with equal amounts of lettuce, tomato and cucumber while the meat is grilling. When the meat is done, transfer it to a cutting board and let stand covered with aluminum foil 2 to 3 minutes to let the juices settle. Thinly slice each piece of meat across the grain ¼- to ½-inch thick.

Assemble the burritos. On a clean flat surface put out one warm tortilla. Spread ¾ cup of the Chimichurri Rice and Beans in a 2 by 5-inch rectangle on the bottom half of the tortilla. Top the rice with equal amounts of meat. Drizzle with 1 tablespoon of Chimichurri Sauce.

Fold the right and left sides of the tortilla towards the center over filling. Then, fold up the bottom edge of the tortilla and gently roll the burrito away from you so the tortilla is completely wrapped around the filling. Put each burrito seam side down on a plate. Spoon a dollop of sour cream on top of each burrito and garnish with a sprig of parsley. Serve immediately.

Grill Times

Two-Sided Contact Grill: 5 to 7 minutes for medium.

Hibachi Grill, Combination Grill or Infusion Grill: 10 to 14 minutes for medium. Turn the pork halfway through the grilling time. Grills with lids may be covered halfway through the grilling time. Infusion grills with lids may be covered for the entire grilling time.

Chimichurri Rice and Beans

Makes 4 (1 cup) servings

1¾ cups water

½ teaspoon light salt

1 cup long grain white rice

1 15 ounce can black eyed peas or black beans

¼ cup Chimichurri Sauce (see recipe page 134)

½ cup diced bell pepper

½ cup thinly sliced celery

1. In a 2- or 3-quart pot with a tight fitting lid, bring the water and salt to a rolling boil over high heat. Stir in the rice, bring back to a rolling boil then cover and immediately reduce the heat to a low simmer. Simmer until all the liquid is absorbed, about 20 minutes.
2. While the rice is cooking, rinse the beans in a strainer under cool running water to remove the preservatives and drain well.
3. When the rice is done, remove the pot from the heat, uncover quickly and fold in the beans using a spatula. Cover immediately and let stand for 10 minutes then fold in the Chimichurri sauce, bell pepper and celery. Cover until serving time.
4. To keep the rice warm until serving time, do not lift the lid. If the rice becomes too cool, transfer it into a microwavable casserole and reheat covered in the microwave for 2 to 4 minutes on high (100% power).

Chimichurri Sauce

Makes 1 cup

1   medium jalapeño pepper or
    2 medium serrano peppers

¼   cup olive oil

¼   cup white wine vinegar or
    distilled vinegar

2   tablespoons lemon juice

¼   cup water

1½ cups packed flat leaf parsley

2   medium green onions, sliced

1   tablespoon chopped fresh
    oregano or 1 teaspoon dried

1½ teaspoon chopped garlic

½   teaspoon finely ground
    black pepper

½   teaspoon light salt

To prepare the fresh peppers for this sauce, put on a pair of kitchen gloves to prevent the essential pepper oil from burning your hands. Use this sauce as both a marinade and finishing sauce for beef, chicken, fish or shellfish.

1. Using a small pairing knife, slice the stem end off of the jalapeño or serrano peppers. Slice the pepper in half lengthwise and use the tip of the knife to remove the seeds. Cut into ¼-inch thick pieces.

2. In a blender, pulse the peppers, olive oil, vinegar, lemon juice, water, parsley, green onions, oregano, garlic, black pepper and salt until well blended.

3. Refrigerate in an airtight container up to 3 days.

Approximate Nutrients Per Serving of Entire Meal

Total Calories 635	Protein 42 g / 26%	Carbohydrate 71 g / 45%
Total Sugar 3 g	Fat Total 18 g / 28%	Saturated Fat 4 g / 6%
Cholesterol 84 mg	Sodium 906 mg	Fiber 14 g Calcium 78 mg

Malaysian-Style Beef and Pear Satays with Lemony Peanut Sauce over Coconut Rice

Whether you spell it satay like the Malaysian or Thai, or saté like the Indonesian, this tasty meal on a stick is a Southeast Asian style kebab. The skewered meat may be thin in strips, or thick and chunky. The main flavoring ingredients in my Malaysian style satay dinner (coconut milk, peanuts and chilies) are used extensively in all 3 ethnic cuisines that dominate Malaysia's culinary potpourri: Malay, Chinese and Southern Indian. Malaysians enjoy coconut rice for breakfast and snacks as well as for dinner. The Lemony Peanut Sauce, a perfect compliment to the rice and satay, is one of my favorites because all you have to do is mix it up in a blender and serve!

Menu Game Plan

Prep & Cooking Time: 1 hour

- Preheat the grill.
- Marinate the meat.
- Make the Coconut Rice.
- Make the Lemony Peanut Sauce.
- Prepare and grill the kebabs.

Cook's Notes

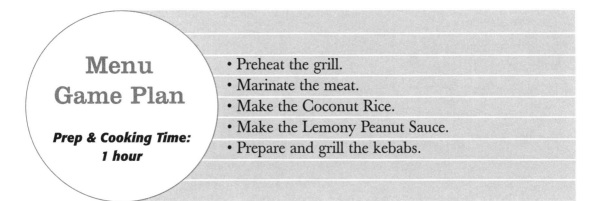

Coconut milk is not the juice found inside the coconut. It is made by boiling grated coconut pulp, pureeing it in a food processor or blender and then straining it to make smooth, pulp-free milk. Fortunately Southeastern Asian cuisine is easier than ever to reproduce because good-quality coconut milk is available in cans. Like cow's milk, the fat content of coconut milk varies. Most canned coconut milk is thicker and has more fat than fresh. "Light" canned coconut milk has half the fat of regular. If the "light" version is unavailable, make your own by blending one can of thick coconut milk and one can of water.

Since coconut milk goes bad within 2 days of refrigeration, freeze leftovers and defrost it in the microwave whenever needed.

Malaysian Satays

Serves 4

1 tablespoon peanut, canola, or your favorite vegetable oil

1 tablespoon light coconut milk

1 cup mild onion, white, Maui, Vidalia, or Walla Walla

2 tablespoons granulated sugar

½ teaspoon ground cumin

¼ teaspoon ground cinnamon

½ teaspoon tumeric

1 tablespoon natural peanut butter

1¼ pounds boneless beef sirloin

1 medium red bell pepper

2 medium size firm pears such as Asian or Bosc

16 8-inch bamboo skewers

Nonfat or canola oil cooking spray

½ cup thinly sliced green onions

¼ cup thinly sliced cucumber

½ cup shredded carrot

¼ cup shredded coconut or coarsely chopped peanuts

1. Preheat the grill to the highest setting.

2. Make the marinade. In a food processor or blender, puree the oil, coconut milk, onion, sugar, cumin, cinnamon, tumeric and peanut butter.

3. Marinate the meat. Cut the beef into 1-inch cubes then put it into a 1-gallon freezer-weight zipper bag or a 1-quart airtight container or non-corrosive shallow dish. Pour the marinade over all. Turn the meat pieces so all the surfaces are coated with the marinade, then squeeze the air out of the bag and zip it closed or cover the container or dish. Refrigerate for 20 minutes or up to 2 hours.

4. Prepare the pears and bell pepper. Leave the peel on the pears. Cut each one in half then remove the stem ends by cutting small V's around them with a sharp pairing knife. Remove the core with a melon baller. Position each pear half, sliced side down on a cutting board, then cut across the meridian into 1-inch-thick half moons.

Cut the bell pepper in half and remove the stem and seeds then cut it into (16 or up to 32) 1-inch square pieces.

5. Make the skewers. Remove the meat from the marinade; discard the marinade unless using an Infusion Grill.

Alternately thread the meat, bell pepper and pear pieces onto 8 (2 skewer) sets of parallel bamboo skewers leaving a ⅛- to ¼-inch space between each piece of food. (See page 192 for double skewering technique.) To allow the pear to lie flat on the grill, skewer it so that the parallel skewers pierce the center first then come out through the peel.

6. Grill the skewers. Spray each prepared skewer lightly with cooking spray before placing on the grill. Grill the skewers according to the Grill Times opposite until the internal temperature reaches the doneness you desire on an instant read thermometer. Consult the grilling chart on page 101 for exact temperatures: 140° to 150° F for medium.

7. To serve, spoon equal amounts of rice onto the center of 4 plates. Arrange 2 skewers on opposite sides of the rice. Garnish around the edges of the rice with even amounts of the cucumber slices and shredded carrot. Top the rice with ¼ cup of the peanut sauce and sprinkle with 1 tablespoon each of the green onion and coconut. Serve immediately, passing around the remaining sauce.

Two-Sided Contact Grill: *5 to 6 minutes for medium.*

Hibachi Grill, Combination Grill or Infusion Grill: *10 to 14 minutes for medium. Turn the skewers 180° halfway through the grilling time. Grills with lids may be covered halfway through the grilling time. Infusion grills with lids may be covered for the entire grilling time.*

Infusion Grill Notes: *For a more intense flavor, pour the leftover marinade into infusion cup before putting the skewers on the grill. If there is not much leftover marinade, combine it with some extra lemon juice to make ½ cup before pouring into infusion cup. Grill covered for entire time if putting extra marinade in infusion cup. Grill either covered or uncovered if infusion cup contains no marinade.*

Substitutions:
Pears are out of season? Substitute jicama, or two 5-ounce cans of whole water chestnuts. To prepare the water chestnuts, rinse them in a colander under cool running water and drain well before using. Skewer the chestnuts through the center of the circle.

Coconut Rice

Makes 4 generous (1 cup) servings

2   cups light coconut milk

1   cup fat-free canned chicken broth

1½ cups long grain white rice

You can make this rice ahead, refrigerate up to 2 days or freeze up to 2 months in an airtight container or zippered freezer bag.

1. In a 2-quart pot over high heat, bring the coconut milk and chicken broth to a boil.
2. Stir in the rice. Reduce heat to low, cover and simmer 20 minutes, or until all liquid is absorbed. Remove the pot from the heat. Do not lift the lid to stir rice as the trapped heat is continuing to steam it. Let stand covered on the counter on a trivet or on a cool stove burner for 10 minutes before fluffing with a fork and serving.

Lemony Peanut Sauce

Makes 8 (¹/₄ cup) servings

½ cup mild onion such as white, Maui, Vidalia, Walla Walla

¾ cup lemon juice

¾ cup natural chunky peanut butter from roasted peanuts or reduced fat peanut butter

1 teaspoon grated gingerroot

1 to 2 teaspoons dried chili flakes

3 tablespoons granulated sugar

If stored in an airtight container, this sauce can be refrigerated up to 3 days or frozen up to 2 months.

1. Cut the onion into chunks and place in a food processor or blender. Add the lemon juice, peanut butter, ginger, chili flakes and sugar. Process to puree.
3. Pour into a 3 or 4 cup decorative bowl. Set aside on the counter until ready to serve.

Approximate Nutrients Per Serving of Entire Meal

Total Calories 786	Protein 46 g / 24%	Carbohydrate 90 g / 46%
Total Sugar 21 g	Fat Total 26 g / 30%	Saturated Fat 5 g / 6%
Cholesterol 95 mg	Sodium 286 mg	Fiber 5 g	Calcium 57 m

(Including 2 satays, 1¹/₄ cups Coconut Rice and ¹/₄ cup Lemony Peanut Sauce made with reduced fat peanut butter.)

Cowboy Kebabs with Easy Ridin' BBQ Sauce and Rootin' Tootin' Texas Tabouli

Texas style pork kebabs and Middle Eastern tabouli salad? A wild menu no Texas Cowboy ever dreamed of. But don't knock it if you haven't tried it. Your taste buds will make the connection when you transform tabouli, a cracked wheat, parsley and tomato salad traditionally made in Lebanon and Syria, into Southwestern fast food. The secret is starting with a packaged tabouli mix, then seasoning it with Texas-style ingredients such as fresh cilantro, jicama, corn, and Tabasco.

Menu Game Plan

Prep & Cooking Time: 50 minutes

- Preheat the grill.
- Make the Rootin' Tootin' Tabouli.
- Make the Rough Ridin' BBQ Sauce.
- Prepare the Cowboy Kebabs.
- Grill the kebabs.

Cook's Notes

Jicama (HEE-ka-ma). When you peel away the unassuming brown skin of this edible tuber with a vegetable peeler or knife, you'll find a delightful white vegetable with the crunch of a water chestnut and the flavor of fresh sweet peas. The part you eat grows underground while the part of the plant that grows above ground produces poisonous pea pods. Diced or sliced, it is a favorite ingredient in Southwest, Mexican, Chinese, Philippine and Asian cuisine for salads, hors d'oeuvres, salsas, soups and stir-frys. I use jicama in the tabouli to give this refreshing salad an unexpected crunch. But, I also love to grill jicama. As it grills it keeps its shape and crispness, yet becomes sweeter as its natural sugars caramelize. (See Arizona Sunrise Grilled Pepper and Roasted Corn Salad on page 260.) I usually grill jicama raw because I like it to crunch. But if you prefer a more tender texture inside, you can steam them first on your stove top or microwave. (See precooking instructions for jicama, page 246).

Cowboy Kebabs

Serves 4

1¼ pounds pork tenderloin

2 medium size bell peppers, red, yellow, or orange

½ pound jicama root

Light salt and freshly ground pepper to taste

16 8-inch bamboo skewers

1 recipe Easy Ridin' BBQ Sauce (see recipe page 150)

Nonfat or canola oil cooking spray

8 large lettuce leaves, Romaine or leaf lettuce

4 lemon wedges

1. **Preheat the grill** to the highest setting.

2. **Prepare the vegetables and meat.** Peel the jicama with a vegetable peeler or sharp pairing knife then cut it into (16 or up to 32) 1-inch cubes (2 to 4 pieces per kabob). Cut the bell pepper in half and remove the stem and seeds, then cut it into (16 or up to 32) 1-inch square pieces. Cut the meat into 1-inch cubes.

(Optional step: Precook the jicama to tenderize it and make it easier to put on the skewers. Steam or boil 4 to 5 minutes, or microwave the jicama with ¼ cup hot water in a covered 1-quart casserole 3 minutes on high (100% power). Cool in a strainer under cold running water. Jicama should be tender but still crisp before it goes on the grill.)

3. **Make the kebabs.** Alternately thread the meat, bell peppers, and jicama onto 8 (2-skewer) sets of parallel bamboo skewers leaving a ⅛- to ¼-inch space between each piece of food. (See page 192 for double skewering technique.)

4. **Grill the kebabs.** Sprinkle each prepared kabob lightly with salt and pepper, then spray with cooking spray. Place the kebabs on the grill, then baste the upper side with the Rough Ridin' Sauce. Grill the kebabs according to the Grill Times below or until the internal temperature reaches the doneness you desire on an instant-read thermometer. Consult the grilling chart on page 102 for exact internal temperatures: 140° to 150°F for medium.

5. **To serve,** arrange 2 leaves of Romaine lettuce leaves on one side of 4 dinner plates. Spoon equal amounts of tabouli on top of the leaves. Place kebabs beside the tabouli. Serve immediately, passing around extra barbecue sauce.

Grill Times

Two-Sided Contact Grill: *5 to 7 minutes for medium. Baste halfway through the grilling time.*

Hibachi Grill, Combination Grill or Infusion Grill: *10 to 14 minutes for medium. Turn the skewers 180° and baste halfway through the grilling time. Grills with lids may be covered halfway through the grilling time. Infusion grills with lids may be covered for the entire grilling time.*

Rootin' Tootin' Texas Tabouli

Makes 4 (1¼ cup) servings

1	5.25-ounce box tabouli mix
½	teaspoon garlic powder
1	tablespoon extra-virgin olive oil
1	cup boiling water
¼	cup green onions, thinly sliced
½	cup finely chopped fresh cilantro (optional)
½	cup thinly sliced or diced cucumber (preferably hothouse)
1	cup coarsely chopped tomatoes
½	cup shredded carrot
½	cup petite corn kernels, canned or frozen

Dressing

2	tablespoons red wine vinegar
⅛	to 2 teaspoons hot pepper sauce such as Tabasco (optional)
1	tablespoon extra-virgin olive oil
	Light salt and freshly ground pepper to taste

This recipe can be refrigerated in an airtight container up to 3 days before serving.

1. Hydrate the tabouli. In a 6-cup bowl or airtight container with a lid, mix the tabouli, seasoning mix from the box, garlic powder, oil and water. Cover with plastic wrap or a lid and let hydrate in the refrigerator for 30 minutes.
2. Prepare the vegetables. While the tabouli is hydrating, use a chef's knife or food processor to slice the green onions, cilantro, cucumber, tomatoes and carrots. Rinse the corn kernels in a strainer under cool running water and drain well. When tabouli has hydrated and cooled, use a rubber spatula to gently fold in the prepared vegetables and thawed corn kernels until thoroughly mixed.
3. Make the dressing. In a 1- to 2-cup measure, whisk the vinegar, hot pepper sauce, oil, salt and pepper with a fork until blended. Drizzle the dressing over the tabouli then fold it in with a rubber spatula to coat all the grains and vegetables. Cover and set aside in the refrigerator until ready to serve.

Easy Ridin' BBQ Sauce

Makes 1 cup BBQ sauce

2 teaspoons extra-virgin olive oil

¼ cup finely chopped white, yellow, or red onion

1 teaspoon pressed garlic

½ cup catsup

1 tablespoon plus 1 teaspoon packed brown sugar

1 tablespoon chili powder

1 teaspoon spicy brown mustard

1 tablespoon fresh lime juice

½ to 2 teaspoons hot pepper sauce such as Tabasco (optional)

2 tablespoons red wine vinegar

This sauce can be refrigerated for up to 1 week or frozen for up to 2 months if stored in an airtight container.

1. In a 6- or 8-inch nonstick skillet over medium heat, heat the olive oil. When it begins to sizzle, add the onion and garlic then sauté, stirring constantly for 4 to 6 minutes until the onions are transparent and tender.
2. Scrape the cooked onion into a 1- or 2-cup bowl or glass measure. With a fork, thoroughly mix in the catsup, brown sugar, chili powder, mustard, lime juice, hot pepper sauce and vinegar until the sugar is dissolved.
3. Measure ¼ cup of the sauce into a small bowl to baste the meat during cooking. Separating the garnish sauce from the basting sauce ahead of grilling prevents cross-contamination by the basting brush that is being used on uncooked meat. Use the remaining sauce to garnish the kebabs when done.

Super Easy BBQ Sauce

Makes 1 cup BBQ sauce

½ cup of your favorite bottled sauce (don't use hickory flavored)

1 tablespoon chili powder

2 tablespoons dehydrated chopped onions

If you don't want to take the time to make my BBQ sauce, mix the bottled sauce, chili powder and onions with a fork in a 1 or 2-cup bowl or glass measure.

Use and store exactly like the "from-scratch" BBQ Sauce above.

Approximate Nutrients Per Serving of Entire Meal

Total Calories 455	Protein 36 g / 32%	Carbohydrate 47 g / 41%
Total Sugar 8 g	Fat Total 13 g / 27%	Saturated Fat 3 g / 6%
Cholesterol 92 mg	Sodium 567 mg	Fiber 11 g Calcium 81 mg

(Calculated with 2 kebabs, 2 tablespoons barbecue sauce, and 1¼ cups tabouli.)

Rockin' Moroccan Lamb Kebabs with Honey Lemon Sauce over Jeweled Couscous

When the Arabs invaded Morocco in the seventh century, they rocked the local culinary world with their highly developed cuisine. Thanks to the Arabs, modern Moroccan dishes are seasoned with ginger, cinnamon, saffron, tumeric, peppercorns, caraway, cloves, allspice, cardamom and cumin. The Arabs also introduced the idea of mixing sweet, sour and savory ingredients, a combination they adapted from Persian cuisine. Moroccan couscous and tagines, which are slow cooking meat or poultry stews, are often seasoned in the Arabic style with sweet ingredients like fresh or dried fruit, cinnamon, cardamom, honey, and sugar, sour lemon and savory vegetables like onion and tomato. I created this menu to capture these sumptuous Moroccan flavors and to help you make a conquest of your own . . . time! Instead of slow cooking lamb in a sweet and sour tagine stew, you'll quickly re-create the flavors with fast grilling lamb, apple and zucchini kebabs drizzled with my easy-to-make Honey Lemon Sauce. Jeweled Couscous adorned with toasted almonds and carrots rounds out the meal. To serve up an authentic bit of Moroccan hospitality, finish the meal by offering a cup of steaming mint tea.

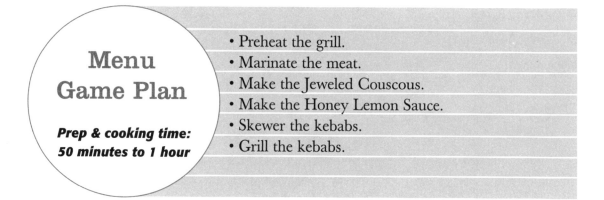

Menu Game Plan

**Prep & cooking time:
50 minutes to 1 hour**

- Preheat the grill.
- Marinate the meat.
- Make the Jeweled Couscous.
- Make the Honey Lemon Sauce.
- Skewer the kebabs.
- Grill the kebabs.

Cook's Notes

In Arabic, they are called "shish kebab." "Shashlik" is the name in Russia and the countries of the Caucasus (Armenia, Azerbaijan and Georgia). In India, they are called "tikka" and in Asia "satay" or "sate." If you want to order them in France, you will ask for a "brochette." In America we put "kebabs" on the grill. Whatever you call them, the meaning is the same . . . small chunks of food grilled on a skewer.

Serves 4

1¼ pounds lean, boneless leg of lamb

⅓ cup lemon juice

¼ cup orange juice

2 teaspoons pressed garlic

1 teaspoon ground cinnamon

1 teaspoon ground cumin

½ teaspoon freshly ground pepper

Pinch ground cloves

2 medium firm apples such as Granny Smith, Fuji or Braeburn

2 medium zucchini

16 8-inch bamboo skewers

Nonfat or olive oil cooking spray

Lamb Kebabs

1. **Preheat the grill** to the highest setting.

2. **Make the marinade.** In a 1-cup bowl or glass measure, mix the lemon juice, orange juice, garlic, cinnamon, cumin, ground pepper and cloves thoroughly with a fork.

3. **Marinate the meat.** Cut the lamb into 1-inch cubes then put it into a 1-gallon freezer-weight zipper bag or a 1-quart airtight container or shallow glass dish (8 x 8 x 2-inch). Pour the marinade over all. Turn the meat pieces so all the surfaces are coated with the marinade, then zip the bag closed or cover the container or dish. Refrigerate for 20 minutes or up to 24 hours.

4. **Prepare the apples and zucchini.** Leave the peel on the apples. Cut each in half through the stem end. Use a pairing knife to remove the stem and core ends from each apple half by cutting a small V at both ends. Use a melon baller to remove the core. Position each apple half, sliced side down, on a cutting board, and then slice each across the meridian into 1-inch thick half moons. Cut the zucchini into 1-inch thick rounds.

5. **Skewer the kebabs.** Remove the meat from the marinade; discard the marinade unless using an infusion grill. Alternately thread the meat, apple pieces, and zucchini onto 8 (2 skewer) sets of parallel bamboo skewers leaving a ⅛- to ¼-inch space between each piece of food. (See page 192 for double skewering technique.) To allow the apple and zucchini slices to lie flat on the grill, skewer the apples so that the parallel skewers pierce the core side then come out through the peel. Skewer the zucchini so that the parallel skewers pierce through the peel on two sides instead of through the center.

6. **Grill the kebabs.** Spray each kabob lightly with cooking spray before placing on the grill. Grill the kebabs according to the Grill Times or until the internal temperature reaches the doneness you desire on an instant-read thermometer. Consult the grilling chart on page 101 for exact temperatures: 140° to 150°F for medium.

7. **To serve,** place equal amounts of the couscous on 4 plates. Arrange two skewers on opposite sides of the couscous. Top the couscous with ¼ cup of the lemon sauce and sprinkle with 1 tablespoon parsley if desired before serving.

Two-Sided Contact Grill: *5 to 7 minutes for medium.*

Hibachi Grill, Combination Grill or Infusion Grill: *10 to 14 minutes for medium. Turn kebabs halfway through the grilling time. Grills with lids may be covered halfway through the grilling time. Infusion grills with lids may be covered for the entire grilling time.*

Infusion Grill Notes: *For more intense flavor, pour the leftover marinade mixture into the infusion cup. If there is not much leftover marinade, combine it with some extra orange juice to make ½ cup. If your grill is equipped with a lid, cover for 5 minutes before cooking the meat to allow the marinade in the cup to warm and grill covered for the entire cooking time.*

Substitutions:
Substitute 1 pound pork tenderloin, center cut pork loin, beef sirloin, skirt or flank steak trimmed of fat, boneless skinless chicken breast or 1 pound of extra-firm tofu for the lamb.

Jeweled Couscous

Makes 4 (1¼) cup servings

2¼ cups canned nonfat chicken broth

1 cup coarsely grated carrot

½ cup dried currants

1⅓ cup plain instant couscous (equivalent to 1 10-ounce box)

½ cup toasted blanched slivered almonds

Substitutions:
Instead of canned chicken broth, try canned vegetable broth or water.
Instead of almonds, try pine nuts or shelled pistachios.

This recipe can be made up to 2 days ahead and refrigerated in an airtight container or zippered freezer bag, or frozen for up to 2 months. Defrost overnight in the refrigerator, or in the microwave. To reheat in the microwave, transfer the couscous to a 2-quart microwavable dish. Cook covered for 2 to 4 minutes on high (100% power) or until hot, stirring halfway through the cooking time.

1. In a 2-quart non-stick saucepan over medium-high heat, bring the broth to a boil.
2. When the liquid reaches a boil, add the carrot and currants then cook for 2 minutes.
3. Stir in the couscous and nuts. Remove from the heat, cover and set aside for 5 minutes until the couscous is hydrated. To keep the couscous warm, do not remove the pot cover until serving time. Fluff with a fork before serving. If the couscous needs reheating, transfer it to a microwavable casserole and follow the directions above.

Honey Lemon Sauce

Makes 7 (¼ cup) servings

1   teaspoon extra-virgin olive oil

½   cup finely chopped onion

¼   teaspoon ground coriander

1   teaspoon pressed garlic

¼   teaspoon ground cinnamon

1   tablespoon honey

1   cup canned nonfat or
     low-fat chicken broth

2   tablespoons cornstarch

½   cup frozen lemonade
     concentrate, thawed

Substitutions:
Instead of olive oil, substitute your favorite vegetable oil. Instead of canned chicken broth, substitute canned vegetable broth.

This recipe can be made up to 2 days in advance and reheated in the microwave. Leftover sauce can be frozen in an airtight container for up to 3 months, then defrosted and reheated in the microwave.

1. In a 1-quart nonstick pot, heat the oil over medium-high heat.
2. When oil is hot, stir in the onion, coriander, garlic and cinnamon. Turn the heat down to medium and cook covered until onions are tender, 4 to 5 minutes. Remove cover once or twice during the cooking time to stir the onions.
4. While the onions are cooking, in a blender or 2-cup bowl or measure, thoroughly mix the honey, broth, cornstarch and lemonade concentrate.
5. When the onions are tender, pour the lemonade mixture into the pot and turn the heat to medium-high. Cook uncovered over medium-high heat, whisking constantly until the sauce is thickened, about 2 to 3 minutes.
6. Remove from the heat, cover and then set aside until serving time. If the sauce cools before serving, reheat over low heat, whisking constantly. If it gets too thick while reheating, whisk in a few teaspoons of broth.

Approximate Nutrients Per Serving of Entire Meal

Calories 674	Protein 41g / 24%	Carbohydrate 91g / 54%
Total sugar 35g	Fat Total 16g / 22%	Saturated Fat 3g / 5%
Cholesterol 72mg	Sodium 203mg	Fiber 10g Calcium 136mg

Perfect Poultry

What's the quickest solution for putting a healthy grilled poultry dinner on the table? Start with boneless-skinless chicken or turkey parts, and you'll have them flying from your grill to table within 15 minutes. Small, bone-in poultry pieces like wings can take over 30 minutes to grill. Thick, large pieces, like turkey thighs and legs, must be pre-cooked (either in the oven or microwave) to ensure the meat at the bone is on its way to being done before the cooking is finished on the electric indoor grill. Skin renders a lot of fat as it grills, creating a huge mess no matter what type of grill you own. And who wants to spend time cleaning splattered fat off counters and cabinets? (Grilled, skinless poultry is also much lower in fat. See the chart.) Boneless-skinless chicken breasts and thighs, and boneless-skinless turkey meat are interchangeable in all the recipes in this chapter.

The following are solutions for purchasing the best quality poultry:

Solution 1: Know How to Interpret the Product Description

Have you ever grilled chicken or turkey to perfection, but when you tasted it the flavor and texture was not as good as you expected? That's because the taste of poultry comes from what it eats and how it is raised. Consider the following to help you make your decision about which brand to purchase.

Natural poultry does not contain any artificial flavoring, coloring ingredients, chemical preservatives or any other synthetic ingredient, and the product is minimally processed. Minimal processing means the meat can be smoked, roasted, frozen, or dried to make it edible or to preserve it for safe consumption. It is legal for poultry producers to raise their chickens and turkeys with antibiotics and still call them "naturally grown."

Antibiotic-free means poultry is free from antibiotics for its entire life (from the hatchery to the

Poultry Nutrient Calculator

Per 4 Ounces	Calories	Total Fat (gm)	Saturated Fat (gm)	Cholesterol (mg)	Protein (gm)
Chicken breast, skinless, boneless	124	1	.4	66	26
Chicken breast, with skin, boneless	195	10	3	73	24
Chicken thigh, skinless, boneless	135	4	1	94	22
Chicken thigh, with skin, boneless	148	9	3	56	15
Turkey breast, skinless, boneless	133	1	.2	82	30
Turkey breast, with skin, boneless	154	6	2	60	24

processing plant). Conventional poultry producers usually feed antibiotics to their chickens or turkeys through the water system to encourage growth, as well as to prevent and treat disease.

Free-range poultry have spent time between enclosed houses and outdoor pens where they can forage and roam freely. Conventional poultry are never allowed to go outdoors and are raised in the confinement of poultry houses. Free-range poultry producers believe that birds able to roam freely outdoors have better-developed, meatier legs. They also believe that free-range birds have better flavor because they eat the fermented grains and seeds available in the grasses and soil in the outdoor pen.

Certified organic chickens and turkeys have been fed certified organic feed for their entire lives. Certified organic feed contains grains grown in soil that has been free of pesticides and chemical fertilizers for a period of 3 years. No drugs of any kind can be used in organic poultry production. In order to be certified organic, an independent, third-party certifier must verify that organic practices were used during all steps of poultry production and distribution. A complete audit trail must be maintained at all times that can trace a chicken or turkey from hatching to the supermarket. USDA labeling regulations require the phrase "certified organic by a third party certifier" on the label.

Hormone-Free: The entire poultry industry has been "hormone-free" since around 1960. Before that time, hormones were being used to make bigger and calmer birds.

Vegetarian diet means the poultry is fed a vegetable diet usually based on corn and soybean meal. Many chickens are fed a diet that includes animal fat and animal by-products. Poultry processors who feed their chickens and turkeys vegetarian diets either put that information on the package or supply the butcher with brochures.

Solution 2: Check the Grade

The USDA requires poultry processors to inspect for signs of disease, but grading for quality is voluntary. To be allowed to put the USDA Grade A shield on poultry packaging, the poultry must have plump meaty bodies, and be free of bruises, discoloration, broken bones, cuts and feathers. If the poultry you are purchasing is sold fresh and unpacked, don't be afraid to ask your butcher if there is any literature available that describes the product.

Solution 3: Check the Package Date

Even though the USDA does not require poultry processors and stores to put a freshness date on their packaging, most voluntarily include one of the following:

- **"Sell-By" date** tells the store how long to display the poultry for sale. It is usually not more than a week from the date that the poultry arrives at the store. I suggest always purchasing poultry before the "sell-by" date expires.
- **"Best if Used By" date** is not a purchase or safety date. It tells you the date the poultry will have the best flavor.
- **"Use-by" date** gives you the last date recommended by the poultry processor for peak quality. After the "use-by" date expires, fresh poultry may not taste great, but it can still be cooked if it smells and looks good. Poultry parts can be frozen for up to 9 months; whole poultry up to 12 months. So if you freeze it before the "use-by" date expires and want to cook it long after the "use-by" date has expired, the poultry can still be used. A store may legally sell fresh poultry beyond the expiration date on the package if they deem it wholesome. It is also legal for meat vendors to change the date on poultry that they cut and wrap themselves. It is illegal, though, for meat vendors to change the date on a container that has been packaged under federal inspection. If a date has expired on packaged poultry and it is still considered safe to eat, the package may be sold but it is illegal to alter or change the expired date, or cover it with a new date.

Whether the date on the package is a "sell-by" or "use-by," the poultry should be cooked or frozen within 1 or 2 days of purchase.

Solution 4: Make Sure Fresh Poultry is Really Fresh and Frozen Poultry is Really Frozen.

According to USDA standards, "fresh" means that raw poultry has never been below 26°F. Fresh poultry can cost more than frozen, so if "fresh" poultry is frozen at the time of purchase, think twice about buying it. Any poultry held at 0°F or below must be labeled "frozen" or "previously frozen."

Solution 5: "Look-and-Feel" Test

• Look to make sure that the poultry has no whitish slime on the surface and no ice crystals are visible whether fresh or frozen.
• Feel the package to make sure that it is cool to the touch.
• The color of raw poultry is not an indicator of its freshness but is a direct result of its age, breed, exercise and/or diet. Raw poultry can range in color from yellow to bluish-white. If the skin has a bluish tint, it is most likely from a young bird because they have less fat under the skin. Poultry fed large amounts of corn and corn gluten has yellow colored skin due to a chemical called xanthophyll that naturally occurs in yellow corn. Birds fed mostly grains like oats, wheat or barley have whiter skin.

Solution 6: Handle Your Poultry Safely

For more tips see Food Safety Precautions page 26.
• Refrigerate raw poultry promptly. Never leave it on a countertop at room temperature or it will instantly become a bacterial breeding ground.
• Packaged fresh chicken may be refrigerated in its original wrappings if kept in the coldest part of the refrigerator.
• Freeze uncooked poultry if it is not to be used within 2 days.
• Refrigerate cooked poultry pieces no longer than 2 days.

Solution 7: Internal Temperature

To prevent salmonella contamination, don't take your poultry off of the grill until it has reached an internal temperature of 160°F.

Chicken or Turkey	Serving size (Raw)	Degree of doneness	Approximate Grilling Time* refrigerator temperature, grilled on highest setting	Chef's Choice Temperature Recommendation	USDA Temperature Recommendation
Boneless, skinless breasts, tenderloins or scallops	4 to 5 ounces	Done	10 to 12 minutes	160°F	160° to 170°F
Kebabs	1-inch cubes	Done	10 to 12 minutes	160°F	160° to 170°F

Divide the grilling time in half for Two-sided Contact Grills.

Chicken Romagna and Rapid Risotto

On a recent visit to the Emiglia-Romagna region of northern Italy, my husband John and I were treated to an unforgettable country-style feast cooked by Ada, one of his energetic 80-year-old cousins. For me, the highpoint of the meal was watching Ada cook a mixed grill of beefsteaks, pork chops and sausages in her kitchen fireplace. Cooks in this region use a limited variety of herbs for seasoning grilled meats, and rosemary is one of the favorites. Instead of rubbing the meat with chopped rosemary, Ada placed several sprigs directly on the grilling rack then put meat seasoned with salt and pepper on top of the rosemary. As it cooked over smoldering wood, the meat became perfumed with the essential oils released from the heated rosemary. A few days after Ada's feast, we visited John's cousin Paolo in Bologna, the capitol of Emiglia-Romagna. Paolo was delighted to teach me how to make his famous risotto in the time honored Italian way . . . standing over the stove and stirring for 30 minutes. This leisurely cooking method creates risotto's characteristic creaminess and its chewy, "al dente" texture. When I returned home, I wanted to recreate the Romagnole recipes I learned. I tried Ada's simple seasoning technique on the electric grill and found it worked beautifully on both meat and poultry. My Chicken Romagna cried out for Paolo's risotto but I didn't want to make it the traditional way. Who has time? So, I created a rapid, no-stir risotto, flavored with an unexpected combination of yellow raisins, almonds and lemon, that mimics the real thing but without the fuss.

Menu Game Plan

**Prep and Cooking Time:
40 to 50 minutes**

- Preheat the grill.
- Flatten and season the chicken breasts.
- Slice the zucchini in half.
- Make the Almond Raisin Risotto.
- Grill the zucchini and chicken breasts.

Cook's Notes

Arborio rice is grown exclusively in the Po and Ticino valleys in Northern Italy. Used solely for making risotto, these short, round grains have been developed with the perfect amount of starch that enables them to absorb large quantities of liquid while remaining firm on the inside and rendering a creamlike sauce on the outside.

Chicken Romagna and Grilled Zucchini

Serves 4

2 tablespoons olive oil

¼ cup lemon juice

1 tablespoon pressed garlic

Light salt and pepper to taste

8 3- or 4-inch sprigs fresh rosemary

1¼ pounds boneless skinless chicken breasts or turkey breast cutlets

2 medium zucchini, sliced lengthwise into ¼-inch to ½-inch pieces

Nonfat or olive oil cooking spray

Scenting poultry, meat or fish with the essential oils of fresh herbs is as simple as placing herbs directly on the grill underneath the food you are cooking. This technique works well for adding flavor to meat and fish as well as your poultry.

1. Preheat the grill. If you have a grill with a variable temperature control, set it to medium-high (one or two steps below high) or to about 350° to 400°F.

2. Make the marinade. In a 1-cup bowl or measure, mix the lemon juice, olive oil, salt and pepper. Set aside.

3. Flatten and season the chicken. Spread a large piece of plastic wrap on a flat work surface. Arrange the chicken breasts in a single layer over the plastic wrap. Cover the breasts with another large piece of plastic wrap. Pound the breasts with the bottom of a large heavy skillet, the flat side of a meat mallet or a rolling pin until flattened to about ¼-inch to ½-inch thick.

Place the chicken in a 1-gallon zippered freezer-weight storage bag, a 1-quart airtight container or a shallow square glass dish (8 x 8 x 2-inches).

Pour the marinade over the chicken, then turn the chicken pieces so all sides have been covered with the marinade. Zip the bag closed, or cover the container or dish and marinate in the refrigerator for 20 minutes or up to 24 hours.

4. Grill the chicken and the zucchini. If you have a grill with a small grilling surface, grill the zucchini first, then the chicken. If you own a larger capacity grill, grill everything simultaneously. Transfer grilled food to a platter covered with aluminum foil to keep it warm until serving time.

Season the zucchini halves lightly with salt and pepper, then spray each piece lightly with the cooking spray before placing on the grill. Grill until tender, but not translucent or limp.

Place 1 or 2 rosemary sprigs directly on the grill and place a piece of the chicken on top. Put another sprig of rosemary on top of the chicken piece. Repeat for all the remaining chicken pieces. Grill the chicken according to the Grill Times below until interior temperature reaches 160°F on an instant-read thermometer. The meat should no longer be pink in the center and all of the juices should run clear when pricked with the tip of a knife. **5. To serve,** artfully arrange equal amounts of risotto, grilled poultry and zucchini on 4 plates. Garnish with fresh rosemary sprigs and serve immediately with crusty Italian or French bread.

Grill Times

Two-Sided Contact Grill: *Zucchini 5 to 6 minutes / chicken 4 to 6 minutes*

Hibachi Grill, Combination Grill or Infusion Grill: *Zucchini 10 to 12 minutes / chicken 8 to 12 minutes. Turn the zucchini and chicken halfway through the grilling time. Grills with lids may be covered halfway through the grilling time. Infusion grills with lids may be covered for the entire grilling time.*

Substitutions:
Instead of scenting your poultry with rosemary, try fresh thyme or lavender sprigs.

Mix & Match

Serve the Almond Raisin Risotto with any of the main dishes in the following menus: Provencal Kissed Veal Chops, page 111; Pick-Me-Up Poultry Piccata, page 175; Amazing Maple Glazed Pork Chops, page 115; A Turkey for All Seasons, page 163.

Almond Raisin Risotto

Makes 4 (1¼ cup) servings

¼ cup toasted slivered blanched almonds or pine nuts

3 cups nonfat canned chicken broth or 2 cups canned chicken broth plus 1 cup white wine

⅓ cup chopped white or yellow onion

1 teaspoon pressed garlic

1 tablespoon olive oil

1⅓ cups Arborio or medium-grain rice

⅓ cup golden raisins

3 tablespoons lemon juice

½ cup shredded Parmesan cheese

Light salt and freshly ground pepper

2 tablespoons chopped fresh parsley, optional

Toasted nuts give this dish a more intense flavor. But if you don't want to take the time to toast them, add them in raw.

1. (Optional step.) Toast the almonds. Put nuts in an 8-inch non-stick fry pan over medium-high heat. Stir constantly for 2 to 3 minutes until lightly browned. Remove immediately from heat to prevent burning and set aside to cool.

2. Put broth in a 1-quart pot and heat to almost boiling. Remove from heat until ready to use.

3. While broth is heating, mix onions, garlic, and olive oil in a covered 2 to 3 quart covered pot. Cook covered over high heat until you hear the onions sizzle. Then, immediately turn the heat down to extra low and sweat the onions until tender, about 4 to 5 minutes.

4. Add the rice and stir to coat with oil. Cover and cook over medium low heat for 2 minutes, or until the rice starts becoming transparent.

5. Stir the heated broth, raisins and lemon juice into the rice mixture, cover and bring to a rapid boil. When broth starts to boil, immediately turn the heat down to extra low. Surface of broth should barely bubble. Keep covered and cook 20 to 25 minutes.

6. When time is up, remove pot from the heat, and stir in the Parmesan cheese, nuts, salt and pepper to taste. Cover and let stand 5 minutes off of the heat for risotto to absorb any excess moisture. Sprinkle with chopped parsley before serving. Risotto can be refrigerated in an airtight container for up to 2 days and frozen for up to 2 months.

Approximate Nutrients Per Serving of Entire Meal

Total Calories 553	Protein 22 g / 16%	Carbohydrate 80 g / 58%
Total Sugar 13 g	Fat Total 16 g / 26%	Saturated Fat 4 g / 7%
Cholesterol 13 mg	Sodium 140 mg	Fiber 4 g Calcium 216 mg

A Turkey for All Seasons

Want to make a Thanksgiving-style dinner without spending long hours in the kitchen? With your electric tabletop grill, you can whip up a super healthy turkey dinner including all the trimmings in under an hour. Instead of roasting a whole turkey, you'll save time by grilling marinated turkey breast tenderloins. My Rosemary Raisin Stovetop Stuffing, a savory "from scratch" delight, can be ready in less than 15 minutes. Mix up a batch of Cranberry Orange Nut Sauce and Petite Pea Salad, two no-cook dishes, and you'll have a perfect meal for any season.

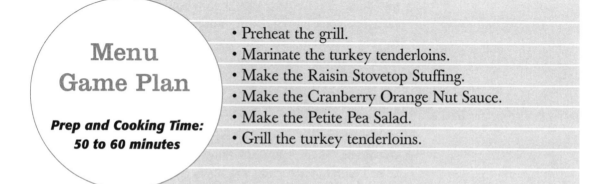

**Menu
Game Plan**

*Prep and Cooking Time:
50 to 60 minutes*

- Preheat the grill.
- Marinate the turkey tenderloins.
- Make the Raisin Stovetop Stuffing.
- Make the Cranberry Orange Nut Sauce.
- Make the Petite Pea Salad.
- Grill the turkey tenderloins.

Cook's Notes

It has not been proven that cranberries were at the first American Thanksgiving. But we are certain that there were plenty of wild cranberry bogs not far from where the Pilgrims first set foot. Cranberries have a high benzoic acid content, and their addition to meat kept it edible for months. Also a good source of vitamin C and potassium, cranberries have been found effective in protecting the urinary tract from infection, and may improve blood circulation and the digestive system. Cultivated in the United States, mainly in Massachusetts, Oregon, Wisconsin, and New Jersey, cranberries are also grown in Canada. The recipes in this menu call for canned whole cranberry sauce because it saves time, is easy to use, and tastes good! If you are purchasing fresh berries to make cranberry sauce from scratch, choose plump, firm and shiny berries.

Cranberry Marinated Turkey Tenderloins

Serves 4

½ cup whole cranberry sauce

¼ cup orange juice concentrate

1 tablespoon poultry seasoning

1 teaspoon pressed garlic

¼ cup chopped shallot or white onion

1 to 2 tablespoons Grand Marnier or orange liqueur (optional)

½ teaspoon light salt or to taste

Freshly ground pepper to taste

1¼ pounds turkey tenderloin

Nonfat or canola oil cooking spray

Substitutions:
For the turkey tenderloin, substitute boneless skinless chicken or duckling breasts or pork tenderloin.

1. **Preheat the grill.** If you have a grill with a variable temperature control, set it to medium-high (one or two steps below high) or to about 350° to 400°F.

2. **Make the marinade.** In a blender, puree all the ingredients except the turkey breast. Pour the marinade into a 1-gallon zippered freezer-weight storage bag, a 1-quart airtight container, or a shallow square glass dish (8 x 8 x 2-inch).

3. **Marinate the turkey tenderloins.** Cut the turkey tenderloin into 3-inch lengths across the grain of the meat. Place the turkey pieces on your cutting board so that the length is perpendicular to your body. Holding your free hand on top, slice the turkey pieces ¾ of the way through, leaving it "hinged" along one side so that it can open up to twice its original size like a book. Be sure that you cut evenly through the middle. With the palms of your hands, press the "hinge" down to evenly flatten the pieces.

Put the turkey in the zippered freezer bag, container or dish containing the marinade, then turn it so all the surfaces are coated with the marinade. Zip the bag closed or cover the container or dish and refrigerate for 20 minutes or up to 24 hours.

5. **Grill the turkey tenderloins.** As you remove each piece of turkey from the marinade, lightly spray it with cooking spray before placing it on the grill. Grill it according to the Grill Times opposite until the interior temperature reaches 160°F on an instant read thermometer. The meat should no longer be pink in the center and all of the juices should run clear when pricked with the tip of a knife.

6. **To serve,** spoon equal amounts of the Rosemary Raisin Stuffing and Petite Pea Salad onto one side of four dinner plates. Arrange a grilled tenderloin on the other side. Spoon 2 tablespoons of the Cranberry Orange Pecan Sauce near the tenderloin. Serve immediately and offer extra Cranberry Orange Pecan Sauce on the side.

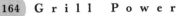

Two-Sided Contact Grill: 6 to 8 minutes.

Hibachi Grill, Combination Grill or Infusion Grill: 12 to 14 minutes. Turn the tenderloins halfway through the grilling time. Grills with lids may be covered halfway through the grilling time. Infusion grills may be covered for the entire grilling time.

Cranberry Orange Nut Sauce

Makes 8 (¼ cup) servings

1   cup whole cranberry sauce

½   cup pecan pieces, coarsely chopped

½   cup all-fruit marmalade

Substitutions:
For the pecans, substitute walnuts or pistachios.

This easy recipe also tastes great on grilled chicken, duck or pork. It will keep in the refrigerator for up to 3 weeks or in the freezer for up to 4 months in an airtight container.

1. Place all ingredients in a 4-cup measure or bowl and mix thoroughly with a fork. Using a spatula, scrape into a decorative dish and cover with plastic wrap, or into an airtight container. Refrigerate or freeze until ready to use.

Variation:
Cranberry Apricot Sauce: Substitute apricot jam for the orange marmalade.

Raisin Cornbread Stuffing

Makes 4 (1 cup) servings

1   tablespoon light butter

½   cup diced shallots

1   teaspoon pressed garlic

1⅓   cups nonfat chicken broth

1   teaspoon dried rosemary

¼   teaspoon dried sage

¼   teaspoon dried thyme

⅓   cup golden raisins

Light salt to taste

Freshly ground pepper to taste

2½   cups seasoned cornbread stuffing mix

This recipe can be made up to 48 hours in advance of serving. It can also be frozen for up to 3 months. .

1. In a 2-quart pot, melt the butter over medium heat.
2. Mix in the shallots and garlic to coat with the butter, turn down the heat to low, cover and cook about 5 minutes until shallots are tender. Lift the cover to stir about every 2 minutes.
3. Add the chicken broth, rosemary, sage, thyme, raisins, salt and pepper. Turn the heat to medium-high and bring to a boil. Cover, reduce the heat to medium low and simmer for 3 minutes.
4. Remove the pot from the heat and fold in the cornbread stuffing mix with a rubber spatula until completely moistened.
5. Cover immediately and let stand for 5 minutes. Fluff with a fork before serving.

Petite Pea Salad

Makes 5 scant (¾ cup) servings

Salad

1   5 ounce can sliced
    water chestnuts

2   cups petite frozen peas

½   cup diced bell pepper, red,
    yellow or orange

½   cup shredded or thinly
    sliced carrots

⅓   cup thinly sliced green
    onions

Dressing

⅓   cup nonfat or low-fat
    mayonnaise

1   teaspoon garlic powder

Light salt and pepper to taste

Substitutions:
For the bell pepper, substitute
⅓ cup diced canned roasted
bell pepper.

This simple salad makes a nice flavor contrast to the more vibrantly seasoned dishes. Make this recipe up to 48 hours before serving.

1. Put the sliced water chestnuts in a strainer and rinse under cool running water; drain well. If desired, make the water chestnut slices a bit smaller by coarsely chopping them. Put them into a 2-quart mixing bowl.

2. Put the frozen peas in a strainer and defrost them under cool running water; drain well. Add them to the bowl with the water chestnuts.

3. Using a rubber spatula, mix in the bell pepper, carrot, and green onions.

4. In a 1-cup measure, mix the mayonnaise, garlic powder, salt and pepper with a fork. Using the rubber spatula fold the dressing into the vegetables to coat evenly. Cover and refrigerate until serving time.

Approximate Nutrients Per Serving of Entire Meal

Total Calories 669	Protein 46 g / 28%	Carbohydrate 101 g / 60%
Total Sugar 44 g	Fat Total 8 g / 11%	Saturated Fat 1 g / 2%
Cholesterol 88 mg	Sodium 1127 mg	Fiber 13 g Calcium 128 mg

Armenian Apricot Sauced Poultry with Grilled Asparagus over Vermicelli Pilaf

Armenian cuisine resonates with the influence of the different cultures that have occupied Armenia throughout the centuries—Tartar, Persian, Russian and Turkish. Armenian cooks adopted the recipes of their invaders using the local ingredients available in the fertile valleys of the Caucasus Mountains. The result is a vast repertoire of meat dishes seasoned with a combination of savory spices and sweet fruits such as allspice, cumin, cinnamon, cayenne, pomegranate, apricots, raisins and plums. This menu pays tribute to the ingenuity of Armenian cooks who usually serve sweet and savory dishes with a pilaf made of rice or bulgur wheat. At Aram's Armenian Café, in Petaluma, California (my hometown), the daily meat or poultry special is always accompanied by such a delicious rice and vermicelli pilaf, that I recreated it for this menu.

Menu Game Plan

Prep & Cooking Time: 50 minutes

- Preheat the grill.
- Marinate the meat.
- Make the Vermicelli Pilaf.
- Make the Armenian Apricot Sauce.
- Prepare the asparagus.
- Grill the meat and asparagus.

Cook's Notes

To peel or not to peel? If you are cooking young, thin asparagus it is not necessary to peel. If you are cooking mature, thick stemmed asparagus, peeling the outer fibrous skin is recommended. Peeling the outer fibers from the stems eliminates getting them stuck in between your teeth. Peeling also helps the asparagus stems cook at the same rate as the tender tips, which will cook faster than an unpeeled stem. To prepare asparagus, first break off the woody ends of the stalks. Then lay each asparagus spear on a cutting board and holding the tip end, remove the outer skin with a sharp vegetable peeler, scraping from beneath the tip away from you to the stem end as you rotate the spear.

Grilled Chicken and Asparagus

Serves 4

2   tablespoons pressed garlic

1   tablespoon white wine

1   teaspoon extra-virgin olive oil

2   teaspoons sweet paprika

1   teaspoon ground cinnamon

Dash cayenne pepper

1¼ pounds boneless skinless chicken breasts

16 fresh asparagus, peeled

Nonfat or canola oil cooking spray

Fresh parsley or cilantro

Substitutions:
Instead of white wine, substitute apple cider, or apple juice.
Instead of olive oil substitute your favorite vegetable oil.
Instead of chicken breast, substitute turkey breast medallions.

1. **Preheat the grill.** If you have a grill with a variable temperature control, set it to medium-high (one or two steps below high) or to about 350° to 400°F.

2. **Marinate the meat.** Measure garlic, wine, olive oil, paprika, cinnamon and cayenne into a 1-cup bowl and mix thoroughly with a fork. Place the chicken in a zippered freezer storage bag, 1-quart air tight container or shallow glass dish (8 x 8 x 2-inch). Using a rubber spatula, scrape the rub onto the chicken. With your fingertips, smear the paste onto all sides of the chicken. Zip the bag closed or cover the container or dish with plastic wrap or a cover and set aside in the refrigerator for 20 minutes or up to 24 hours until ready to grill.

3. **Wash and prepare the asparagus.** (See page 167 for peeling instructions.)

4. **Grill the chicken and asparagus.** If you have a small grill, grill meat first and then asparagus. Keep grilled food warm on a covered platter. If you have a larger grill, grill the asparagus and chicken simultaneously. Spray the asparagus and chicken breasts lightly with the cooking spray and place on the grill. Grill according to the Grill Times opposite until the interior temperature reaches 160°F on an instant read thermometer. Meat should no longer be pink in the center, and all of the juices should run clear when pricked with the tip of a knife.

5. **To serve,** spoon equal portions of the pilaf in the center of 4 plates. Allow the chicken to rest 2 to 3 minutes after coming off the grill (this allows the juices to settle). Slice each chicken breast across the grain of the meat into ½-inch slices and place it, reassembled, on top of the rice. Surround the rice on 4 sides with 4 asparagus spears. Drizzle 2 tablespoons of the apricot sauce over the chicken. Garnish with parsley or fresh cilantro sprigs and serve immediately.

Two-Sided Contact Grill: *Chicken 5 to 6 minutes / asparagus 5 to 6 minutes.*

Hibachi Grill, Combination Grill or Infusion Grill: *Chicken and asparagus 10 to 12 minutes. Turn both chicken and asparagus halfway through the grilling time. Grills with lids may be covered halfway through the grilling time. Infusion grills with lids may be covered for the entire grilling time.*

Infusion Grill Notes: *For a more intense flavor, pour ½ cup wine, apple cider, apple juice or a combination of wine and juice into infusion cup before preheating grill.*

Vermicelli Pilaf

Makes 4 (1 cup) servings

3 tablespoons salted butter

4 ounces (¼ package) vermicelli noodles broken into 1- or 2-inch pieces

1½ cups long grain white rice

3 cups very hot tap water or canned nonfat chicken broth, heated

⅓ cup dried cranberries, currants or yellow raisins (optional)

¼ cup finely chopped fresh parsley or cilantro (optional)

This recipe can be made up to 2 days in advance. It freezes well stored in zippered freezer bags for up to 2 months. It can be defrosted and reheated in a microwave oven. To reheat, microwave covered on high (100% power) for 2 to 5 minutes. Stir halfway through cooking time.

1. Melt butter in a 3-quart pot, covered for 2 minutes over low heat.
2. Stir in the vermicelli coating all surfaces with butter. Cook, stirring constantly, over medium heat until noodles begin to brown, about 3 minutes.
3. Stir in the rice and cook, stirring constantly, over medium-heat an additional 3 minutes until rice becomes well coated with the fat and slightly transparent.
4. Stir in the hot water or chicken broth and bring to a boil. Cover and immediately reduce heat to low. Cook 20 minutes. Remove the cover briefly to stir in the optional dried cranberries, currants, or raisins, then cover immediately. If not adding dried fruit, do not remove cover. Let stand covered 10 minutes off the heat. Remove cover, fluff with a fork and sprinkle with optional chopped parsley or cilantro before serving.

Mix & Match

Serve the Vermicelli Pilaf with the main dishes in any of the following menus: Amazing Maple Glazed Pork Chops, page 115; Smart and Saucy Rosemary-Cherry Lamb Chops, page 119.

Armenian Apricot Sauce

Makes 4 (¼ cup) servings

2   teaspoons extra-virgin olive oil or your favorite vegetable oil

¼   cup chopped white or yellow onion

½   teaspoon pressed garlic

⅛   teaspoon ground cumin

½   teaspoon ground thyme

Pinch cayenne pepper

½   cup all-fruit apricot jam

½   cup plus 2 tablespoons canned, nonfat chicken broth

2   teaspoons cornstarch

1. In a 1-quart pot, heat the olive oil over medium-low heat. Stir in the onions, garlic, cumin, thyme and cayenne pepper. Cover, turn down the heat to low and cook 10 minutes, stirring occasionally until the onions are translucent and tender.

2. Whisk the apricot jam and ½ cup of the chicken broth into the onions. Turn the heat up and bring to a boil.

3. Meanwhile, in a 1-cup measure or small bowl, whisk the 2 tablespoons of chicken broth and the cornstarch. When the broth comes to a boil, whisk in the cornstarch mixture. Continue whisking until the sauce is thickened, 1 to 2 minutes.

4. Remove from the heat, cover and set aside until serving time. If the sauce becomes too cool before serving, reheat, covered, over low heat on the stove. If it gets too thick while reheating, whisk in a few teaspoons of chicken broth.

Variation:

Apricot Brandy Sauce: If you would like to give your sauce a bit of a zing, substitute 2 tablespoons or up to ¼ cup of apricot brandy for part of the chicken broth in the sauce recipe.

Approximate Nutrients Per Serving of Entire Meal

Total Calories 755	Protein 38g / 20%	Carbohydrate 117g / 63%
Total Sugar 16g	Fat 14g / 17%	Saturated Fat 6g / 8%
Cholesterol 89 mg	Sodium 186 mg	Fiber 7g Calcium 85mg

Cantonese Lemon Chicken Sez Me!

It is hard to resist Cantonese-style Lemon Chicken with its deep-fried golden-brown crust flavored with sweet/sour lemon sauce. Before putting the chicken on the grill, you'll dip each marinated piece into a sesame seed and breadcrumb mixture. As it cooks, the crust gets crispy enough on the grill to give the taste of its high-fat cousin minus the calories and excess fat. My lip-smacking lemon sauce is flavored with honey instead of sugar to smooth the sourness of the lemon juice. Steamed jade green sugar peas brighten the plate. To save you time and effort, you don't need an extra pot to steam them. Just add them on top of the rice immediately after it has cooked. By putting the lid on, the peas will steam in the moisture released from the cooked rice as it rests for 10 minutes off the burner.

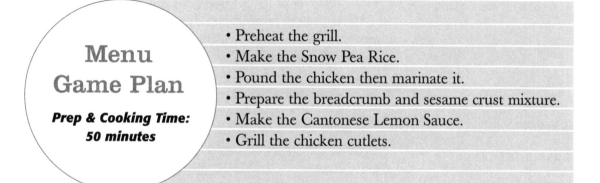

Menu Game Plan

Prep & Cooking Time: 50 minutes

- Preheat the grill.
- Make the Snow Pea Rice.
- Pound the chicken then marinate it.
- Prepare the breadcrumb and sesame crust mixture.
- Make the Cantonese Lemon Sauce.
- Grill the chicken cutlets.

Cook's Notes

Notes

In ancient Egyptian, "sesemt" meant sesame seed, and it is one of the few ancient Egyptian words still in use today. Sesame plants, prized both for the seeds and the oil expressed from them, were also cultivated in ancient Ethiopia, Mesopotamia, Greece, Rome and India. Sesame seeds remain an important ingredient in many cuisines where the seeds are ground into a pasty condiment known as tahini (see page 81 for Tahini Sauce recipe) used to flavor dips, sauces, main dishes and desserts. There is evidence that sesame seeds were grown in China as early as the fifth century A.D. The Chinese name for sesame oil means fragrant oil, and it is used for frying, in marinades, and as a seasoning. The Chinese use whole black or white sesame seeds in cakes, cookies and candies and in savory dishes for sauces or garnishing.

Sesame Chicken Cutlets

Serves 4

Chicken

1¼ pounds boneless, skinless chicken breasts

Nonfat or canola oil cooking spray

Marinade

2 large egg whites or ¼ cup nonfat egg substitute

1 tablespoon low-sodium soy sauce

1 tablespoon dry Sherry

1 teaspoon pressed garlic

1 teaspoon grated gingerroot

¼ cup cornstarch

Crust Mixture

1 cup dry breadcrumbs

¼ cup sesame seeds

4 tablespoons thinly sliced green onion

1. Preheat the grill. If you have a grill with a variable temperature control, set it to medium-high (1 or 2 steps below high) or to about 350° to 400°F.

2. Make the marinade. In a 1- or 2-cup bowl or measure, whisk the egg, soy sauce, Sherry, garlic, ginger and cornstarch. Pour it into a zippered freezer storage bag, 1 quart airtight container or shallow glass dish (8 x 8 x 2-inch).

3. Flatten the chicken breasts and marinate them. Arrange the chicken breasts in a single layer over a large piece of plastic wrap. Cover the chicken breasts with another large piece of plastic wrap. Pound the breasts with the bottom of a large heavy skillet, the flat side of a meat mallet or a rolling pin until flattened to about ¼- to ½-inch thick.

Put the chicken pieces in the bag or dish containing the marinade, then turn them so all the surfaces are coated with the marinade. Zip the bag closed or cover the container or dish and refrigerate for 20 minutes or up to 24 hours.

4. Mix the coating. If you are making breadcrumbs from scratch, see page 46 for instructions. In a shallow dish, mix the breadcrumbs and sesame seeds, then place near the grill.

5. Grill the chicken. Dip each chicken breast into the coating mixture so all sides are covered. As you finish coating each piece, put it on a large plate. Spray each piece lightly on both sides with the cooking spray before putting it on the grill. Grill the chicken according to the Grill Times opposite until the interior temperature reaches 160°F on an instant read thermometer. The meat should no longer be pink in the center, and all of the juices should run clear when pricked with the tip of a knife.

6. To serve, place equal amounts of Snow Pea Rice on each plate. Place a chicken cutlet beside the rice then drizzle it with 2 tablespoons of the Cantonese Lemon Sauce. Sprinkle with about 1 tablespoon of thinly sliced green onion and serve immediately.

Two-Sided Contact Grill: 5 minutes.

Hibachi Grill, Combination Grill or Infusion Grill: 10 to 11 minutes. Turn the chicken halfway through the grilling time. For a crispier crust, do not cover the grill.

Cantonese Lemon Sauce

Makes 8 (2 tablespoon) servings

½ cup canned, low-fat chicken broth

¼ cup honey

¼ cup lemon juice

1 tablespoon brown sugar

2 tablespoons seasoned rice vinegar

1 teaspoon pressed garlic

1 teaspoon finely minced gingerroot

1 teaspoon grated lemon zest

2 teaspoons canola or peanut oil

1 tablespoon cornstarch

This sauce can be made up to 2 days in advance of serving if kept in an airtight container in the refrigerator. You can also freeze it for up to 2 months and then defrost and reheat it in the microwave. If you love lemon sauce, this recipe is easily doubled.

1. In a blender, mix all the ingredients until they are evenly blended. Pour into a 1-quart saucepan.
2. Heat over medium heat until just boiling, whisking constantly until slightly thickened, about 4 minutes.
3. Remove from heat and set aside on a cool burner until serving time. If making ahead let cool to room temperature, then cover tightly and store in the refrigerator.

Snow Pea Rice

Makes 4 generous (1 1/3 cup) servings

2³⁄₄ cups water

1 tablespoon canola oil

³⁄₄ teaspoon light salt or to taste (optional)

1½ cups white long-grain rice

2 cups (½ pound) snow pea pods

Substitutions:

Instead of snow pea pods, substitute equal amounts of sugar snap peas, broccoli florets, sliced bok choy, or 1 cup of frozen petite peas or frozen, shelled edamame (green soybeans). Thaw the frozen peas or beans in a strainer under cool running water and drain well before using.

1. In a 2- or 3-quart pot with a tight fitting lid, bring the water, oil and salt to a rolling boil over high heat. Stir in the rice, bring back to a rolling boil, then cover and immediately reduce the heat to a low simmer. Simmer until all the liquid is absorbed, about 20 minutes.

2. While the rice is cooking, remove the stems and strings from the pea pods.

3. When the rice is done, remove the pot from the heat, uncover quickly and put the pea pods on top of the rice. Cover immediately and let stand for 10 minutes. Just before serving, use a rubber spatula to fluff the rice and fold the pea pods evenly into the rice. To keep the rice warm until serving time, do not lift the lid. If the rice becomes too cool, transfer it into a microwavable casserole and reheat covered in the microwave for 2 to 4 minutes on high (100% power).

Approximate Nutrients Per Serving of Entire Meal

Total Calories 736	Protein 46 g/ 26%	Carbohydrate 103 g/ 57%
Total Sugar 12 g	Fat Total 13 g/ 17%	Saturated Fat 2 g/ 2%
Cholesterol 82 mg	Sodium 574 mg	Fiber 4 g Calcium 127 mg

Pick-Me-Up Poultry Piccata

In the good old days, BEG (Before Electric Grills), just thinking about the classic Italian dish "Piccata al limone" (or scallops in lemon), started a craving that wouldn't stop until I broke down and made it. The sheer amount of butter involved in this recipe makes my fat meter go berserk, so I've always restrained myself from making it often...until now because I can serve my guilt-free grilled version whenever the mood grips me. The secret to getting this recipe right is making sure all the "piccata" or scallops are of equal thickness so they will cook fast and evenly. I do it the Italian way by pounding the poultry with a heavy metal meat mallet called a "batticarne" (literally meat pounder in Italian). A few sharp whacks with my trusty kitchen hammer, and the day's frustrations melt away with the promise of succulent, tenderized meat.

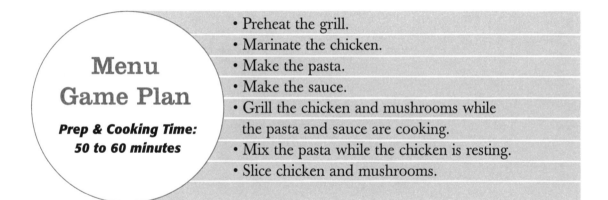

Menu Game Plan

**Prep & Cooking Time:
50 to 60 minutes**

- Preheat the grill.
- Marinate the chicken.
- Make the pasta.
- Make the sauce.
- Grill the chicken and mushrooms while the pasta and sauce are cooking.
- Mix the pasta while the chicken is resting.
- Slice chicken and mushrooms.

Cook's Notes

Capers are the pickled flower buds of a creeping shrub native to the Mediterranean and have been used as a condiment since ancient times. Today they are cultivated in France, Spain and Italy and range in size from petite to grape-size. The buds are pickled in brine, vinegar or wine before they open. Capers can be costly because they are handpicked daily as the buds form. Believed to improve digestion, capers are used in cold sauces, spreads, salads, sandwiches, pizza, hors d'oeuvres and as garnishes for meat, poultry and fish. Before using, I rinse my capers in a strainer under cool running water to eliminate excess salt. Capers will disintegrate if you cook them too long, so if using them in a hot dish, add them at the very end of the cooking time.

Lemon Caper Chicken Piccata and Portobello Mushrooms

Serves 4

1½ cups lemon juice

2 tablespoons extra-virgin olive oil

2 tablespoons Dijon-style mustard

1 tablespoon pressed garlic

1 teaspoon freshly ground pepper

1½ teaspoons light salt

1¼ pounds boneless, skinless chicken breasts

2 medium portobello mushrooms

Nonfat or olive oil cooking spray

Lemon Cream Capellini (see recipe on page 178)

2 tablespoons capers

⅓ cup finely chopped parsley

1 whole lemon

1. Preheat the grill. If you have a grill with a variable temperature control, set it to medium-high (1 or 2 steps below high) or to about 350° to 400°F.

2. Mix the marinade. In a blender, mix the lemon juice, oil, Dijon-style mustard, garlic, pepper and salt.

Divide the marinade between two (1-gallon) zippered freezer-weight storage bags, 1-quart airtight containers or shallow square glass dishes (8 x 8 x 2-inch). Set aside while you prepare the chicken and mushrooms.

3. Pound and marinate the chicken. Spread a large piece of plastic wrap on a flat work surface. Arrange the chicken breasts in a single layer over the plastic wrap. Cover the breasts with another large piece of plastic wrap. Pound the breasts with the flat side of a meat mallet, bottom of a large heavy skillet or rolling pin until evenly flattened to about ¼- to ½-inch thick.

Put the pounded breasts into one of the marinade-filled bags, containers or dishes. Turn the chicken so all surfaces are coated with the marinade. Zip the bag closed, or cover the container or dish and marinate in the refrigerator for 20 minutes or up to 24 hours.

4. Prepare and marinate the portobello mushrooms. Using a small pairing knife cut the stems from the portobello mushrooms and slice the caps into 1-inch thick strips.

Put the mushrooms into the remaining marinade-filled bag, container or dish.
(Note: If you are marinating the chicken overnight, do not put the mushroom slices in the marinade filled bag or container until up to 2 hours before cooking. The mushrooms will get too soggy if marinated longer.)

With your fingertips, gently turn the mushroom pieces so all surfaces are coated with the marinade. Zip the bag closed, or cover the container or dish and marinate in the refrigerator for 20 minutes or up to 2 hours.

5. Grill the chicken and mushrooms. If you have a grill with a small grilling surface, grill the mushrooms first, then the chicken.

Substitutions:
Substitute turkey breast
scallops for chicken.

If you own a larger capacity grill, grill everything simultaneously. Transfer the grilled food to a platter covered with aluminum foil to keep it warm until serving time.

Spray all surfaces of the mushrooms and chicken with cooking spray before putting them on the grill. Grill the mushrooms according to the Grill Times until grill marks appear, they are cooked through and a little over half their size when raw. Grill the chicken according to the Grill Times until the interior temperature reaches 160°F on an instant-read thermometer. The meat should no longer be pink in the center, and all the juices should run clear when pricked with the tip of a knife.

6. **To serve,** slice the lemon into very thin rounds. Place equal amounts of pasta on four dinner plates. Slice the chicken breasts across the grain into 1/4- to 1/2-inch slices. Arrange equal amounts of the chicken and the grilled mushrooms on top of the pasta on each plate.

Sprinkle each plate with equal amounts of the capers, and parsley. Garnish with the thinly sliced lemon. Serve immediately with hot garlic bread and a Caesar salad.

Grill Times

Two-Sided Contact Grill: Mushrooms 6 to 8 minutes / chicken 4 to 6 minutes.

Hibachi Grill, Combination Grill or Infusion Grill: Mushrooms 12 to 16 minutes / chicken 8 to 12 minutes. Turn the chicken and mushrooms halfway through the grilling time. Grills with lids may be covered halfway through the grilling time. Infusion grills with lids may be covered for the entire grilling time.

Lemon Cream Cappellini

Makes 4 scant (1 cup) servings

Pasta

½   pound capellini or spaghetti

2   teaspoons olive oil

½   teaspoon salt

Sauce

2   tablespoons light butter

⅛   teaspoon white pepper

¼   teaspoon light salt

Pinch of nutmeg

1   cup low-fat or nonfat sour cream

1   tablespoon lemon juice

½   cup shredded Parmesan cheese

1. In a 4- to 5-quart pot, bring very hot tap water, salt and oil to a rolling boil over high heat with the cover on. (The cover helps the water boil faster because the steam is trapped.)

2. When water is boiling, add the pasta. Part of the pasta will be sticking out of the pot. Stir gently until the pasta softens and all the noodles fit in the pot. Cover the pot and bring the water back up to a boil, about 1 to 3 minutes. When the water begins to boil again, take the cover off, and cook for 8 to 12 minutes until tender but slightly chewy (al dente). Since cooking times vary per brand, read the package for exact timing.

3. When pasta is done, drain immediately in a large colander.

4. While the pasta is cooking, melt the butter in a 1-quart saucepan over medium low heat. Whisk in the pepper, salt and nutmeg. Cook for 1 to 2 minutes.

5. Measure the sour cream, lemon juice and Parmesan into a 2- or 3-cup bowl or measure. Whisk the butter mixture into the sour cream.

6. Using a rubber spatula, fold the lemon cream sauce into the hot pasta right before serving. Cover to keep warm if chicken and mushrooms are not quite done.

Approximate Nutrients Per Serving of Entire Meal

Total Calories 619	Protein 53 g / 35%	Carbohydrate 69 g / 45%	
Total Sugar 8 g	Fat 14 g / 20%	Saturated Fat 6 g / 9%	
Cholesterol 104 mg	Sodium 873 mg	Fiber 4 g	Calcium 240 mg

Chicken Lo-Fat Mein

In Chinese, "Lo" means "tossed or mixed" and "Mein" means noodles. The noodles in classic Lo Mein are boiled to "al dente" and then tossed into a hot wok that is filled with saucy stir-fried vegetables and/or bits of meat, poultry or fish. Instead of stir frying the vegetables, I add them to the noodles at the end of their boiling time. Just a couple of minutes in the boiling pasta water will parboil the vegetables so that they are tender but still colorful and crisp. Boiling also reduces the fat usually required for stir-frying. The sauce is easy too! All the ingredients first get pureed in the blender, then go into a pot with the mushrooms where the mixture cooks on the stove into a thickened sauce within 3 minutes. If you time it right, you'll be tossing the noodles and vegetables with the sauce just before the chicken comes off of the grill for a dish that tastes just like it came from your favorite Chinese restaurant.

Menu Game Plan

Prep & Cooking Time: 50 minutes

- Preheat the grill.
- Marinate the Chef's Special Chicken.
- Make the Mushroom Sauce.
- Prepare the Lo Mein.
- Grill the chicken and onions while the noodles are cooking.

Cook's Notes

Bok Choy (also known as Pak Choy) is a cabbage that was introduced to America by Chinese gold prospectors in the late 1800's. With its wide bright green leaves and whitish fleshy ribs, it looks like a cross between celery and Swiss chard. But that is where the similarity ends. Its mild, sweet tasting leaves and stalks are tender enough for raw salads or can be quickly cooked in stir-fry or steamed dishes. Try steamed bok choy drizzled with a little rice vinegar and a dash of sesame oil as an easy side dish to your grilled favorites. Or slice it into 1-inch strips and add it to just-cooked rice. (See Snow Pea Rice recipe page 174 for the method.) Bok Choy is also loaded with nutrients. It is a good source of calcium, vitamins A, C, B6, iron, folic acid and potassium.

Chef's Special Chicken and Grilled Onions

Serves 4

Marinade

2   tablespoons oyster sauce

2   tablespoons low sodium soy sauce

1   teaspoon sugar

1   teaspoon finely minced gingerroot

1   teaspoon pressed garlic

2   tablespoons cornstarch

Chicken

1¼ pounds boneless skinless chicken or turkey breasts

1   small onion

Nonfat or canola oil cooking spray

2   medium ripe tomatoes, thinly sliced

4   tablespoons thinly sliced green onion

Fresh cilantro

Substitutions:
Instead of chicken, substitute equal amounts of turkey tenderloin, pork tenderloin, beef tenderloin, shrimps, scallops, or 1 pound firm tofu.

1. **Preheat the grill.** If you have a grill with a variable temperature control, set it to medium-high (one or two steps below high) or to about 350° to 400°F.

2. **Make the marinade.** In a 1- or 2-cup bowl or measure, whisk the oyster sauce, soy sauce, sugar, ginger, garlic and cornstarch. Pour it into a 1-gallon zippered freezer-weight storage bag, shallow square dish (8 x 8 x 2-inch) or an airtight container with a lid.

3. **Flatten the chicken breasts and marinate them.** Arrange the chicken breasts in a single layer over the plastic wrap. Cover the chicken breasts with another large piece of plastic wrap. Pound the breasts with the bottom of a large heavy skillet, flat side of a meat mallet or rolling pin until flattened to about ¼- to ½-inch thick.

   Put the chicken in the zippered bag, container or dish containing the marinade, then turn it so all the surfaces are coated with the marinade. Zip the bag closed or cover the container or dish and refrigerate for 20 minutes or up to 24 hours.

4. **Prepare the onion.** Peel the onion and cut off the ends. Cut the onion in half, then cut across the meridian into 1-inch-thick half moons.

5. **Grill the onions and chicken.** If you have a small grill, grill the onions first. If you have a larger grill, put the onions on a couple of minutes before adding the chicken because onions take slightly longer. Spray the onions liberally with cooking spray as you toss them with your fingers to evenly distribute the oil. Grill according to the Grill Times opposite until they are browned around the edges, tender yet slightly crisp.

   As you remove each piece of chicken from the marinade, lightly spray it with cooking spray before placing it on the grill. Grill the poultry according to the Grill Times opposite until the interior temperature reaches 160°F on an instant read thermometer. The meat should no longer be pink in the center, and all the juices should run clear when pricked with the tip of a knife.

6. **To serve,** spoon equal amounts of noodles onto one side of 4 plates. Arrange a grilled breast on the other side. Garnish with a sprinkle of thinly sliced tomatoes, green onions, and/or fresh cilantro leaves. Serve immediately.

Grill Times

Two-Sided Contact Grill: Onions 6 to 7 minutes / chicken 5 to 6 minutes.

Hibachi Grill, Combination Grill or Infusion Grill: Onions 12 to 14 minutes / chicken 10 to 12 minutes. Turn onions and chicken halfway through the grilling time. Cover combination grill halfway through the grilling time. The infusion grill may be covered for the entire grilling time.

Mushroom Sauce

Makes 2¾ cups, enough for ¾ to 1 pound pasta

- ½ cup canned low-fat or nonfat chicken broth
- 1 teaspoon chopped garlic
- 1 teaspoon finely minced gingerroot
- ¼ cup hoisin sauce
- ¼ cup oyster sauce
- 1 tablespoon sesame oil
- 1 tablespoon low-sodium soy sauce
- 1 tablespoon dry Sherry
- 2 teaspoons sugar
- 1 tablespoon cornstarch
- 2 cups sliced fresh mushrooms, any type
- 1 15-ounce can straw mushrooms, rinsed in a strainer under cool running water, well drained

This recipe can be made up to 2 days in advance if refrigerated in an airtight container.

1. In a blender, puree all the ingredients except the mushrooms. Pour into a 2-quart saucepan. Stir in the fresh mushrooms.
2. Bring to a boil over high heat, whisking constantly, until the sauce thickens, about 3 to 5 minutes.
3. Stir in the canned straw mushrooms, then cover and set aside until ready to dress the noodles.

Substitutions:
If straw mushrooms are unavailable, add another cup of sliced fresh mushrooms to the sauce, or substitute a 15-ounce can of common sliced mushrooms.

If you don't want to use fresh mushrooms, substitute three 10-ounce cans of mushrooms for the entire amount of mushrooms. Make sure they are rinsed in a strainer under cool water and well drained before using.

Variation:
Garlic Mushroom Sauce: If you are a garlic lover, don't put the garlic and sesame oil in the blender with the rest of the ingredients. Instead, sauté a larger amount, 2 to 3 teaspoons of chopped garlic in the sesame oil until fragrant before adding the blended ingredients and mushrooms to the pot. Follow steps 2 and 3 above to complete the recipe.

Lo Mein

Makes 4 (2 cup) servings

3   quarts water

1   tablespoon vegetable oil

¼   cup pine nuts

¾   pound spaghetti noodles

1   15-ounce can baby corn, well drained

1   cup thinly sliced or shredded carrots

1   cup broccoli florets

1   small baby Bok Choy about ½ pound or 1¼ cups sliced

Thinly sliced green onions

Fresh cilantro

Substitutions:
For baby Bok Choy, substitute 1 cup of sliced Napa cabbage, fresh baby spinach leaves, cabbage or celery.
For spaghetti noodles, substitute ¾ pound fresh or dried Chinese wheat noodles, 8 ounces Mung bean (cellophane) or rice noodles.

This recipe, which makes enough for leftovers or to feed hearty eaters, is enhanced by the flavor of the toasted pine nuts, but tastes just as good if you add them raw to the cooked pasta.

1. In a large pot, bring the water and oil to a boil.
2. (Optional step.) While the water is coming to a boil, toast the pine nuts in an 8-inch nonstick fry pan over medium-high heat Stir constantly for 2 to 3 minutes until lightly browned. Remove immediately from heat to prevent burning and set aside to cool.
3. Add the noodles and bring the water back to a boil.
4. Cook uncovered stirring occasionally; about 11 to 12 minutes until tender but slightly chewy.
5. While the noodles are cooking, rinse the baby corn in a strainer under cool running water and cut into 1-inch-long pieces. Slice the carrots; cut the broccoli florets into bite-sized pieces; slice the baby Bok Choy into 1-inch thick pieces.
6. Three minutes before the noodles are done, add the carrot and broccoli. Bring the water back to a boil.
7. Add the baby corn and the bok choy and cook for 1 minute longer until the Bok Choy leaves are slightly wilted.
8. Drain the pasta immediately in a large colander. Fold in the mushroom sauce, the pine nuts and the grilled onions when they are ready. Cover to keep warm. Serve as soon as the chicken comes off of the grill.

Approximate Nutrients Per Serving of Entire Meal

Total Calories 504	Protein 44 g / 35%	Carbohydrate 64 g / 51%
Total Sugar 16 g	Fat Total 7 g / 13%	Saturated Fat 1 g / 2%
Cholesterol 82 mg	Sodium 1809 mg	Fiber 6 g Calcium 61 mg

Buffalo Chicken Salad with Homemade Blue Cheese Dressing

The first time I tasted Buffalo Chicken Wings, those super spicy deep-fried goodies that you dip into blue cheese dressing to cut the fire, I thought, "What a weird name. This is chicken–not buffalo!" Silly me. After a little research, I discovered that Teressa Bellissimo invented Buffalo Chicken Wings in 1964 at the Anchor Bar in Buffalo, New York. But the events that skyrocketed this appetizer to fame happened almost 30 years later. It was during 4 consecutive Super Bowl games starring the Buffalo Bills from 1991 through 1994 that football fans nationwide honored the team by making Buffalo Wings for their home Super Bowl parties. If you have a thing for hot and spicy Buffalo Wings but would like a lower fat, healthier version, this salad is for you. Instead of deep frying chicken wings, I grill boneless-skinless chicken breasts that have been marinated in the same type hot pepper sauce as the real McCoy. I am leaving the brand of hot pepper sauce up to you, dear reader, since some like it hotter than others.

Menu Game Plan

Prep & Cooking Time: 45 minutes

- Preheat the grill.
- Marinate the chicken.
- Make the Blue Cheese Dressing.
- Make the salad.
- Grill the chicken.

Cook's Notes

Notes

Blue Cheese: English Stilton, Irish Cashel Blue, French Bleu de Gex, German Cambazola, Italian Gorgonzola, or Danish Blue, all of these wonderfully piquant cheeses with blue or green veins are lumped into a category called "blue." All Blue cheeses begin as uncooked, white, crumbly cheese. A blue mold is dusted onto formed wheels of the cheese via holes punched with wire needles. As the cheese cures in a humid cellar environment, it ripens from the center out toward the crust to form an even distribution of blue veins. The flavor and texture of blue cheese depend on the type of milk used, the ripening environment and the length of time the cheese is ripened. A 1-ounce serving of blue cheese contains 8 grams of fat (about 73%).

Buffalo Chicken Salad

Serves 4

Chicken

1¼ pounds boneless skinless chicken breasts

4 tablespoons of your favorite hot sauce

1 tablespoon lemon juice

½ teaspoon light salt

Nonfat or canola oil cooking spray

Salad

6 cups iceburg or Romaine lettuce, cut into bite-size pieces

1 cup thinly sliced cucumber (preferably hothouse)

1 cup thinly sliced celery

1 cup diced bell pepper, red, yellow, orange or green

1 cup shredded carrot

2 cups cherry tomatoes

4 tablespoons finely chopped parsley (optional)

2 cups garlic croutons (optional)

Substitutions:
If you don't want to take the time to make my blue cheese dressing from scratch, substitute your favorite bottled brand.

1. **Preheat the grill.** If you have a grill with a variable temperature control, set it to medium-high (one or two steps below high) or to about 350° to 400°F.

2. **Make the marinade.** In a 1-cup bowl, mix the hot pepper sauce, lemon juice and salt thoroughly with a fork. Pour the marinade into a 1-gallon zippered freezer-weight storage bag, a 1-quart airtight container or a shallow square glass dish (8 x 8 x 2-inch).

3. **Flatten and marinate the chicken.** Spread a large piece of plastic wrap on a flat work surface. Arrange the chicken breasts in a single layer over the plastic wrap. Cover the breasts with another large piece of plastic wrap. Pound the breasts with the bottom of a large heavy skillet, the flat side of a meat mallet, or a rolling pin until flattened to about ¼-inch to ½-inch thick.

Place the chicken in the bag, container or dish, then turn it so all surfaces are coated with the marinade.

Zip the bag closed, or cover the container or dish and marinate in the refrigerator for 20 minutes or up to 24 hours.

4. **Prepare the salads.** Put equal amounts of the lettuce on 4 dinner plates. Arrange equal amounts of all the sliced vegetables and the cherry tomatoes on top of the lettuce, leaving the center free for the chicken. If not serving immediately, cover each plate tightly with plastic wrap and store in the refrigerator for up to 8 hours.

Chop the parsley (optional) and refrigerate in a tightly covered dish until serving time.

5. **Grill the chicken.** As you remove each piece of chicken from the marinade, spray it lightly with the cooking spray and place it on the grill. Grill the chicken according to the Grill Times opposite until interior temperature reaches 160°F on an instant-read thermometer. The meat should no longer be pink in the center and all the juices should run clear when pricked with the tip of a knife.

6. **To serve,** allow the chicken to rest for 2 to 3 minutes after coming off of the grill (this allows the juices to settle), then cut each piece across the grain into ¼- to ½-inch wide strips. Lay equal amounts of chicken in the center of the lettuce on each plate and sprinkle with garlic croutons and onions. Drizzle each salad with ⅓ cup of the dressing, and sprinkle with 1 tablespoon of chopped parsley. Serve immediately with corn bread or corn muffins.

Two-Sided Contact Grill: *Chicken 4 to 6 minutes.*

Hibachi Grill, Combination Grill or Infusion Grill: *Chicken 8 to 12 minutes. Turn the chicken halfway through the grilling time. Grills with lids may be covered halfway through the grilling time. Infusion grills with lids may be covered for the entire grilling time.*

Variation:

Drunken Buffalo Chicken: Instead of lemon juice in the marinade, substitute 1 or 2 tablespoons of Bourbon or Whisky.

Blue Cheese Dressing

Makes 7 (¹/₃ cup) servings

- ¾ cup low-fat or nonfat mayonnaise
- ½ cup low-fat or nonfat sour cream
- ¼ cup low-fat buttermilk
- ½ teaspoon garlic powder
- 1 tablespoon red wine vinegar
- 1 tablespoon lemon juice
- 2 tablespoons thinly sliced green onions
- ½ cup crumbled blue cheese

Light salt and freshly ground pepper to taste

This dressing can be made up to 5 days in advance of serving if refrigerated in an airtight container.

1. In a 3-cup bowl, whisk the mayonnaise, sour cream, buttermilk, garlic powder, vinegar, lemon juice, green onions, blue cheese and salt and pepper to taste.
2. Cover and refrigerate until serving time.

Approximate Nutrients Per Serving of Entire Meal

Total Calories 338	Protein 41 g / 50%	Carbohydrate 25 g / 30%
Total Sugar 8 g	Fat Total 7 g / 20%	Saturated Fat 3 g / 10%
Cholesterol 96 mg	Sodium 873 mg	Fiber 5 g Calcium 217 mg

Kitchen Sink Chicken Caesar Salad

I love Caesar salad, but there are times when I want something more substantial than the classic recipe–Romaine lettuce, Caesar dressing, croutons and Parmesan cheese. One of those occasions was the day I came home ravenous after teaching two aerobic classes. I opened my refrigerator, scanned my vegetable drawer and then proceeded to put everything but the kitchen sink into the salad. My Caesar dressing doubles as a marinade for the chicken. If you don't want to take the time to make my dressing from scratch, substitute one of your favorite bottled dressings.

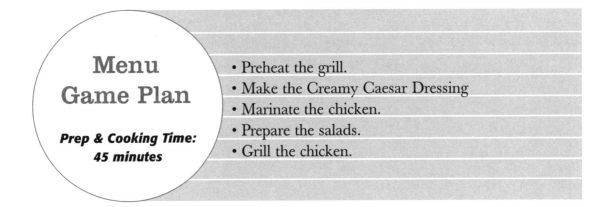

Menu Game Plan

Prep & Cooking Time: 45 minutes

- Preheat the grill.
- Make the Creamy Caesar Dressing
- Marinate the chicken.
- Prepare the salads.
- Grill the chicken.

Cook's Notes

Who was Caesar? Caesar Cardini invented Caesar salad in 1924 at his restaurant in Tijuana, Mexico. He wanted diners to eat his salad with their fingers so he left the Romaine leaves whole, sprinkled them with croutons and Parmesan, then drizzled them with a dressing made of olive oil, garlic and Worcestershire sauce. Later, some creative chef added anchovy slices. Still later, Caesar dressings laced with anchovy paste and mayonnaise became popular.

Chicken Caesar Salad

Serves 4

Chicken

1¼ pounds boneless skinless chicken breasts

½ cup creamy Caesar Dressing (see recipe on page 188)

Salad

6 cups chopped Romaine lettuce

1 cup thinly sliced cucumber (preferably hothouse)

1 cup thinly sliced bell pepper

1 cup thinly sliced fennel or celery

1 cup thinly sliced radish

½ cup thinly sliced green onion

1 cup thinly sliced or shredded carrot

2 medium navel oranges

2 cups garlic croutons

½ cup shredded Parmesan or Romano cheese

Substitutions:
Instead of fresh oranges, substitute tangelos when in season or canned Mandarin oranges. Make sure the canned Mandarin oranges are well drained before putting on the salad.

1. Preheat the grill. If you have a grill with a variable temperature control, set it to medium-high (one or two steps below high) or to about 350° to 400°F.

2. Flatten and marinate the chicken. Spread a large piece of plastic wrap on a flat work surface. Arrange the chicken breasts in a single layer over the plastic wrap. Cover the breasts with another large piece of plastic wrap. Pound the breasts with the bottom of a large heavy skillet, the flat side of a meat mallet, or a rolling pin until flattened to about ¼- to ½-inch thick.

Place the chicken in a 1-gallon zippered freezer-weight storage bag, a 1-quart airtight container or a shallow square glass dish (8 x 8 x 2-inch).

With your fingertips, smear ½ cup of the dressing onto all sides of the flattened meat. Zip the bag closed, or cover the container or dish and marinate in the refrigerator for 20 minutes or up to 24 hours.

3. Prepare the salads. Put equal amounts of the Romaine lettuce on 4 dinner plates.

Peel the oranges and cut them in half; then cut each half across the meridian into ¼-inch thick half moons.

Artistically arrange equal amounts of all the vegetables on top of the lettuce, leaving the center free for the chicken. If not serving immediately, cover each plate tightly with plastic wrap and store in the refrigerator for up to 8 hours.

4. Grill the chicken. Remove each piece of chicken from the marinade and place it on the grill. Grill the chicken according to the Grill Times on page 188 until the interior temperature reaches 160°F on an instant-read thermometer. The meat should no longer be pink in the center, and all the juices should run clear when pricked with the tip of a knife.

6. To serve, allow the chicken to rest for 2 to 3 minutes after coming off of the grill (this allows the juices to settle) and then cut each piece across the grain into ¼- to ½-inch wide strips. Lay equal amounts of chicken in the center of the lettuce and sprinkle with garlic croutons and onions. Drizzle with 3 tablespoons of the dressing and sprinkle with chopped parsley. Serve immediately with hot garlic bread.

Grill Times

Two-Sided Contact Grill: *4 to 6 minutes*

Hibachi Grill, Combination Grill or Infusion Grill: *8 to 12 minutes. Turn the chicken halfway through the grilling time. Grills with lids may be covered halfway through the grilling time. Infusion grills with lids may be covered for the entire grilling time.*

Creamy Caesar Dressing

Makes 6 (3 tablespoon) servings

- ¾ cup low-fat or nonfat mayonnaise
- ¼ cup extra-virgin olive oil
- ¼ cup seasoned red wine vinegar
- ¼ cup fresh lemon juice
- ½ teaspoon pressed garlic
- ½ teaspoon Worcestershire sauce
- 2 teaspoons Dijon-style mustard
- 1 to 2 teaspoons anchovy paste (from a tube)
- ¼ teaspoon light salt or to taste
- ¼ teaspoon freshly ground pepper

This dressing will keep up to 2 weeks if refrigerated in an airtight container.

1. In a blender, mix the mayonnaise, olive oil, vinegar, lemon juice, garlic, Worcestershire sauce, mustard, anchovy paste, salt and pepper to taste.
2. Reserve ½ cup to marinate the chicken.

Variation:

Creamy Balsamic Caesar Dressing: Instead of red wine vinegar, lemon juice and Worcestershire, substitute ½ cup balsamic vinegar.

Approximate Nutrients Per Serving of Entire Meal

Total Calories 440	Protein 40 g/ 36%	Carbohydrate 32 g/ 29%
Total Sugar 13 g	Fat Total 17 g/ 35%	Saturated Fat 3 g/ 7%
Cholesterol 88 mg	Sodium 872 mg	Fiber 6 g Calcium 186 mg

Oasis Pitas Stuffed with Aromatic Turkey Tenderloins and Quick Tabouli Salad

Like an oasis in the desert, this easy-to-make menu is a refreshing change for a tired culinary repertoire. Scented with a harmonious blend of fresh mint, dill, parsley and lemon, the tabouli and grilled turkey filling for these Middle Eastern make-it-yourself sandwiches provides a soothing respite from busy schedules. Like the Rootin' Tootin' Texas Tabouli on page 149, you'll start this Quick Tabouli Salad recipe with a timesaving packaged mix and finish by adding fresh vegetables. Better yet, a pita filled with turkey and a heaping helping of grain and vegetable rich tabouli is a hassle-free way to meet your daily requirement of carbohydrates, protein, fiber, vitamins and minerals.

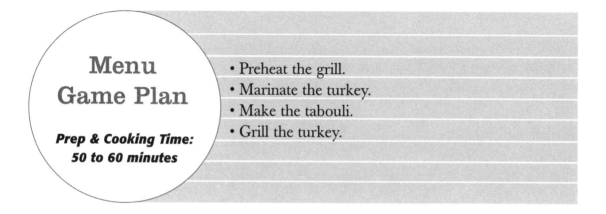

Menu Game Plan

**Prep & Cooking Time:
50 to 60 minutes**

• Preheat the grill.
• Marinate the turkey.
• Make the tabouli.
• Grill the turkey.

Cook's Notes

Notes

Pita bread is one of the oldest flat breads in existence. Legend has it that these round, little breads with a pocket in the middle were introduced to the Mediterranean, Middle East and Africa by nomads. After a long day wandering, they would bake their pitas over an open fire in the evenings. Each culture that adopted the bread gave it a different name. Moroccans and Syrians call it khubiz, Lebanese kemaj, Turks pide and Algerians kesra. The Greeks called this bread pita like we do, but their version has no pocket. In Italy, some creative ancient Etruscan topped a pita with vegetables and sauce and pizza was born.

Aromatic Turkey Tenderloins

Serves 4

1 teaspoon pressed garlic

⅓ cup lemon juice

1 tablespoon olive oil

1 tablespoon finely chopped fresh dill or 1 teaspoon dried

1 tablespoon finely chopped fresh mint or 1 teaspoon dried

½ teaspoon ground cumin

½ teaspoon light salt

1¼ pounds turkey tenderloin

4 to 8 butter lettuce leaves

4 6- to 7-inch pita breads, white or whole wheat

Nonfat or canola oil cooking spray

Substitutions:
Instead of turkey, substitute boneless skinless chicken breasts, or a firm fleshed fish, like tuna or swordfish.

1. **Preheat the grill.** If you have a grill with a variable temperature control, set it to medium-high (1 or 2 steps below high) or to about 350° to 400°F.

2. **Make the marinade.** In a blender, blend the garlic, lemon juice, olive oil, dill, mint, cumin and salt until smooth. Pour the marinade into a 1-gallon zippered storage bag, 1-quart airtight container or shallow square glass dish (8 x 8 x 2-inch). Set aside while you prepare the turkey.

3. **Marinate the turkey tenderloins.** Cut the turkey tenderloin into 3-inch lengths. Place them on your cutting board so that the length is perpendicular to your body. Holding your free hand on top, slice the turkey pieces ¾ of the way through, leaving them "hinged" along one side so that they can open up to twice their original size like a book. Be sure that you cut evenly through the middle. With the palms of your hands, press the "hinge" down to evenly flatten the pieces.

Put the turkey pieces in the zippered bag, container or dish containing the marinade, then turn it so all the surfaces are coated with the marinade. Zip the bag closed or cover the container or dish and refrigerate for 20 minutes or up to 24 hours.

4. **Grill the turkey tenderloins.** As you remove each piece of turkey from the marinade, lightly spray it with cooking spray before placing it on the grill. Grill the poultry according to the Grill Times opposite until the interior temperature reaches 160°F on an instant read thermometer. The meat should no longer be pink in the center, and all the juices should run clear when pricked with the tip of a knife.

5. **To serve,** place 2 butter lettuce leaves on each of 4 dinner plates. Spoon equal amounts of the Quick Tabouli Salad on top of the lettuce. Cut the pita bread into half moons and put two halves onto each plate. When the turkey is done, let it rest 2 to 3 minutes before slicing it across the grain into ¼ to ½-inch wide strips. Put equal amounts of the strips on each plate beside the tabouli and serve immediately, allowing diners to stuff their own pita breads with the turkey and tabouli.

Grill Times

Two-Sided Contact Grill: *6 to 8 minutes*

Hibachi Grill, Combination Grill or Infusion Grill: *12 to 14 minutes. Turn the tenderloins halfway through the grilling time. Grills with lids may be covered halfway through the grilling time. Infusion grills with lids may be covered for the entire grilling time.*

Quick Tabouli Salad

Makes 4 (1½ cup servings)

1	6-ounce box tabouli mix
2	tablespoons olive oil
¼	cup plus 2 tablespoons lemon juice
1	cup boiling water
½	teaspoon ground cumin
½	cup finely chopped fresh parsley
2	tablespoons finely chopped fresh dill or 2 teaspoons dried
2	tablespoons finely chopped fresh mint or 2 teaspoons dried
½	cup thinly sliced green onion
1	cup diced ripe tomatoes or sliced cherry tomatoes
1	cup diced cucumber (preferably hothouse)
1	cup shredded or thinly sliced carrot

This salad can be made up to 48 hours in advance of serving if refrigerated in an airtight container.

1. In a 2-quart airtight container or bowl, mix the contents of the tabouli box, the seasoning package, the oil, lemon juice, boiling water, and cumin. If using dry dill and mint, mix them in. Cover with plastic wrap or a lid, and let hydrate in the refrigerator for 30 minutes.
2. Prepare the vegetables while the tabouli is hydrating.
3. When the tabouli has hydrated and cooled, use a rubber spatula to gently fold in the prepared vegetables until thoroughly mixed. Store tightly covered in the refrigerator until ready to serve.

Mix & Match

Serve the Tabouli Salad with any of the main dishes in the following menus: Memories of Manhattan Moroccan Burgers, page 79; Pita the Great Lamb Burgers, page 92; Rockin' Moroccan Lamb Kebabs, page 151; Fetadillas, page 251.

How to Create High Security Skewers

Does the food on your skewers cook unevenly . . . some pieces are tough and overdone while others are underdone? You can remedy these problems with a little skewering savvy.

1. Cut all pieces of food uniformly. Smaller pieces of food grill faster than larger pieces. So, if you have skewered pieces of food that are not even in size, the small pieces will become overcooked while waiting for the larger ones to grill.

2. Double skewer. Food pierced through the center by one skewer tends to cook unevenly because it spins around when you turn the kebabs on the grill. Here's why: The high grill heat causes evaporation, shrinking the food just enough to make the skewer hole too large for a tight hold on the skewer. To prevent this, I double skewer my kebabs. Hold two 8-inch bamboo skewers firmly in one hand with a finger between the two skewers holding them about 1/2 inch apart. Then thread the pieces of food on both skewers at once.

3. Thread the food evenly on each skewer for more even grilling. Try to thread the skewers so that each piece of food touches the grilling rack on two opposite sides. Since the food pieces are small, kebabs grill perfectly with one turn halfway through the cooking time.

4. Leave space between the pieces of food on each skewer. Skewered foods that are tightly pushed together steam instead of grill. This makes them take longer to cook than foods that have 1/8 to 1/4 inch of "breathing room" between each piece.

5. For even cooking, choose foods that require the same grilling times. For example, chicken, orange, and jicama slices all take about 10 minutes to grill, so they can all be grouped together on the same skewer.

Approximate Nutrients Per Serving of Entire Meal

Total Calories 602	Protein 46 g / 31%	Carbohydrate 76 g / 50%
Total Sugar 8 g	Fat Total 13 g / 19%	Saturated Fat 2 g / 3%
Cholesterol 82 mg	Sodium 946 mg	Fiber 11 g Calcium 149 mg

(Nutritional analysis for menu on pages 189 to 191.)

Uncle Mannie's BBQ Chicken Sandwich with Waldorf Slaw

When I am in the mood for comfort food, I make my Uncle Mannie's BBQ Chicken Sandwich. Until I discovered electric indoor grills, it used to be a recipe that I made only in summer like my Uncle Mannie. He used to serve it as a special Sunday supper treat at his Los Angeles home during my family's annual summer visit from Northern California. The best part of the sandwich was Uncle Mannie's secret sauce. As a child, I would scramble out of his swimming pool where I had been playing all afternoon with my sister and cousins, to stand at his elbow and watch him grill chicken breasts slathered with his lip-smacking "Secret BBQ Sauce." As I got older, Uncle Mannie let me help him make his sauce, stirring the ingredients with a long handled spoon as he added them to the pot. Since my favorite side dish for Uncle Mannie's BBQ Chicken Sandwich has always been coleslaw, I created a Waldorf-style recipe studded with grapes and walnuts that I hope will become as popular with your family as it is with mine.

Menu Game Plan

Prep & Cooking Time: 45 minutes

- Preheat the grill.
- Flatten and season the chicken.
- Make Uncle Mannie's Secret BBQ Sauce.
- Make the Waldorf Coleslaw.
- Prepare the sandwich garnishes.
- Grill the chicken.
- Assemble the sandwiches.

Cook's Notes

I love coleslaw in just about any form. The cabbage can be finely shredded or coarsely chopped. Vegetables and/or fruit may be mixed in. The dressing may simply be mayonnaise, or a more complex combination of mayonnaise, sour cream, vinegar or lemon juice and seasonings. Coleslaw has been an American favorite since at least the late 1700s. Early Americans adapted the name of the salad from the Dutch, Americanizing the words "kool" meaning cabbage and "sla" meaning salad into "coleslaw." Some call it "cold slaw" because it is usually served cold.

BBQ Chicken Sandwich

Serves 4

1¼ pounds boneless skinless chicken breasts (4 breast halves)

Light salt and pepper to taste

½ cup Uncle Mannie's Secret Sauce (see recipe on page 195)

Nonfat or canola oil cooking spray

4 sourdough or French sandwich rolls

2 medium tomatoes

Crisp lettuce leaves such as Romaine or iceburg

Low-fat or nonfat mayonnaise

1. Preheat the grill. If you have a grill with a variable temperature control, set it to medium-high (1 or 2 steps below high) or to about 350° to 400°F.

2. Flatten and season the chicken. Spread a large piece of plastic wrap on a flat work surface. Arrange the chicken breasts in a single layer over the plastic wrap. Cover the breasts with another large piece of plastic wrap. Pound the breasts with the bottom of a large heavy skillet, the flat side of a meat mallet or a rolling pin until flattened to about ¼- to ½-inch thick.

Put the chicken on a plate and season with salt and pepper to taste. Cover with plastic wrap and refrigerate up to 24 hours.

3. Grill the chicken. Put ¼ of Uncle Mannie's Secret Sauce into a separate bowl for basting and set it near the grill with a basting brush. Reserve the remaining sauce for the finished sandwiches. Spray all surfaces of the chicken with the cooking spray. Place the chicken on the grill, then baste the upper side with Uncle Mannie's Secret Sauce. Grill the chicken according to the Grill Times below until interior temperature reaches 160°F on an instant-read thermometer. The meat should no longer be pink in the center, and all the juices should run clear when pricked with the tip of a knife.

4. To serve, slice the sourdough rolls open and toast in a preheated 350°F oven if desired. Put equal amounts of coleslaw on 4 plates.

Spread 1 tablespoon of the reserved Uncle Mannie's Secret Sauce on half of the roll and top with a piece of chicken and the remaining half a roll. Place the sandwich on the plate next to the coleslaw. Offer low-fat or nonfat mayonnaise, lettuce and tomatoes to complete the sandwich.

Grill Times

Two-Sided Contact Grill: 4 to 6 minutes. Baste halfway through the grilling time.

Hibachi Grill, Combination Grill or Infusion Grill: 8 to 12 minutes. Turn the chicken and baste halfway through the grilling time. Grills with lids may be covered halfway through the grilling time. Infusion grills with lids may be covered for the entire grilling time.

Uncle Mannie's Secret BBQ Sauce

Makes 1½ cups

1   tablespoon olive oil

½   cup finely chopped white or red onion

2   teaspoons pressed garlic

1   cup ketchup

¼   cup molasses

2   tablespoons apple cider vinegar

2   tablespoons Worcestershire sauce

½   cup currant jelly

1   teaspoon paprika

1   teaspoon chili powder

Pinch ground cayenne pepper

This menu calls for ½ cup of BBQ sauce. But since it is so good and will last up to 1 month in the refrigerator, I tripled the recipe for you. Use it as a baste or finishing sauce for poultry, meat, fish, or tofu. It tastes even better after it has sat in the refrigerator overnight.

1. In a 2-quart saucepan, heat the oil over medium-high heat.
2. When the oil sizzles, stir in the onions and garlic. Turn the heat down to medium-low and sauté the onions and garlic for 1 or 2 minutes. Cover and cook an additional 5 to 6 minutes until onions are tender, lifting the cover to stir once or twice during the cooking time.
3. While the onions are cooking, whisk the ketchup, molasses, vinegar, Worcestershire sauce, currant jelly, paprika, chili powder and cayenne pepper in a 1-quart bowl or measure.
4. When onions are done, stir in the catsup mixture. Raise the heat to medium and bring to a soft boil.
5. Turn the heat down to a low simmer and cook uncovered for 10 minutes, stirring occasionally.
6. Remove the sauce from the heat and let stand to cool.

Variations:
Spirited BBQ Sauce: Add 2 to 3 tablespoons bourbon, rum or sweet Sherry.
Pineapple BBQ Sauce: Substitute pineapple jam for the currant jelly.
Spirited Orange BBQ Sauce: Substitute orange marmalade for the current jelly and add 3 tablespoons Grand Marnier.

Waldorf Slaw

Makes 4 (1 cup) servings

⅓ cup low-fat or nonfat mayonnaise

⅓ cup low-fat or nonfat sour cream

3 tablespoons seasoned rice vinegar

1 tablespoon honey

3 cups cabbage

⅓ cup thinly sliced green onion

1 cup peeled, chopped apple

1 cup seedless grapes sliced in half

½ cup chopped walnuts

Light salt to taste

1. In the bottom of a 2-quart mixing bowl, whisk the mayonnaise, sour cream, vinegar, and honey.
2. Using a rubber spatula, fold in the cabbage, green onion, apple, grapes and walnuts. Season with salt to taste. Serve at once or refrigerate tightly covered for up to 3 days.

Substitutions:
For the green grapes, substitute yellow raisins.
Make the slaw colorful by using 2 cups of green cabbage and 1 cup of red cabbage.

Mix & Match

Serve the Waldorf Slaw with any of the main dishes in the following menus: Double Whammy Texas BBQ Burger, page 76; Grandma Jennie's Burger, page 39; Farmhouse Steaks, page 103; Amazing Maple Glazed Pork Chops, page 115; Cowboy Kebabs with Easy Ridin' BBQ Sauce, page 147; A Turkey for All Seasons, page 163; How's Bayou? Louisiana Shrimp and Orange Brochettes, page 235.

Approximate Nutrients Per Serving of Entire Meal

Total Calories 613	Protein 46 g / 30%	Carbohydrate 75 g / 49%
Total Sugar 32 g	Fat Total 14 g / 20%	Saturated Fat 2 g / 2%
Cholesterol 90 mg	Sodium 1,021 mg	Fiber 5 g Calcium 132 mg

Ah So! Sweet and Sour Pineapple Chicken Kebabs

One of the most memorable experiences of my career was working with my friend Martin Yan as his assistant during a season's taping of the *Yan Can Cook* show for Public Television in San Francisco. Among the many Chinese recipes I learned at his elbow, Sweet and Sour Chicken is still one of my favorites. Unfortunately, this delightful dish is not on my menu often because each tasty tidbit of chicken is traditionally battered and deep-fried. To create a healthier version, suitable for waistline watchers like myself, I turned to my electric tabletop grill. Instead of deep-frying, I skewer the marinated chicken along with bell pepper and fresh pineapple to make colorful kebabs. Topped with my easy-to-make Pineapple Sweet and Sour Sauce and served over sticky rice, this menu delivers the flavor you expect without the fat.

Menu Game Plan

Prep and Cooking Time: 50 minutes

- Preheat the grill.
- Marinate the meat.
- Make the rice.
- Make the Sweet and Sour Sauce.
- Prepare optional vegetable garnishes.
- Grill the kebabs.

Cook's Notes

Notes

When Columbus sailed to the New World in search of gold, he didn't find the metallic kind. He did discover it, though, in the sweet, golden fruit of the pineapple. Pineapples originated in Pre-Incan Peru and made their way to the West Indies where islanders placed them in front of their huts to tell visitors they were welcome. Spanish explorers not only introduced the fruit to Europe, but also brought it to Hawaii, where it is now one of the state's most important commercial crops.

Pineapple Chicken Kebabs

Serves 4

2 tablespoons dry Sherry

1 tablespoon light or low-sodium soy sauce

½ teaspoon sesame, peanut or canola oil

1¼ pounds boneless, skinless chicken breasts

1 medium bell pepper, red, yellow or orange

½ small ripe pineapple or 1 12-ounce package fresh pineapple chunks

Nonfat or canola cooking spray

½ cup thinly sliced green onions

¼ cup thinly sliced cucumber

¼ cup thinly sliced red radish

Substitutions:
Substitute turkey tenderloin, pork tenderloin or extra firm tofu for the chicken.

1. **Preheat the grill.** If you have a grill with a variable temperature control, set it to medium-high (1 or 2 steps below high) or to about 350° to 400°F.

2. **Marinate the meat.** In a 1-cup bowl or glass measure, mix the dry Sherry, soy sauce, and oil thoroughly with a fork. Cut the chicken into 1 x 1 x 1-inch or 1 x 1 x 2-inch cubes. Put it into a 1-quart zippered freezer bag, 1-quart airtight container or or shallow square glass dish (8 x 8 x 2-inch) and then pour the marinade over all. Turn the meat pieces so all surfaces are coated with the marinade. Squeeze the air out of the bag and zip it closed or cover the container with a lid or plastic wrap. Marinate in the refrigerator for 20 minutes or up to 24 hours until ready to grill.

3. **Prepare the pepper and the pineapple.** Remove the seeds from the bell peppers, then cut them into 1 x 1 x 1-inch pieces. Leave the rind on the pineapple and cut it into 1-inch thick triangles.

4. **Skewer and grill** the kebabs. Remove the chicken from the marinade. Discard the marinade unless using an Infusion Grill. Alternately thread the meat, bell pepper and pineapple onto 8 (2 skewer) sets of parallel bamboo skewers leaving a ⅛ to ¼ inch space between each piece of food. (See page 192 for double skewering technique.) To allow the pineapple to lie flat on the grill, skewer it so that the double skewers first pierce the flesh then come out through the rind.

Spray each skewer lightly with the cooking spray for faster browning and to encourage grill marks before placing on the grill. Cook the kebabs according to the Grill Times opposite until the internal temperature reaches 160°F on an instant-read thermometer.

5. **To serve,** spoon equal amounts of rice onto the center of 4 plates. Arrange 2 skewers on opposite sides of the rice. Garnish around the edges of the rice with equal amounts of the fresh cucumber and radish slices (optional). Top the rice with ¼ cup of the Sweet and Sour Sauce, and sprinkle with 1 tablespoon of the thinly sliced green onion. Serve immediately, passing around the remaining sauce.

Two-Sided Contact Grill: 5 to 6 minutes.

Hibachi Grill, Combination Grill or Infusion Grill: 10 to 12 minutes. Turn the kebabs 180° halfway through the grilling time. Grills with lids may be covered halfway through the grilling time. Infusion grills with lids may be covered for the entire grilling time.

Infusion Grill Notes: For a more intense flavor, pour the leftover marinade mixture into infusion cup. If there is not enough marinade left, combine it with some extra soy sauce to make ½ cup before pouring into infusion cup.

Sticky Rice

Makes 4 generous (1 cup) servings

1½ cups medium grain rice, known also as Japanese or pearl rice

2 cups water

This basic recipe can be kept in the refrigerator for up to 3 days or in the freezer for up to 2 months if stored in an airtight container or a zippered freezer bag.

1. In a 4-quart pot, mix the rice and water and bring to a boil.
2. Reduce heat to low and simmer covered 20 minutes, or until all the water is absorbed. Remove from heat and let stand covered 10 minutes. Stir with a fork to fluff up rice before serving.

Sweet and Sour Sauce

Makes 4 generous (¹/₃ cup) servings

1 tablespoon light or low-sodium soy sauce

1 tablespoon white vinegar

2½ teaspoons cornstarch

1 8-ounce can crushed pineapple including juice

½ teaspoon grated gingerroot

2 tablespoons brown sugar

3 tablespoons ketchup (low sodium, if desired)

This will keep in your refrigerator in an airtight container up to 2 weeks.

1. In a 1-quart saucepan thoroughly whisk the soy sauce, vinegar and cornstarch to make a smooth paste.

2. Whisk in the pineapple, ginger, brown sugar and ketchup. Put the pot over medium heat and bring to a boil whisking constantly. Continue whisking until the sauce is thickened, about 1 to 2 minutes. Remove from the stove, cover and set aside until serving time. If the sauce cools before serving, reheat over low heat whisking constantly. If it gets too thick while reheating, whisk in a few teaspoons of hot water.

Approximate Nutrients Per Serving of Entire Meal

Total Calories 563	Protein 35 g / 25%	Carbohydrate 92 g / 66%
Total Sugar 22 g	Fat Total 5 g / 8%	Saturated Fat 1 g / 2%
Cholesterol 78 mg	Sodium 527 mg	Fiber 3 g Calcium 52 mg

Port Royale Chicken Fajitas with Buccaneer Black Beans and Caribbean Fruit Salsa

Yo-ho-ho and a marinade of rum! My Jamaican rum marinade transforms traditional Tex-Mex fajitas to a Caribbean tour de force honoring the original Grill Gods of the Caribbean…the Buccaneers. This motley collection of ruthless seventeenth century escapees—runaway bondsmen, castaways, escaped criminals, political and religious refugees—originally found sanctuary on the Spanish Island of Hispanola (now occupied by Santo Domingo and Haiti). They became known as buccaneers because they used a wooden frame called a "boucan" (a French adaptation of a Carib-Indian word) to cure and cook the meat they sold.

This wickedly delicious menu features ingredients that were available during Port Royale's pirate heyday: chicken, onions, pineapple, mango, hot peppers, beans, allspice and avocado. Since the pirates loved grilled food, it would not be too far-fetched to imagine the infamous brigand, Captain Morgan, supping on a similar meal, a wench on either side assembling his fajitas.

Menu Game Plan

Prep & Cooking Time: 50 to 60 minutes

- Preheat the grill.
- Preheat the oven for the tortillas.
- Marinate the chicken and the pineapple.
- Make the Buccaneer Black Beans.
- Make the Quick Caribbean Fruit Salsa.
- Put the optional garnishes into serving bowls.
- Grill the peppers and onions.
- Grill the chicken and pineapple
- Warm the tortillas while the chicken is grilling.

Cook's Notes

There are over 1,000 varieties of mangoes ranging in shape from round to kidney and in skin color from greenish yellow to orange with a bright red blush. Ripe mangoes yield to gentle pressure, like ripe avocados, and will keep in the refrigerator for up to 2 weeks. To make sure that a mango will be flavorful, smell the stem. If it has no fragrance, it will be flavorless. If it has a chemical smell, it is fermented and should be rejected. Overripe mangoes actually contain kerosene. Use mangoes in salads, salsas, blender drinks, yogurt, ice cream, sorbet, chutney, jam, appetizers, soups and sauces. An excellent source of vitamins A, C and potassium, one cup of diced mango weighs in at only 107 calories.

Chicken Fajitas

Serves 4

Marinade

2 tablespoons lime juice

1 tablespoon low-sodium soy sauce

2 tablespoons rum or pineapple juice

1 teaspoon pressed garlic

2 teaspoons grated gingerroot

2 tablespoons prepared jerk sauce or 1 to 2 teaspoons prepared jerk paste*

Fajitas

1¼ pounds boneles, skinless chicken breasts

¼ fresh pineapple or 1 8-ounce can pineapple rings, well drained

2 medium bell peppers, red, yellow, orange or green

1 medium red onion

Nonfat or canola oil cooking spray

8 6- to 10-inch low-fat flour or corn tortillas

Grated coconut

Sliced tomatoes

Sliced fresh mango or papaya

---

1. **Preheat the grill.** If you have a grill with a variable temperature control, set it to medium-high (1 or 2 steps below high) or to about 350° to 400°F.

2. **Preheat the oven to 350°F** for warming the fajitas.

3. **Make the marinade paste.** In a 1-cup bowl, mix the lime juice, soy sauce, rum or pineapple juice, garlic, ginger and jerk seasoning thoroughly with a fork. Reserve 1 teaspoon for marinating the pineapple. Set aside until ready to use.

4. **Flatten and marinate the chicken.** Spread a large piece of plastic wrap on a flat work surface. Arrange the chicken breasts in a single layer over the plastic wrap. Cover the breasts with another large piece of plastic wrap. Pound the breasts with the bottom of a large heavy skillet, the flat side of a meat mallet or a rolling pin until flattened to about ¼- to ½-inch thick.

Place the chicken in a 1-gallon zippered freezer-weight storage bag, a 1-quart airtight container, or a shallow square glass dish (8 x 8 x 2-inch). With your fingertips, smear the marinade paste onto all sides of the flattened meat. Zip the bag closed and press out the air, or cover the container or dish and marinate in the refrigerator for 20 minutes or up to 24 hours.

5. **Prepare and marinate the pineapple.** Leave the rind on and slice the pineapple into about 8 1-inch-thick triangles. Place the pineapple in a shallow dish. With your fingertips, smear the reserved paste onto all sides of the pineapple. Cover the dish tightly with plastic wrap and marinate in the refrigerator for 20 minutes or up to 24 hours.

6. **Grill the bell peppers and the onion.** Slice each bell pepper in half lengthwise and remove the stem and seeds. Cut each half lengthwise into ½-inch strips. Slice onion across the meridian into ½-inch rings. Put the vegetables into a 3- or 4-cup bowl, and spray all surfaces lightly with cooking spray. Start grilling the vegetables as soon as the grill has reached the set temperature. Grill according to the Grill Times opposite until the peppers are cooked through yet tender-crisp and the onion slices are tender. When the vegetables are done, keep them warm until serving time on a serving platter covered with aluminum foil.

7. **Grill the chicken and pineapple.** As you remove each piece of chicken from the marinade, spray it lightly with the cooking spray and place it on the grill. Do the same with the pineapple.

Avocado slices, prepared
    guacamole or recipe on
    page 72

Nonfat or low-fat sour cream

Quick Caribbean Salsa (see recipe
    page 204) or prepared
    Mango Chutney

*If unavailable, use my recipe on
page 54.

Substitutions:
Instead of chicken substitute
equal amounts of flank steak,
pork tenderloin; a firm fleshed
fish like tuna, swordfish; shellfish like shrimp, scallops or
extra-firm tofu.

Grill the pineapple according to the Grill Times until it has distinct grill marks on either side. Grill the chicken according to the Grill Times below until the internal temperature reaches 160°F on an instant-read thermometer. The meat should no longer be pink in the center, and all the juices should run clear when pricked with the tip of a knife.

8. Warm the tortillas while the chicken is grilling. Place the tortillas on a nonstick baking sheet and cover with a damp color-free paper towel. Cover with aluminum foil then place in a preheated 350°F oven for 4 to 5 minutes until tortillas are warmed.

(Microwave Method: Place the tortillas on a dinner plate and cover with a color-free paper towel. Sprinkle the towel with about 2 teaspoons water. The towel should be damp, not wet. Microwave 20 to 30 seconds on high (100% power).)

9. To serve, transfer the grilled chicken to a cutting board, and let it stand covered 2 to 3 minutes. Slice each piece of chicken across the grain into 1/4- to 1/2-inch strips. Arrange the chicken strips and grilled pineapple on a serving platter with the grilled peppers and onions. Put the warmed tortillas on a plate. Set out the optional garnishes. Let diners assemble their own fajitas by putting a warm tortilla in the middle of their plate, then topping with a couple of strips of chicken, grilled onions, peppers, avocado slices or prepared guacamole, sliced mango, or papaya, a sprinkle of grated coconut, nonfat sour cream and salsa. Fold 2 sides of the tortilla over one another to make a long tube. Then, before eating, fold up the bottom end so the food doesn't slip out when you pick up the filled tortilla. Serve the Buccaneer Beans on the side.

Grill Times

Two-Sided Contact Grill: Peppers and onions 7 to 10 minutes / pineapple 3 to 4 minutes / chicken 4 to 6 minutes.

Hibachi Grill, Combination Grill or Infusion Grill: Peppers and onions 14 to 20 minutes / pineapple 6 to 8 minutes/ chicken 8 to 12 minutes. Turn the vegetables, chicken and pineapple halfway through the grilling time. Grills with lids may be covered halfway through the grilling time. Infusion grills with lids may be covered for the entire grilling time.

Infusion Grill Notes: For a more intense flavor, mix 1 tablespoon garlic purée from a jar, or pressed garlic with 2 tablespoons orange juice and 1/4 cup rum or lime juice in a 1-cup measure or bowl. Pour it into the infusion cup before preheating.

Buccaneer Black Beans

Makes 4 (½ cup) servings

1   tablespoon canola or corn oil

½   cup chopped onion

1   teaspoon pressed garlic

1   tablespoon grated gingerroot

1   tablespoon chili powder

½   teaspoon allspice

3   tablespoons diced canned chilies, mild or hot

2   16-ounce cans black beans, rinsed in a colander, drained

½   cup nonfat chicken broth

½   teaspoon light salt

1   to 2 tablespoons rum (optional)

1. In a 1- or 2-quart nonstick pot, heat the canola oil over a low flame. Add the onion, garlic, ginger, chili powder, allspice and canned chilies.

2. Cook onion mixture covered over a low flame, 10 to 15 minutes, lifting the lid to stir occasionally, until the onions are tender.

3. In a food processor fitted with the metal chopping blade or a blender, puree the beans, chicken broth, salt and optional rum.

4. When the onions are done, scrape the bean mixture into the pot using a rubber spatula. Mix the beans thoroughly with the onions using a heatproof spoon or spatula. Heat, covered, over a low flame until hot, about 5 to 6 minutes, stirring every 2 minutes to prevent burning. Remove from the flame, cover and set aside until serving.

Reheat over a low flame stirring constantly. Or, transfer the beans to a microwavable casserole and microwave covered for 3 to 4 minutes on high (100% power), stirring halfway through the cooking time. If the mixture becomes too thick as it reheats, stir in 1 or 2 tablespoons of chicken broth.

Quick Caribbean Fruit Salsa

Makes 16 (2 tablespoon) servings

1   cup fresh pineapple, chopped

½   cup chopped fresh mango

1   11-ounce jar thick and chunky fat-free salsa, mild or hot

½   teaspoon grated gingerroot

½   teaspoon allspice

1. Mix all ingredients in a 2-quart bowl.
2. Cover tightly and refrigerate for up to 10 days.

Substitutions:
For the pineapple substitute an 8-ounce can of drained crushed pineapple. For the mango substitute ½ cup peeled, chopped kiwi fruit or papaya, ½ cup chopped jicama root or an 8-ounce can of drained crushed pineapple.

Approximate Nutrients Per Serving of Entire Meal

Total Calories 738	Protein 63 g / 31%	Carbohydrate 112 g / 56%
Total Sugar 15 g	Fat Total 10 g / 11%	Saturated Fat 2 g / 2%
Cholesterol 84 mg	Sodium 1849 mg	Fiber 24 g Calcium 164 mg

Sublime Seafood

If you've cast your net for some new grilled seafood ideas, you've come to the right place. Your electric tabletop grill gives you the power to make basic grilled seafood recipes, like my Basic Salmon Fillet with Simple Pineapple Soy Marinade (page 55), as well as recipes you normally wouldn't make on the grill. Did you know you could use your tabletop grill to make fish cakes? Learn how as you make my Mac Nut Crab Cake Salad (page 223). How about using your grill to make delicate stuffed fish rolls? Follow the step-by-step instructions in Sole Food Florentine (page 231), and you'll be an expert at grilling flat fish with style. The following are solutions for choosing the best quality fish available. You will also learn solutions for keeping your catch in good shape up until it hits the grill.

Solution 1: Find a Reliable Fish Vendor

My first step in finding the finest fresh or frozen fish is choosing vendors that are actively involved in a Hazard Analysis and Critical Control Point food safety program (HACCP). The best of these programs is monitored by a third party, which certifies that the fish is being handled properly all the way from the water to the supermarket and that food safety procedures at the vendor exceed government food safety standards. A full-scale HACCP program ensures that:
• The fish and shellfish comes from government approved noncontaminated waters. Particularly shellfish.
• The seafood distributors are certified and com-

ply with manufacturing and sanitation guidelines set by the U.S. Food and Drug Administration.
• The fish is transported at a constant temperature of between 38° to 40°F to prevent bacterial growth. (Live shellfish must be kept at 45°F.)
• The store monitors and documents the temperature of their fish cases and employs strict sanitation practices to prevent product cross-contamination.

Solution 2: Do the Smell and Eyeball Test

Upon entering a fish store or fish department in a grocery store, I recommend doing the smell and eyeball test:
• If the store or area around the department smells fishy, try a cleaner smelling establishment.
• If sliced fish, like fillets or steaks, is displayed directly on ice, do not purchase it. If the fish sits on top of a barrier nestled in ice, like a plastic plate or a piece of plastic wrap, it is ok to purchase. According to Wilfred Sumner, USDA Food Safety Consultant and Technical Director for NutriClean, based in Oakland, California, "Ice is a sponge for bacterial contamination. If one piece of sliced contaminated fish is placed directly on ice within a large case, that contamination will leech into the ice and spread to all the uncontaminated fish in the case." This is extremely important if you are purchasing fish to grill rare or eat raw, like Ahi tuna. Ice also pulls moisture out of sliced fish, leaving the fish dry and tough even before you grill it.

Solution 3: Don't be Afraid to Ask Questions

I prefer to purchase fresh fish from a refrigerated case rather than from a shrink-wrapped package. It is much easier to check for freshness when you can ask your fish seller to take the pieces directly out of the display cooler rather then trying to determine freshness by looking through the plastic on fresh or thawed prewrapped pieces. Don't be afraid to ask your fishmonger the following questions:

• Is the store involved in a HACCP program? Does a third party monitor the program 2 to 4 times per year? If it is monitored only once per year, I would choose another store.
• When did the fish arrive at the store and how long has the fish been in the display cooler? If it has been in the store and cooler more than 2 days, try another variety.
• Was the fish frozen? If so, how long ago was it defrosted? More than 2 days is too long. Since freezing slightly alters the taste and texture of fish, U.S. regulations require that defrosted fish be clearly labeled as such.
• Ask to have the fish taken out of the cooler so you can smell it. A strong "fishy" aroma can mean the fish is more than 3 days old. Also the fishy aroma only becomes stronger when it is cooked.
• Check to make sure the flesh is firm, elastic and shiny. Don't consider purchasing it if the flesh is brownish, yellowish or dried out.

Solution 4: Can't Find Fresh Fish? Buy Frozen

Flash-frozen or cryogenically frozen fish is surprisingly delicious and many times better quality than fresh. Caught at sea by ships equipped with high-powered freezers, then processed, this fish is frozen immediately to retain freshness at –60°F or colder. Flash-frozen fish may taste fresher and has firmer flesh than fresh fish because once frozen at extremely low temperatures, it has not had time to deteriorate like naturally happens to fresh fish once it is caught. Fish should be eaten as soon as possible after it has been defrosted and should never be refrozen unless it has been cooked. Shrimp is always frozen at sea immediately upon catching, or frozen

at the farm. Purchase flash-frozen fish either in bags or vacuum wrapping. It is safe to purchase if:

• The fish looks firm and has shiny flesh
• The fish is completely frozen.
• The packaging is unbroken.
• The "sell-by" date is not past.
• There are no frost or ice crystals on the fish, and it does not show signs of dryness or freezer burn. These could mean that the fish may be old, or that it could have slightly thawed in transit and then been refrozen.
• There is no pooled ice in the bag.
• The fish has no freezer burn.

Solution 5: Be Picky about How Your Fish is Packed

If the fish you purchase is raw or defrosted, the way your fish vendor packs it to go home can affect the quality of the fish.

• Always ask your fish vendor to wrap your fish loosely in paper, especially long, thin fish fillets. Fish is extremely delicate, and any bending of fillets or tight packing will damage the flesh.
• Always ask to have the paper package put into a plastic bag. This prevents any cross contamination from juices that may leak from raw meat or poultry. (I always put raw meat and poultry packages in plastic bags as well.)
• Make sure that the grocery clerk always puts your fish on top of the bag so that heavy boxes and cans don't ruin the delicate flesh. Better yet, ask to put your fish in a bag with delicate groceries, like herbs.

Solution 6: Be a Responsible Fish Consumer

While wild fish stocks are dwindling, commercial fishing and fish farming has become more efficient. If you want more information on the state of world fisheries, visit www.montereybayaquarium.org on the World Wide Web for a consumer's guide to seafood availability.

Solution 7: Learn to Grill Fish to Perfection

It is extremely easy to overcook fish and shellfish because they are so delicate. For perfectly grilled

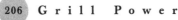

fish and shellfish, cook just until the flesh becomes opaque, just starts to flake, and there is no translucence in the center.

While there is no USDA internal temperature recommendation for cooking fish and shellfish, I discovered while grilling my way through pounds and pounds of both, fish is cooked through yet still tender and juicy at an internal temperature of between 135° to 140° F. For the best results, preheat your grill to medium-high (1 or 2 steps below high) or at about 350° to 400° F. If the grill is hotter than that, the fish's delicate flesh can become dry and tough on the outside before the inside reaches a cooked temperature.

No fish is free of external bacteria. To eliminate it, the exterior temperature of the fish should reach 160° F. If your grill is set at medium high, as suggested above, and you cook the fish so the outside is opaque and grill marks have formed, your fish will have reached the proper exterior temperature. Freshly caught, noncommercial fish could contain internal bacteria or parasites if it comes from mildly contaminated waters, or if it was not kept at a cool enough temperature from the boat to the kitchen. If you suspect this, grill the fish to an internal temperature of 160° F, and all bacteria and parasites will be killed.

For fish cooked rare, like tuna, select fish that is 1 to 2 inches thick. Preheat your grill to the highest setting. Grill just until distinct grill marks appear on both sides of the fish, and the outer edge is still slightly translucent in the middle.

Omega 3's A Good Reason to Eat Fish

I have always believed that eating real food is healthier and far more satisfying than taking supplements. In the case of fish, researchers agree with me. Fish are the richest source of Omega-3 fats and its derivative acids EPA (eicosapentanoic acid) and DHA (docosahexanoic acid). Researchers have found that high consumption of Omega 3's may be linked to a reduced risk of inflammatory diseases such as arthritis and colitis, as well as heart disease, cancer, Alzheimer's disease, moodiness and depression.

Americans now get 700 to 1,400 milligrams weekly. Although there is no official recommendation for Omega-3s, the estimate for therapeutic benefits is about 3,500 milligrams weekly. The fish highest in Omega-3's include swordfish, turbot, tuna, salmon, pacific halibut, sardines, shark and trout.

One Last Word Before You Begin Grilling My Fish Recipes

You may not always be able to find the exact fish I suggest for each of the menus in this chapter. So, for example, if a recipe calls for swordfish, don't be afraid to substitute any other firm fleshed fish.

	Serving size	Degree of doneness	Approximate Grilling Time* refrigerator temperature, grilled on highest setting	Chef's Choice temperature recommendation	USDA temperature recommendation
Fish fillets and steaks all types	4 to 5 ounces, 1/2- to 1-inch thick	Medium	10 to 12 minutes	135° to 140°F	No recommendation
Fresh scallops or shrimp	Medium Large	Medium	4 to 6 minutes	135° to 140°F	No recommendation

Divide the grilling time in half for Two-sided Contact Grills

Grilled Greek Tuna with Pasta of the Gods Salad

According to Greek myth, Zeus, king of the gods, had his mortal weaknesses. He was passionately fond of female charms and lavish cuisine. One taste of this menu might have caused Zeus to serve it to his paramours instead of his usual ambrosia and nectar. I am certain though, that once mortals make my Greek-style grilled tuna and pasta salad, they can't help but fall in love with them because they are deliciously easy to make. As the tuna marinates briefly in oregano, garlic and lemon juice, you'll throw together the pasta salad in the blink of an eye. Freshly cooked pasta is mixed with a delightful combination of feta cheese, Kalamata olives, diced ripe tomatoes, cucumbers and dressing, then rests in the refrigerator to allow the flavors to marry. Meanwhile, you'll grill the tuna to a sizzling succulence fit for any god.

Menu Game Plan

Prep & Cooking Time: 45 minutes

- Preheat the grill.
- Marinate the tuna.
- Boil the pasta.
- Make the pasta salad.
- Grill the tuna.

Cook's Notes

Since tuna is so low in fat, it can easily dry out on the grill. I keep the moisture in and the fat down by lightly spraying it with extra-virgin olive oil before pouring marinade over it. According to food scientist Shirley Corriher, an oil marinade is the best tenderizer for a tuna steak. It works very much like the natural marbling in beef because it coats the strands of protein, allowing the tuna to feel moist in your mouth even after most of the moisture has been cooked out. Corriher explains that the extra-virgin olive oil penetrates the fish more quickly than other types of olive oil.

Marinated Greek Tuna Steaks

Serves 4

4 tablespoons finely chopped fresh oregano or 4 teaspoons dried

2 teaspoons pressed garlic

¼ cup fresh lemon juice

1¼ pounds tuna steaks, about ¾- to 1-inch thick, cut into 4 equal pieces

Nonfat or olive oil cooking spray

Light salt and freshly ground pepper to taste

Romaine lettuce leaves

Thinly sliced lemon rounds

1. **Preheat the grill.** If you have a grill with a variable temperature control, set it to medium-high (1 or 2 steps below high) or to about 350° to 400°F.

2. **Make the marinade.** In a 1-cup bowl or measure, mix the oregano, garlic and lemon juice with a fork or small wire whisk. Set aside.

3. **Marinate the fish.** Rinse the fish and pat it dry with a paper towel. Spray both sides of the fish lightly with olive oil spray. Put the fish into a 1-gallon freezer weight zipper bag or a 1-quart airtight container, or shallow square glass or ceramic pan (8 x 8 x 2-inch). Pour the marinade over the fish, then turn it to coat all surfaces with the marinade. Squeeze the air out of the bag and zip it closed, or cover the container or pan and marinate in your refrigerator for 20 minutes or up to 1 hour.

4. **Grill the tuna steaks.** Place the tuna steaks on the grill and cook according to the times below or until the interior temperature reaches 135° to 140°F on an instant-read thermometer. The fish should be opaque yet still moist in the center when checked with the point of a sharp knife. Do not overcook or it will dry out.

5. **To serve,** arrange 4 romaine lettuce leaves on 4 plates and place equal amounts of pasta on top of the lettuce. Place the grilled tuna steak beside the pasta and garnish each dish with thinly sliced lemons.

Grill Times

Two-Sided Contact Grill: *5 to 6 minutes.*

Hibachi Grill, Combination Grill or Infusion Grill: *10 to 12 minutes. Turn the fish halfway through the grilling time. Grills with lids may be covered halfway through the grilling time. Infusion grills with lids may be covered for the entire grilling time.*

Infusion Grill Notes: *For a more intense flavor, pour the leftover marinade mixture into the infusion cup. If there is not much leftover marinade, combine it with some extra lemon juice or hot water to make ½ cup before pouring it into the infusion cup.*

Mix & Match

Serve the Pasta of the Gods Salad with any of the main dishes in the following menus: Provencal Kissed Veal Chops, page 103, Fetadillas, page 253 and Pick-Me-Up Poultry Piccata, page 175.

 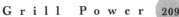

Pasta of the Gods Salad

Makes 4 (2 cup) servings

Salad

8   ounces dried pasta such as fusilli, elbows, shells, bows

¼   cup Kalamata olives

½   cup diced cucumber (preferably hothouse)

1   cup diced tomato

¼   cup thinly sliced green onion

2   tablespoons chopped fresh oregano or 2 teaspoons dried

¼   cup chopped fresh parsley

1   8¾-ounce can garbanzo beans, rinsed, drained

⅓   cup crumbled feta cheese

Lemon Dressing

¼   cup fresh lemon juice

1   to 2 tablespoons extra-virgin olive oil

¼   teaspoon pressed garlic

Light salt and freshly ground pepper to taste

1. Bring 10 cups of water to a boil in a 4- to 5-quart pot. Put the noodles into the boiling water. The water will stop boiling. When it comes back to a boil, start timing and cook noodles for 10 to 12 minutes until al dente (meaning "to the teeth" in Italian, or cooked but still slightly chewy). Pour noodles into a colander and cool immediately under cold running water. Drain well.

2. While water is boiling and pasta is cooking, combine the olives, cucumber, tomato and green onion. Chop the oregano (if you are using fresh) and parsley. Toss these vegetables and herbs with all remaining pasta ingredients in a 6- to 8-cup bowl. Set aside until pasta is ready.

3. In a 1-cup measure, whisk the lemon juice, olive oil, garlic, salt and freshly ground pepper to taste.

4. Put the cooled pasta on top of the vegetables. Drizzle with the dressing, and toss to evenly distribute all the ingredients.

Approximate Nutrients Per Serving of Entire Meal

Calories 527	Protein 51 g / 40%	Carbohydrate 34 g / 26%
Total Sugar 4 g	Fat 19g / 34%	Saturated 5g / 9%
Cholesterol 77 mg	Sodium 412 mg	Fiber 4 g Calcium 144 mg

Nordic Amazon Salmon and Asparagus with Creamy Mustard Dilled Pasta

"Eating salmon the night before a cross-country ski race will give you strength and power because it is full of protein and rich in Omega-3 fats," confided one of the fittest seventy-something women I have ever met. I looked around the room and saw that the tall stunning women packed into the posh restaurant in Lillehammer, Norway were all feasting on the same delectable salmon dinner that I was eating. The next morning I would be the first American contestant in the world's largest all-women's cross-country ski race...all for the sake of writing a magazine article. Was I nuts!?!? At 4 foot 10½ inches, I was a munchkin compared to the Amazonian blond beauties surrounding me. I was already having nightmares of being skied down by tall women who couldn't see me because I was too short.

The next day under a crystalline blue March sky, I interviewed participants before the start of the race and found that most were there to leisurely ski the track with their girlfriends. I was relieved, but still worried that I might not make it. Several hours later, wildly pumping my arms and legs in a surge of Amazonian strength, I finished the race unscathed and with one happy thought: "It must have been the salmon!"

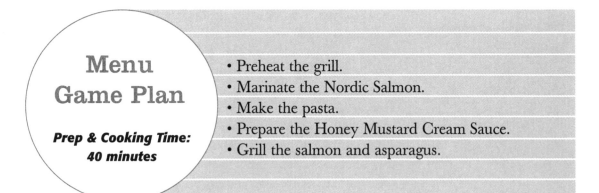

Menu Game Plan

**Prep & Cooking Time:
40 minutes**

• Preheat the grill.
• Marinate the Nordic Salmon.
• Make the pasta.
• Prepare the Honey Mustard Cream Sauce.
• Grill the salmon and asparagus.

Cook's Notes

Fresh, frozen, wild, farm-raised, Pacific or Atlantic? If the quality of the fish is good, any of these will taste great grilled. When purchasing salmon fillets and steaks look for flesh that is uniformly colored, moist and firm with no separations.

Salmon is grouped into either Pacific or Atlantic. Pacific salmon are grouped into five species: King (AKA Chinook), Coho (AKA Silver), Chum (AKA Dog, Keta, Silver Brite), Sockeye (AKA Red or Blueback), and Pink (AKA hump-back, humpy). Which species is the best choice for grilling? If you like a milder tasting salmon try Atlantic. For a stronger, more robust flavor, try Pacific salmon.

Nordic Salmon

Serves 4

1 tablespoon fresh dill

1 tablespoon honey Dijon-style mustard

¼ cup lemon juice

1¼ pounds salmon fillets, about 1-inch in the thickest parts, cut into 4 pieces

2½ quarts (10 cups) very hot tap water

¾ pound (4½ cups) dried pasta, such as fusilli, elbows, shells, bows

12 medium fresh asparagus spears

Nonfat or canola oil cooking spray

Light salt and freshly ground pepper to taste

1 recipe Creamy Mustard Dill Sauce (see recipe page 214)

1. Preheat the grill. If you have a grill with a variable temperature control, set it to medium (2 steps below high) or to about 350°F.

2. Marinate the fish. In a 1-cup measure mix chopped dill, honey Dijon-style mustard and lemon juice with a fork or small wire whisk. Pour it into a shallow glass or ceramic pan (8 x 8 x 2-inch). Rinse the fish, pat it dry with a paper towel. Using tweezers or needle nose pliers, pull out any visible bones running down the center of the fillet. Place fillets skin-side-up in the shallow dish so that the pink meat is resting in the marinade.

Cover with plastic wrap and marinate in your refrigerator for 20 minutes or up to 1 hour.

3. Boil the water and cook the pasta noodles. Bring 10 cups of water to a boil in a 4- to 5-quart pot. Put the noodles into the boiling water. The water will stop boiling. When it comes back to a boil, start timing and cook the noodles for 10 to 12 minutes until al dente (meaning "to the teeth" in Italian, or cooked but still slightly chewy). Pour the noodles into a colander and cool immediately under cold running water. Drain well. When pasta is cooked and drained, put it into a 2-quart bowl. As you toss the pasta, spray it lightly with canola oil spray or fat-free cooking spray to lightly coat it. Cover the bowl with aluminum foil to keep the pasta hot until serving time. Just before serving mix ¾ cup of the sauce into the pasta.

4. Clean the asparagus. Wash the asparagus thoroughly under cold running water to remove any sand from the tips, slice or break off the woody stem end and peel off any spines or tough skin on the stem end with a sharp vegetable peeler. Set them aside on a plate until ready to grill.

5. Grill the salmon and asparagus. If your grill is not large enough to hold both the asparagus and the fish, grill the asparagus first and then the fish. Spray the asparagus and both sides of each fish fillet lightly with cooking spray. Season the asparagus with lite salt and freshly ground pepper to taste. If fillet has skin, place on the grill skin side up. Grill according to the Grill Times opposite. The interior temperature of the fish should reach 135° to 140°F on an instant-read thermometer. The fish should be opaque yet still moist in the center and flake when checked with the point of a sharp knife. The asparagus is done when it is fork-tender but still crisp and bright green. Do not overcook either the asparagus or the fish. The asparagus will become gray and mushy, and the fish will become dry.

6. Remove the fish from the grill. If the fillet has skin, use 2 spatulas. Place one on top of the fillet and the other underneath between the cooked flesh and skin. As you lift the fish, the skin will remain on the grill. Remove it after the grill cools during the cleaning.

7. To serve, artfully arrange equal amounts of pasta, fish and asparagus on each plate. Spoon 1 tablespoon of the Creamy Mustard Dill Sauce over each piece of fish, and garnish with sprigs of fresh dill if you have them. Serve immediately.

Grill Times

Two-Sided Contact Grill: Salmon and asparagus 5 to 6 minutes.

Hibachi Grill, Combination Grill or Infusion Grill: Salmon and asparagus 10 to 12 minutes. Turn both the salmon and asparagus halfway through the grilling time. Grills with lids may be covered halfway through the grilling time. Infusion grills with lids may be covered for the entire grilling time.

Infusion Grill Notes: For a more intense flavor, pour the leftover marinade mixture into infusion cup. If there is not much leftover marinade, combine it with some extra lemon juice to make ½ cup before preheating grill.

Substitutions:
Instead of grilling the asparagus, cut them into 2-inch lengths and blanch by adding them to the pasta during the last 2 to 4 minutes of the cooking time. Asparagus is cooked when it is tender, yet still bright green and crispy.
If asparagus is out of season, substitute 2 medium zucchini sliced lengthwise down the middle.
Substitute long-grain rice for the pasta.

Creamy Mustard Dill Sauce

Makes 1 cup

¾ cup low-fat or nonfat sour cream

¼ cup low-fat or nonfat whipped cream cheese

1 tablespoon plus 1 teaspoon honey Dijon-style mustard

1 tablespoon fresh chopped dill or 1 teaspoon dried

1 tablespoon lemon juice

Substitutions:
Try the Creamy Mustard Dill Sauce over long grain white rice.

Heat this sauce just as the pasta is finished boiling.

1. In a small saucepan, whisk the sour cream, cream cheese, mustard, dill and lemon juice.
2. Cook over medium-low heat, whisking constantly until heated through but not bubbling.
3. Mix ¾ cup of the sauce into the hot pasta. Use the remaining ¼ cup to garnish the salmon when serving.

Approximate Nutrients Per Serving of Entire Meal

Total Calories 636	Protein 46 g / 30%	Carbohydrate 83 g / 54%
Total Sugar 8 g	Fat Total 11 g / 16%	Saturated Fat 2 g / 2%
Cholesterol 79 mg	Sodium 390 mg	Fiber 4 g	Calcium 152 mg

Mardi Gras Wrap Cajun Shrimp and Black-Eyed Pea Spread

I like to serve these wraps open-faced, because the bright Mardi Gras colored filling immediately puts my family and friends in a party mood. As everyone wraps up their sizzling shrimp, bright bell peppers and spicy spread, we toast each other with the Cajun motto, "Laissez le bon temps rouler!" *"Let the good times roll"* and eat with gusto.

Menu Game Plan

Prep & Cooking Time: 40 minutes

- Preheat the grill.
- Preheat the oven for the tortillas.
- Marinate the shrimp.
- Make the Black Eyed Pea Spread.
- Prepare the bell peppers.
- Grill the peppers.
- Warm the tortillas and assemble the wraps.
- Grill the shrimp.

Cook's Notes

Notes

Forrest Gump had the right idea when he decided to go into the shrimp business. Americans love shrimp. They consume about 5 million pounds per year, more than any other country in the world. Shrimp are low in calories and are a good source of iron, magnesium and zinc. Most of the shrimp we purchase is wild, caught in the Gulf of Mexico. We also get shrimp from Asia, Central and South America, 80 percent of which is farmed. Whether wild or farmed, only about 2 percent of the shrimp available is fresh, so purchasing frozen is always a good choice. When I say frozen, I don't mean shrimp that was previously frozen and then thawed by your fish vendor. I mean the hard stuff. Choose unpeeled frozen shrimp if available. Shrimp that are shelled before freezing are not as flavorful and may have a mushy texture. When thawed, the shell should be tight around the meat. Loose shells mean poor quality and the shrimp should be returned to the vendor. What kind of shrimp should you buy for the grill? The best quality and largest you can find and afford. Of the over 300 individual species in the world, only six are usually available in U.S. markets: gulf white, Mexican white, gulf pink or brown, Chinese white or black tiger.

Cajun Shrimp

Serves 4

Shrimp

12 to 16 medium or 8 to 12 extra large shrimp (about 1¼ to 1½ pounds)

2 small bell peppers, red, yellow or orange

4 to 8 Romaine lettuce leaves

4 large 10- to 12-inch diameter flour tortillas

Rub

1 tablespoon Cajun seasoning mix*

2 teaspoons olive oil

1 teaspoon pressed garlic

2 teaspoons ketchup

Black-Eyed Pea Spread (see recipe on page 216)

Low-fat or nonfat sour cream

Sliced tomatoes or cherry tomatoes

Seedless watermelon (if in season) or fresh pineapple slices

* If unavailable, use homemade recipe on page 54.

1. Preheat the grill. If you have a grill with a variable temperature control, set it to medium-high (1 or 2 steps below high) or to about 350° to 400°F.

2. Mix the marinade. In a 1-cup bowl or measure, mix the Cajun seasoning mix, olive oil, garlic and catsup. Set aside.

3. Clean and marinate the shrimp. Pull the legs apart and gently slip your finger under the shell of each shrimp and peel off the shells and tails.

With a sharp knife, make a shallow ¼-inch slit down the back. Lift out the vein with the tip of the knife or a toothpick. Rinse the shrimp and wrap them in a double layer of paper towel to absorb excess moisture.

Put the shrimp into a 1-gallon freezer-weight zipper bag or a 1-quart airtight container or glass or ceramic dish (8 x 8 x 2-inch). Scrape the marinade paste over the shrimp, then use your fingers to coat all surfaces with the paste. Squeeze the air out of the bag, and zip it closed or cover the container or dish. Marinate in your refrigerator for 20 minutes or up to 1 hour.

4. Prepare the bell peppers. Cut the peppers in half and remove the seeds and stems. Slice each half lengthwise into 1-inch thick strips.

5. Grill the bell peppers. Put the peppers in a large bowl and coat them with cooking spray, light salt and pepper to taste as you toss them.

Grill the peppers according to the Grill Times opposite until dark grill marks appear on the peppers, and they are cooked through yet tender-crisp. Keep the grilled peppers warm on a covered platter until serving time.

6. Grill the shrimp. If your grill is large enough, put the shrimp on during the last 2 to 5 minutes of the peppers' grilling time. Grill shrimp according to the Grill Times opposite until they just turn opaque white and pink. Do not overcook or your shrimp will be tough.

7. Warm the tortillas while the peppers and shrimp are grilling. Place the tortillas on a nonstick baking sheet, and cover with a damp color-free paper towel. Cover with aluminum foil, then place in a preheated 350°F oven for 4 to 5 minutes until tortillas are warmed.

(Microwave Method: Place the tortillas on a dinner plate and cover with a color-free paper towel. Sprinkle the towel with about 2 teaspoons water. The towel should be damp, not wet. Microwave 20 to 30 seconds on high (100% power).)

8. To serve, put 1 warm flour tortilla on each of 4 dinner plates. Arrange 2 large lettuce leaves down the middle of each wrap. In the middle of each leaf, place ⅓ cup of the black-eyed pea spread.

Artfully arrange even amounts of the grilled bell pepper and fresh tomato slices around the spread on each plate. Top the spread with the grilled shrimp. Put watermelon or pineapple slices on a separate plate on the side. Serve this colorful presentation with the tortilla flat and let your family or guests roll their own wrap. Show them how to fold the 2 sides of the tortilla over one another to make a long tube. Then, before eating, fold up the bottom end so the food doesn't slip out when they pick up the filled tortilla. This wrap is so full, they may want to eat it with a fork and knife.

Grill Times

Two-Sided Contact Grill: Peppers 7 to 10 minutes / shrimp 2 to 3 minutes.

Hibachi Grill, Combination Grill or Infusion Grill: Peppers 14 to 20 minutes / shrimp 4 to 5 minutes. Turn the peppers and shrimp halfway through the grilling time. Grills with lids may be covered halfway through the grilling time. Infusion grills with lids may be covered for the entire grilling time.

Black-Eyed Pea Spread

Makes 4 generous (¹/₃ cup) servings

¼   cup packed parsley

2   or 3 medium green onions cut into 1-inch pieces

1   teaspoon pressed garlic

1   to 2 tablespoons diced canned mild chilies

3   tablespoons low-fat or nonfat sour cream

2   to 3 teaspoons Cajun seasoning

¼   cup ketchup

¼   cup thinly sliced celery

¼   cup shredded carrot

1   15-ounce can black-eyed peas, rinsed, drained

½   teaspoon light salt or to taste

Substitution:
For the black-eyed peas, substitute black, pinto or pink beans.

You can make this spread up to 48 hours in advance of serving if refrigerated in an airtight container.

1. In the work bowl of the food processor fitted with the metal chopping blade or in a blender, process the parsley, green onions, garlic, chilies, sour cream, Cajun seasoning and ketchup until vegetables are finely chopped. Occasionally scrape down the work-bowl with a spatula to incorporate any ingredients that fly up on the side of the bowl.

2. Add the celery, shredded carrot and black-eyed peas and pulse a few times to coarsely chop. Do not overprocess, or you will get a baby food consistency. The resulting spread should have a variety of textures, including almost whole and partially mashed peas. Scrape the spread into a bowl or airtight container, season with extra salt if desired and set aside until ready to serve.

Approximate Nutrients Per Serving of Entire Meal

Total Calories 359	Protein 30 g / 33%	Carbohydrate 49 g / 56%
Total Sugar 3 g	Fat Total 3 g / 11%	Saturated Fat .8 g / 3%
Cholesterol 168 mg	Sodium 1,246 mg	Fiber 15 g Calcium 102 mg

The Legend of Louis Seafood Salad...Monterrey Bay Style

When I get a hankering for a Seafood Salad, I long for a Louis. I love the creamy piquant dressing drizzled over succulent shellfish, mounds of crispy vegetables, tomatoes and hard-cooked egg. I also love the story behind the salad just as much as the recipe itself. Legend has it that the famous opera singer, Enrico Caruso, named this salad during a concert tour of the West in 1906. A renowned gourmet, Caruso would drop 3 pounds during a performance, then afterward search out the best restaurants to satisfy his insatiable appetite. One story places him in a Seattle eating establishment after a night of filling the Opera House there with high C's. Famished, he consulted the chef and ordered the Specialty of the House, a crab salad with a creamy pink dressing. Caruso enjoyed the salad immensely, but was disappointed when he ordered a fifth serving. The chef had to come out of the kitchen to tell Caruso that he had exhausted all the available ingredients. The name of the restaurant was never recorded, and one can only assume that the chef's name was Louis because during the remainder of his tour, Caruso continued to sing the praises of the Crab Louis Salad.

Menu Game Plan

Prep & Cooking Time: 45 to 55 minutes

- Preheat the grill.
- Hard cook the eggs (optional).
- Prepare and marinate the shellfish.
- Prepare and steam the artichokes (optional).
- Make the Louis Dressing.
- Prepare the salad vegetables and assemble the salads.
- Grill the artichokes and then the shellfish.
- Dress the salads.

Cook's Notes

My favorite version of Louis Salad, served in and around Monterey Bay, California, the largest artichoke-growing region in the United States, includes artichokes and avocados. All artichokes must be steamed, then sliced in half before grilling. Use baby artichokes for grilled salads whenever available. The entire artichoke can be eaten, choke and all. They also require less preparation and grill faster. Trim any discolored ends of the stems but leave an inch of stem on before steaming. Mature artichokes are also easy to grill, but require a little more preparation. Use kitchen shears to trim off the thorny tips of the leaves.

Grilled Scallops and Shrimp

Serves 4

4   large eggs (optional)

Seafood

½   cup chili sauce

1   tablespoon olive oil

¾   pound large sea scallops

½   to ¾ pound large shrimp

Salad

1   10-ounce bag ready-to-eat Romaine lettuce

1   cup shredded carrot

8   baby or 4 small to medium fresh artichokes (optional)

2   medium fresh tomatoes

1   small avocado

½   cup thinly sliced red radish

¾   cup thinly sliced red, yellow or green bell pepper

⅓   cup thinly sliced green onions

1. **Preheat the grill.** If you have a grill with a variable temperature control, set it to medium-high (1 or 2 steps below high) or to about 350° to 400°F.

2. **Hard cook the eggs** (optional step). Put the eggs into a 1 or 2-quart pot and cover them with 1 inch of cold tap water and ½ teaspoon salt.

Partially cover the pot and bring to a rolling boil over high heat. Turn the heat down to low and leave on the heat for 30 seconds. Remove the pot from the heat and let stand covered for 15 minutes.

Rinse eggs in a strainer under cool running water for 5 minutes before peeling and slicing. Eggs can be made up to 5 days in advance and stored in the refrigerator.

3. **Make the marinade.** In a 1-cup bowl or measure, mix the chili sauce and olive oil thoroughly with a fork. Using a rubber spatula, scrape it into a 1-gallon zippered freezer-weight storage bag, or an airtight container with a lid or a shallow glass or ceramic dish (8 x 8 x 2-inch).

4. **Prepare and marinate the shellfish.** Rinse the scallops in a strainer under cool running water to cleanse and drain well. Wrap them in a double layer of paper towel to absorb excess moisture.

Shell and devein the shrimp. Pull the legs apart and gently slip your finger under the shell of each shrimp. Peel off the shells but leave tails on. With a sharp knife, make a shallow ¼-inch slit down the back. Lift out the vein with the tip of the knife or a toothpick. Rinse the shrimp and wrap them in a double layer of paper towel to absorb excess moisture.

Put the dried shellfish into the marinade-filled bag or container, then turn it so all the surfaces are coated with the marinade. Zip the bag closed or cover the container or dish and refrigerate for 20 minutes or up to 1 hour.

5. **Prepare the artichokes if you are using fresh** (optional). For baby artichokes: Trim off any discolored ends of the artichoke stems, leaving about an inch of stem on each artichoke. For small artichokes: Using a sharp knife, cut off the stems so they are flush with the base of the vegetable; pull off the coarse outer leaves at the bottom; use kitchen shears to trim off thorny tips of the leaves.

Substitutions:

If fresh artichokes are out of season or you just don't want to take the time to prepare them, substitute 1 or 2 13-ounce cans of water-packed quartered artichoke hearts. Rinse the artichokes in a strainer under cool running water to rinse off preservatives and drain well before using.

6. Precook the artichokes. Put a steamer basket into a 3- to 4-quart pot large enough to hold the artichokes and with a tight fitting lid. Fill with water to cover the bottom of the pot but not rising above the bottom of the basket. Cover and bring to a boil over high heat. Add the artichokes and steam, covered, 6 to 7 minutes for baby artichokes and 15 to 20 minutes for small to medium artichokes until tender but not falling apart. Remove artichokes with tongs and put on paper towel or on a cooling rack to drain and become cool enough to handle.

7. **Prepare the salads** while the artichokes precook and cool. On 4 large dinner plates, put equal amounts of lettuce.

Slice each tomato into 8 equal wedges and the avocado into 8 equal wedges. Slice each cooled egg in half.

Artfully arrange equal amounts of the carrots, tomato, avocado, eggs, radish, bell pepper and green onion on each plate over the lettuce, leaving a space in the center for the grilled shellfish and artichokes. If not serving immediately, cover tightly with plastic wrap and store in the refrigerator for up to 8 hours.

8. Grill the artichokes. Cut each cooled artichoke in half. Spray each artichoke lightly with cooking spray then grill according to the Grill Times below. When done, set grilled artichokes aside on a plate to cool as you grill the shellfish.

9. Grill the shellfish. Grill the shrimp and scallops according to the Grill Times below or until they become opaque. Be careful not to overcook or the shellfish will become tough.

10. To serve, as soon as the scallops and shrimp come off of the grill, put equal amounts in the middle of each prepared plate. Arrange the cooled artichokes near the grilled seafood and serve immediately.

Pass around the Louis Dressing. Serve with slices of crusty San Francisco-style sourdough bread, sweet Italian bread, French-style baguette or focaccia.

Grill Times

Two-Sided Contact Grill: Baby artichokes 2 ½ minutes; small artichokes 3 to 5 minutes / shellfish 2 to 3 minutes.

Hibachi Grill, Combination Grill or Infusion Grill: Baby artichokes 5 minutes; small artichokes 6 to 8 minutes / shellfish 4 to 6 minutes. Turn the artichokes and shellfish halfway through the grilling time. Grills with lids may be covered halfway through the grilling time. Infusion grills with lids may be covered for the entire grilling time.

Louis Dressing

Makes 16 (1 tablespoon) servings

⅓ cup nonfat or low-fat mayonnaise

⅓ cup nonfat or low-fat sour cream

⅓ cup chili sauce

1 teaspoon Worcestershire sauce

Dash ground nutmeg

¼ cup chopped green onions

Light salt and freshly ground pepper to taste

This dressing tastes great on any type of a green salad, as an artichoke dip, mixed into tuna or salmon salad, egg salad or as spread for sandwiches. It will keep refrigerated in an airtight container for up to 2 weeks.

In a 2-cup bowl, mix all the ingredients with a fork until well blended. Scrape into an attractive serving bowl cover and set aside in the refrigerator until serving time.

Nutritional Note:

The original Louis dressing recipe called for high-octane, full fat sour cream and mayonnaise. It gives a richer flavor but can play havoc with your waistline. To reduce the fat, I make my version with either low-fat or nonfat sour cream and mayonnaise. Take your pick!

Approximate Nutrients Per Serving of Entire Meal

Total Calories 512	Protein 43 g / 32%	Carbohydrate 49 g / 37%
Total Sugar 16 g	Fat Total 18 g / 31%	Saturated Fat 3 g / 6%
Cholesterol 327 mg	Sodium 1,168 mg	Fiber 15 g Calcium 227 mg

(Calculated with optional egg, fresh artichokes and 2 tablespoons Louis dressing made with low-fat mayonnaise and sour cream.)

Mac Nut Crab Cake Salad with Roasted Red Pepper and Pineapple Vinaigrette

If you love crab cakes but are watching your waistline, you will love making them healthy-style on your electric tabletop grill. Instead of frying them in loads of fat, you simply spray each formed crab cake lightly with cooking spray, then put them on the grill to crisp the outside and cook the inside to juicy tenderness. These crab cakes were inspired by 2 of my favorite Hawaiian ingredients–macadamia nuts and pineapple. In this recipe, I hid chopped macadamia nuts in the crab cake mixture so no one suspects the crunchy surprise until the first bite. Displayed on a colorful salad and drizzled with my sweet and savory Roasted Red Pepper and Pineapple Vinaigrette, these crab cakes are simply "ono" which means "delicious" in Hawaiian.

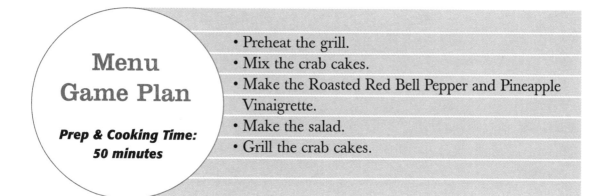

Menu Game Plan

Prep & Cooking Time: 50 minutes

- Preheat the grill.
- Mix the crab cakes.
- Make the Roasted Red Bell Pepper and Pineapple Vinaigrette.
- Make the salad.
- Grill the crab cakes.

Cook's Notes

Notes

Surimi, developed in Japan over a thousand years ago, is also known as "imitation" shellfish. But don't reject it because of its imitation label. Surimi, which means minced fish in Japanese, is the real thing. Made from a mixture of high-quality seafood, including Alaskan pollack and other white fish, surimi mimics the taste, texture, flavor and shape of crab, lobster, scallops and shrimp. Surimi has gained in popularity for several reasons. It won't bust your grocery budget because it is a fraction of the cost of real shellfish. Nutritionally, surimi has only 2 percent fat, no cholesterol (3 ounces of real shellfish packs between 55 to 65 mg of cholesterol) and is high in protein. Surimi requires no preparation because it is pre-cooked. However, it is high in sodium. So when using it, I suggest lowering the sodium in your recipe if you are cooking for sodium-sensitive people.

Mac Nut Crab Cakes

Crab Cakes

½ cup chopped macadamia nuts or blanched, slivered almonds

2 large eggs or ½ cup egg substitute

¾ cup low-fat or nonfat mayonnaise

¼ cup lemon juice

1 teaspoon pressed garlic

2 teaspoons finely minced gingerroot

2 teaspoons Dijon-style honey mustard

1 tablespoon Worcestershire sauce

1 to 2 teaspoons hot sauce

½ teaspoon light salt (optional)

1 cup ground garlic cheese croutons

¼ cup thinly sliced green onion

1 pound lump crabmeat or surimi (imitation fish)

Nonfat or canola oil cooking spray

Salad

4 cups mixed field greens

1 cup shredded carrot

1 cup thinly sliced red bell pepper

¼ cup thinly sliced green onion

½ cup julienned jicama

2 cups fresh or canned pineapple pieces

1. Preheat the grill. If you have a grill with a variable temperature control, set it to medium-high (1 or 2 steps below high) or to about 350° to 400°F.

2. Toast the macadamia nuts (optional step). Put nuts in an 8-inch nonstick frying pan over medium-high heat. Stir constantly for 2 to 3 minutes until lightly browned. Remove immediately from heat and set aside to cool.

3. Mix and form the crab cakes. In a 2-quart bowl whisk the eggs, mayonnaise, lemon juice, garlic, ginger, mustard, Worcestershire sauce, hot sauce and salt. Thoroughly mix in the crushed croutons with a fork. With a rubber spatula fold in the green onion, crabmeat and nuts until evenly mixed.

With wet hands, form the mixture into 8 (3 inches in diameter) cakes. Place the cakes on a large plate, cover with plastic wrap and refrigerate for 20 minutes or up to 24 hours.

4. Prepare the salads while the crab cakes set in the refrigerator. Divide the field greens among 4 dinner plates. Shred the carrot in the food processor using the medium shredding disk or using a hand grater. Using a chef's knife, slice the bell pepper and green onion, peel and julienne the jicama. Artfully arrange equal amounts of all of the prepared vegetables on top of the greens leaving the center free for the crab cakes. Prepare the fresh pineapple by cutting off the rind and cutting it into bite-sized pieces, or drain the canned pineapple and set it aside in a covered bowl in the refrigerator. Do not put it on the salad until just before serving because its natural acid will wilt the lettuce. If not serving immediately, cover each plate tightly with plastic wrap, and store in the refrigerator for up to 8 hours.

5. Grill the crab cakes. Spray each cake lightly with canola oil spray or fat-free cooking spray before placing it on the grill. Grill according to the Grill Times opposite until the cakes are firm and the exteriors are crisp.

6. To serve, place 2 crab cakes in the center of each salad and arrange the pineapple slices around the cakes. Drizzle with 2 to 3 tablespoons of the Roasted Red Pepper and Pineapple Vinaigrette. Serve immediately with a loaf of crusty sourdough bread to mop up any leftover dressing. Pass around extra dressing for those who would like more.

Two-Sided Contact Grill: *6 to 7 minutes.*

Hibachi Grill, Combination Grill or Infusion Grill: *12 to 14 minutes. Turn the crab cakes halfway through the grilling time. Grills with lids may be covered halfway through the grilling time. Infusion grills with lids may be covered for the entire grilling time.*

Roasted Red Pepper and Pineapple Vinaigrette

Makes 16 (1 tablespoon) servings

- ¼ cup roasted red bell peppers from a jar, well drained
- ¼ cup seasoned rice vinegar
- ¼ cup lowfat or nonfat mayonnaise
- ¼ teaspoon pressed garlic
- ¼ teaspoon finely minced gingerroot
- ¼ teaspoon hot pepper sauce
- ¼ cup canned crushed pineapple in its own juice
- ½ teaspoon granulated sugar
- ¼ teaspoon light salt

This dressing will keep in an airtight container in the refrigerator for up to 1 month. It tastes great as a sauce or dressing on any type of grilled fish, shellfish or poultry.

Put all ingredients in the blender or food processor fitted with the metal chopping blade and blend or process until smooth. Pour into a decorative serving cruet or in an airtight container and refrigerate until ready to serve.

Nutrition Notes:

Macadamia nuts are high in fat, but a study conducted in 1995 by the University of Hawaii has proven that cholesterol conscious people don't necessarily have to avoid them. Macadamia nuts, like olive oil, are high in oleic acid, a monounsaturated fatty acid believed to be beneficial in cutting cholesterol. The research study showed that a diet in which 37 percent of the total fat calories were derived from macadamia nuts produced lower triglyceride levels and similar cholesterol levels to the American Heart Association's Diet in which 30 percent of the calories are derived from fat. Mac nuts are also rich in calcium, iron, magnesium and potassium. But keep in mind that ¼ cup of macadamia nuts weighs in at 235 calories and contains 24 grams of fat.

Mix & Match

Serve the Vinaigrette over a small side salad with Mighty Maui Burgers, page 74.

Well Composed Salads

Most of the salads in this book are what the French call "salade composé" or composed salads. Instead of making a huge bowl of salad, I like to arrange or compose just the amount of salad ingredients on each salad plate to satisfy the appetite and tastes of individual family members and guests. How many times have you been forced to throw out salad fixings that someone didn't like or the remains of a large tossed salad soggy with dressing?

Create Salad Sensations

Would you like to make salads that will excite your family? Why not give good old iceberg lettuce and tomato slices a rest and try some unexpected ingredients. Top some mixed field greens or thinly sliced cabbage with your favorite sliced vegetables like carrots, bell peppers, and cucumbers, then add some surprises. How about some thinly sliced fruit like strawberries, orange, kiwi, or apple, a sprinkling of nuts like macadamia, almond, walnuts or pumpkin seeds, and a dusting of chopped fresh herbs like basil, oregano, mint, dill or thyme? An elegant salad like this can become a colorful treat that your family will look forward to eating. And a little bit of fresh salad goes a long way to ensure everyone is eating some of the 5 fresh fruits and vegetables they need each day for the natural fiber, vitamins, and minerals that are essential for good health.

Dress Your Salads with Homemade Creations

For even more of a treat, why not try making some of my homemade dressings? They all blend up in minutes, last in your refrigerator up to two weeks, and have a fresher taste than bottled or packaged products because they are free of preservatives and fillers. For a great everyday dressing, try my Lemon Herb Vinaigrette (page 253) or Creamy Caesar Dressing (page 188). Complement a piquant main dish with a salad dressed in Salsa Salad Dressing (page 134) or Roasted Red Pepper and Pineapple Vinaigrette (page 225).

Approximate Nutrients Per Serving of Entire Meal

Total Calories 373	Protein 32 g / 33%	Carbohydrate 39 g / 41%
Total Sugar 16 g	Fat Total 11 g / 26%	Saturated Fat 2 g / 5%
Cholesterol 81 mg	Sodium 1,227 mg	Fiber 6 g — Calcium 160 mg

(Calculated with 2 crab cakes with Dungeness crabmeat, nonfat mayonnaise, fat-free egg substitute, salad, and 2 tablespoons of dressing.)

The "Irie" Dinner—Swordfish Steaks with Grilled Banana, Sweet Potatoes and Orange Pineapple Slaw

O-lay, O-Lay! This "Feeling Hot, Hot, Hot" menu was inspired by a meal I ate in Jamaica with my husband, John, on our first anniversary vacation many years ago. Sitting at a table in the sand under a large palm tree, we were served paper plates piled with spicy jerked grilled fish, grilled banana, sweet potato and slaw. When we were halfway through our dinner, the chef, a large barefooted woman wearing a calico bib apron, sashayed over to us with a big smile on her face. "Everyt'ing irie?" she asked us. Our forks poised with another piece her irresistible jerked fish, we looked blankly at each other then returned her smile. "Irie?" we asked simultaneously. "Ja mon," she laughed good-naturedly, "In Jamaican dat means goooood!" We laughed too and said her cooking was some of the best we had on the island. (It really was!) Now whenever I make my version of her meal, my husband comments with a sigh of delight, "Oh, we're having the 'Irie Dinner'!"

Menu Game Plan

Prep & Cooking Time: 50 to 60 minutes

- Preheat the grill.
- Marinate the swordfish and bananas.
- Precook the sweet potatoes.
- Make the Orange Pineapple Slaw.
- Grill the sweet potatoes, bananas, and fish.

Cook's Notes

Swordfish is as perfect on the grill as it is in the water. Weighing from 200 to 1,000 pounds, the streamlined swordfish can swim up to 60 miles an hour in chase of prey. All that power means lots of muscle meat, which is why this fish has been a favorite since antiquity. Its compact flesh is delicious lightly seasoned or can embrace a bold marinade without losing its innate flavor. On the grill, it holds together like a beefsteak, yet stays juicy if you don't overcook it. When choosing swordfish steaks, the flesh should be moist, bright and tightly swirled. A good source of niacin, potassium, and phosphorous, a 4-ounce serving of cooked swordfish is low in calories (175) and moderate in fat (6 grams).

Swordfish Steaks with Grilled Bananas and Sweet Potatoes

Serves 4

Marinade

4   tablespoons pineapple or pineapple-orange frozen juice concentrate, thawed

2   teaspoons canola oil or vegetable oil

½   teaspoon ground allspice

1   teaspoon pressed garlic

2   teaspoons grated gingerroot

4   tablespoons prepared jerk sauce, or 1 to 2 teaspoons prepared jerk paste* mixed with 2 tablespoons of low sodium soy sauce

Fish

1¼ pounds swordfish cut about 1-inch thick

2   small firm bananas, peel left on

1½ pounds sweet potatoes (about 2 to 3 medium)

Nonfat or canola oil cooking spray

Butter lettuce leaves

Green onion, thinly sliced or parsley, finely chopped

1. Preheat the grill. If you have a grill with a variable temperature control, set it to medium-high (1 or 2 steps below high) or to about 350° to 400°F.

2. Make the marinade. In a 1-cup bowl or measure, mix the pineapple juice concentrate, oil, allspice, garlic, ginger and jerk sauce with a fork until well blended. Reserve 2 tablespoons of marinade for the banana and potato slices, then pour the rest into a 1-gallon freezer-weight zipper bag or a 1-quart airtight container or shallow glass or ceramic dish (8 x 8 x 2-inch).

3. Marinate the fish and bananas. Cut the fish into 4 equal size pieces and put them into the bag or container with the marinade. Then, using your fingertips, smear the marinade onto all sides of the fish. Squeeze the air out of the bag and zip it closed or cover the container or dish and set aside in the refrigerator for 20 minutes or up to 1 hour.

Leaving the skin on the bananas, slice each banana in half, then slice each half lengthwise. Put them in a shallow bowl, then using your fingertips, smear the cut surfaces with 1 tablespoon of the reserved marinade. Cover the dish and set aside on the counter until grilling time.

4. Precook the sweet potatoes. Peel the potatoes then slice them into 1-inch thick pieces. Put a steamer basket into a 3- to 4-quart pot large enough to hold the potatoes with a tight fitting lid . Fill with water to cover the bottom of the pot but not rising above the bottom of the basket. Cover and bring to a boil over high heat. Put the potato slices into the pot and cover. Steam for 7 to 10 minutes until the potatoes are tender but not mushy. Drain the potatoes in a strainer and set aside until cool enough to handle, about 5 to 10 minutes. When cooled, put the potatoes into a 2-quart bowl. Then with your fingertips, lightly smear the remaining tablespoon of marinade over the pieces. Allow to stand 5 to 20 minutes before grilling.

5. Grill the sweet potatoes, fish and bananas. Since they retain heat longer, grill the sweet potatoes first. As you toss the potatoes with your fingers, lightly spray them with cooking spray. Grill them according to the Grill Times opposite. When they are

* If you can't find jerk sauce or paste in the international or condiment section of your grocery store, see page 54 for homemade recipe.

Substitutions:
Instead of swordfish, substitute any firm flesh fish like tuna, mahi mahi, halibut, or shark.

finished, put them on a platter and cover with aluminum foil to keep warm until serving.

If your grill is small, grill the bananas next. If it is larger, grill the bananas and the fish at the same time. Remember to take the bananas off the grill sooner than the fish as they take less time to grill and will get mushy. Spray the cut side of the bananas with cooking spray. Leave the skin on the bananas. It keeps them from melting on the grill. Grill them according to the times and methods below.

Remove the fish from the marinade; discard it unless using an infusion grill. Spray each piece of fish lightly with cooking spray before placing on the grill. Grill the fish according to the Grill Times below or until the interior temperature reaches 135° to 140°F on an instant-read thermometer.

6. **To serve,** arrange 2 butter lettuce leaves on the side of 4 dinner plates. Spoon equal amounts of slaw on the lettuce then place equal amounts of fish, banana and sweet potato on the opposite side of each plate. Sprinkle with thinly sliced green onion or parsley if desired before serving.

Grill Times

Two-Sided Contact Grill: *Sweet potatoes 6 to 7 minutes / bananas 2 to 3 minutes / fish 6 to 7 minutes.*

Hibachi Grill, Combination Grill or Infusion Grill: *Sweet potatoes 12 to 14 minutes / bananas 4 to 6 minutes / fish 12 to 14 minutes. Turn the potatoes, fish and banana halfway through the grilling time. Grills with lids may be covered halfway through the grilling time. Infusion grills with lids may be covered for the entire grilling time.*

Infusion Grill Notes: *For a more intense flavor, pour the leftover marinade into the infusion cup. If there is not much leftover marinade, combine it with some extra soy sauce to make ½ cup.*

Mix & Match

Serve the Orange Pineapple Slaw with any of the main dishes in the following menus: Port Royale Chicken Fajitas, page 201; Calypso Chicken Burgers, page 96.

Orange Pineapple Slaw

Makes 4 (1¼ cup) servings

Slaw

1 8-ounce can crushed pineapple

4 cups shredded cabbage

1 cup shredded carrot

¼ cup thinly sliced green onion

¼ cup chopped walnuts

¼ cup shredded coconut

Dressing

½ cup low-fat or nonfat mayonnaise

¼ cup low-fat or nonfat sour cream

2 tablespoons frozen orange juice concentrate, thawed

2 teaspoons prepared jerk sauce or ½ teaspoon prepared jerk seasoning (see page 54 for homemade version)

You can make this slaw up to 24 hours in advance of serving if you refrigerate it in an airtight container.

1. Put the pineapple in a strainer and drain well.
2. In a 2-quart bowl or airtight container with a lid, mix the cabbage, shredded carrot, pineapple, green onion, walnuts and coconut with a rubber spatula.
3. In a 2-cup bowl or measure, using a fork, mix the mayonnaise, sour cream, frozen orange juice concentrate and jerk sauce or seasoning.
4. Using a rubber spatula, scrape the dressing on top of the slaw and fold it in so that all the ingredients are evenly coated. Cover tightly and refrigerate until ready to serve.

Approximate Nutrients Per Serving of Entire Meal

Total Calories 514	Protein 27 g / 21%	Carbohydrate 73 g / 57%
Total Sugar 42 g	Fat Total 13 g / 23%	Saturated Fat 3 g / 6%
Cholesterol 39 mg	Sodium 770 mg	Fiber 10 g Calcium 127 mg

Sole Food Florentine

Sometime during the sixteenth century, it is believed that cooks from Florence, Italy, introduced spinach to the French. The name stuck, because French cuisine still honors the Italians who made the initial introduction. Whenever a dish includes spinach in the ingredients, the French add "à la florentine" at the end of the title. Most French dishes with this moniker nestle fish or eggs atop a bed of lightly sautéed spinach leaves and finish with a cheese sauce. In keeping with the tradition, my Florentine Sole Rolls are stuffed with a savory spinach, Parmesan cheese and pine nut mixture reminiscent of the stuffings still used today in Italy for meat, poultry and fish. Presented on a bed of rice-shaped orzo pasta and accented with my Lemon Velouté sauce, these fish rolls make an elegant dinner for special occasions.

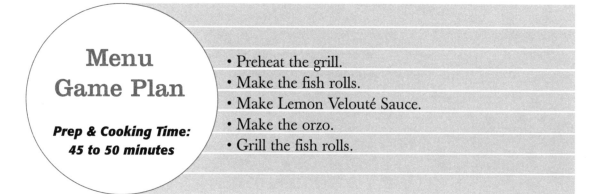

Menu Game Plan

Prep & Cooking Time: 45 to 50 minutes

- Preheat the grill.
- Make the fish rolls.
- Make Lemon Velouté Sauce.
- Make the orzo.
- Grill the fish rolls.

Cook's Notes

Sole, flounder, and dab . . . flatfish are masters of disguise. In order to eat and to avoid being eaten, they burrow their flat bodies into the sandy sea bottom, then change their color to match their surroundings. The only thing that gives away their camouflage is their periscope . . . bulbous eyes placed strategically on one side of their head so they can peer out of the sand. The fillets are so thin and delicate that they easily fall apart when grilled flat. Rolled and secured with toothpicks or skewers, they become lovely bundles that help retain their shape and stay moist on the grill. Seasoned and stuffed like my Florentine Sole Rolls, rolled flat fish make an easy and stylish entrée. Fresh fillets should look moist and smell fresh. A 4-ounce serving of cooked flat fish is extremely low in calories (132), low in fat (2 grams or 12 percent) and a good source of potassium and phosphorous.

Florentine Fish Rolls

Serves 4

Florentine Filling

½   cup finely ground cheese croutons

½   cup low-fat or nonfat mayonnaise

2   teaspoons finely grated lemon zest

1   teaspoon pressed garlic

¼   cup grated Parmesan cheese

¼   cup thinly sliced green onions

1   10-ounce box frozen chopped spinach, thawed and squeezed dry

¼   cup pine nuts

Fish

1⅓ pounds Petrale sole or another flat fish (8 pieces)

4   teaspoons grainy Dijon-style mustard

Light salt and freshly ground pepper to taste

Nonfat or canola oil cooking spray

1. **Preheat the grill.** If you have a grill with a variable temperature control, set it to medium-high (1 or 2 steps below high) or to about 350° to 400ºF.

2. **Make the Florentine Filling.** In a food processor or blender, put the croutons, mayonnaise, lemon zest, garlic, Parmesan cheese, green onions and spinach. Chop by short pulses until mixed but not pureed. Add the pine nuts and pulse to incorporate them into the mixture. Do not over process.

3. **Make the fish rolls.** Place 1 fish fillet on a flat surface. Smear the upper surface with ½ teaspoon of the Dijon-style mustard. Place ¼ cup of the spinach filling on the widest end of the fillet, then gently roll the fish around it and secure with a toothpick. Place on a plate or in a container with an airtight lid. Repeat with the remaining fillets. Cover tightly and refrigerate for 20 minutes to set the filling, or up to 24 hours.

4. **Grill the fish rolls.** Lightly salt and pepper the outside of each fish roll. Spray each fish roll liberally with cooking spray before placing on the grill. Put the fish rolls on the grill seam side up (the side with the toothpick), and grill according to the Grill Times below or until the interior temperature reaches 135° to 140°F on an instant-read thermometer. When turning the fish rolls or removing them from the grill, handle them gently with tongs or 2 spatulas so they won't fall apart.

5. **To serve,** place equal amounts of orzo in the middle of each of 4 dinner plates. Carefully remove the fish rolls from the grill and gently remove the toothpicks from each. Place 2 fish rolls, seam side down on top of the orzo. Drizzle ¼ to ⅓ cup of the Lemon Velouté Sauce over the fish rolls and serve immediately with slices of French bread and a side salad of mixed field greens.

Grill Times

Two-Sided Contact Grill: *5 to 6 minutes.*

Hibachi Grill, Combination Grill or Infusion Grill: *10 to 12 minutes. Turn the rolls halfway through the grilling time. Grills with lids may be covered halfway through the grilling time. Infusion grills with lids may be covered for the entire grilling time.*

Lemon Velouté Sauce

Makes 6 (¼ cup) servings

- 1 cup low-fat milk
- 3 tablespoons light butter
- 3 tablespoons flour
- ½ cup bottled clam juice
- 1 teaspoon finely grated lemon zest
- 2 tablespoons lemon juice
- ¼ teaspoon light salt or to taste
- ⅛ teaspoon ground white pepper

Dash freshly ground nutmeg to taste (optional)

Save time by making this sauce up to 72 hours in advance of serving. Reheat using instructions in Step 5.

1. In a small saucepan over medium heat, bring the milk to a simmer. You can also warm the milk in the microwave by heating it in a 1-quart microwavable pan uncovered for 2 minutes on high (100% power).

2. While the milk is warming, in a 1-quart pot over medium-high heat, melt the butter. Whisk in the flour and cook for 1 minute until the mixture foams. Be careful not to allow it to brown.

3. Remove the pot from the heat. When the bubbling stops, vigorously whisk in the clam juice, then the warm milk. Return to medium-low heat and whisk slowly until the sauce comes to a simmer. Simmer for 2 to 3 minutes, continuing to whisk until the sauce thickens enough to coat a spoon.

4. Remove from the heat and whisk in the lemon zest, lemon juice, salt, pepper and nutmeg to taste. If you are making this sauce ahead of time, prevent a skin from forming on the surface of the sauce by lightly pressing a piece of plastic wrap onto the surface. Allow to cool before refrigerating for up to 3 days.

5. To reheat a sauce made in advance, whisk the sauce over medium-low heat until it is warmed through, being careful not to burn the bottom. If it has thickened too much, add a few tablespoons of milk as you whisk. You can also reheat the sauce in the microwave, covered, for 2 to 4 minutes on high (100% power), whisking halfway through the cooking time.

Mix & Match

Serve the Lemon Velouté Sauce and Orzo Pasta with the main dishes in the following menus: Chicken Romagna, page 159; Nordic Amazon Salmon, page 211.

Orzo Pasta

Makes 4 (⅔ cup) servings

3   to 5 quarts water

¾   to 1 pound Orzo pasta

2   tablespoons light stick butter

⅓   cup finely chopped parsley

To save time make the pasta up to 24 hours in advance of serving. Reheat using the instructions in step number 4.

1. In a 4- or 5-quart pot over high heat, bring the water to a rolling boil.
2. Stir in the orzo then return to a boil.
3. Cook pasta uncovered 9 to 11 minutes until al dente (tender but slightly chewy). Do not overcook.
4. Drain well in a strainer, and then put the pasta into a 2-quart ovenproof or microwavable casserole. Toss with the butter, then sprinkle with the chopped parsley. Keep covered in a 300°F oven until serving time. Or reheat covered in the microwave for 2 to 4 minutes on high (100% power).

Approximate Nutrients Per Serving of Entire Meal

Total Calories 617	Protein 46 g / 31%	Carbohydrate 82 g / 56%
Total Sugar 4 g	Fat Total 8 g / 13%	Saturated Fat 2 g / 3%
Cholesterol 75 mg	Sodium 541 mg	Fiber 5 g Calcium 155 mg

(Calculated with 2 fish rolls made with nonfat mayonnaise, ⅔ cup Orzo Pasta and ¼ cup Lemon Velouté Sauce made with 1% fat milk and light stick butter.)

How's Bayou? Louisiana Shrimp and Orange Brochettes with Red Beans and Rice

The day I wrote this menu I was struggling for a catchy title. After tasting it, I remembered I had to call my father about a family matter. "How's by you?" he cheerfully answered the phone. "That's perfect!" I cried. "You're psychic!" "Of course," he replied. "I'm your Dad!" So Dad, this one is dedicated to you and to Chef Paul Prudhomme, whose cooking tips helped me develop the menu. "People don't miss the fat when there is sweetness in the recipe because it rounds out the flavors," he told me as we both waited to go on the air during a QVC Local Flavors Tour in New Orleans. Taking his advice, I added just enough frozen orange juice concentrate to both the Roasted Bell Pepper and Orange Sauce and the Louisiana Baste to embellish the sizzling Southern Louisiana flavors in this menu without overpowering them.

Menu Game Plan

Prep & Cooking Time: 40 to 45 minutes

- Preheat the grill.
- Make the Red Beans and Rice.
- Make the Roasted Red Pepper and Orange Sauce while the rice is cooking.
- Make the baste.
- Prepare the Shrimp and Orange Brochettes.
- Grill the Brochettes.

Cook's Notes

There are numerous types of chili sauces available in the grocery store these days. The kind I suggest using for this recipe contains mild chilies in a ketchup base, and is usually found in a 12-ounce bottle where the ketchup is sold in the supermarket. If you can't find it in your grocery store, make the following substitution for each 1/4 cup of chili sauce: 3 tablespoons ketchup, 1 tablespoon diced canned mild chilies, 1/2 teaspoon dehydrated onions, 1/4 teaspoon garlic powder, dash allspice and dash of your favorite hot sauce (optional). Allow the mixture to stand for 10 to 15 minutes to hydrate the onions before using.

Louisiana Shrimp and Orange Brochettes

Serves 4

Baste

¼ cup mild ketchup-style chili sauce

2 tablespoons frozen orange juice concentrate, thawed

1 teaspoon pressed garlic

1 tablespoon olive oil

½ to 1 teaspoon prepared Cajun seasoning*

Brochettes

2 medium navel oranges

1¼ to 1½ pounds raw shrimp (12 to 16 medium or 8 to 10 extra large)

16 8-inch bamboo skewers

Nonfat or olive oil cooking spray

¼ cup finely chopped parsley

* If Cajun seasoning is not available, use my recipe on page 54 to make your own.

Substitutions:
Instead of shrimp try 1¼ pounds large sea scallops, boneless skinless chicken breasts or 1¼ pounds extra-firm tofu.

1. **Preheat the grill.** If you have a grill with a variable temperature control, set it to medium-high (1 or 2 steps below high) or to about 350° to 400°F.

2. **Make the baste.** In a small shallow glass bowl or in an airtight 2- to 3-cup container, mix the chili sauce, orange juice concentrate, garlic, olive oil and Cajun seasoning with a fork. Cover and set aside on the counter until ready to grill. This baste can be made up to 1 week in advance if refrigerated in an airtight container.

3. **Prepare the brochettes.** Leave the peel on the oranges, then quarter them, and cut each quarter into 1-inch thick triangular shaped slices.

Shell and devein the shrimp. Pull the legs apart and gently slip your finger under the shell of each shrimp. Peel off the shells but leave the tails on. With a sharp knife, make a shallow ¼-inch slit down the back. Lift out the vein with the tip of the knife or a toothpick. Rinse the shrimp and wrap them in a double layer of paper towel to absorb excess moisture.

Alternately thread the shrimp and orange pieces onto 8 (2 skewer) sets of parallel bamboo skewers leaving a ⅛- to ¼-inch space between each piece of food. (See page 192 for double skewering technique.) Skewer the oranges so that the skewers first pierce the flesh, then come out through the peel.

Spray each brochette lightly with cooking spray. Put each skewer on the grill and baste the upper side. Grill the brochettes according to the Grill Times opposite or until the shrimp becomes opaque. Be careful not to overcook or the shrimp will become tough.

5. **To serve,** spoon equal amounts of rice onto the center of 4 plates. Arrange 2 brochettes on opposite sides of the rice. Top the rice with ⅓ to ½ cup of the Roasted Red Pepper and Orange Sauce sauce and sprinkle with 1 tablespoon of parsley. Serve immediately, passing around the remaining sauce.

Two-Sided Contact Grill: *2 to 3 minutes. Baste halfway through cooking time.*

Hibachi Grill, Combination Grill or Infusion Grill: *4 to 6 minutes. Turn 180° and baste halfway through the grilling time. Grills with lids may be covered halfway through the grilling time. Infusion grills with lids may be covered for the entire grilling time.*

Red Beans and Rice

Makes 4 (1½ cup) servings

2½ cups plus 2 tablespoons water

1½ cups long grain white rice

2 teaspoons canola oil, safflower oil or your favorite vegetable oil

1 teaspoon Cajun spice mix

1 14½-ounce can stewed diced tomatoes well drained (Cajun recipe if you can find them)

1 15-ounce can red kidney or black beans, rinsed, well drained

1 4-ounce can diced mild green chili peppers, well drained

½ cup thinly sliced green onion

You can make this recipe up to 2 days in advance if refrigerated in an airtight container, or you can freeze it for up to 2 months. To greatly decrease the sodium in this recipe, use low sodium or sodium-free canned beans or tomatoes.

1. In a 2-quart pot bring the water to a boil.
2. Stir in the rice, oil and Cajun spice mix. Reduce heat to low, cover and simmer 20 minutes, or until all liquid is absorbed. Remove from heat and let stand, covered, 5 minutes to absorb any remaining liquid.
3. While the rice is about 5 minutes from being done, stir together the tomatoes, beans, chili peppers and green onion in a 1-quart pot over medium heat. When the mixture is hot and the rice is cooked and has stood for 5 minutes off of the heat, fold the beans into the cooked rice with a spatula and serve immediately.

Serve the Roasted Red Pepper Sauce and the Red Beans and Rice with the main dishes in the following menus: Crazy Cajun Burgers, page 85, Pride of Texas Chili Lime Pork, page 123.

Roasted Red Pepper and Orange Sauce

Makes 4 generous (¹/₂ cup) servings

1¹/₂ cups chili sauce

2 cups roasted red peppers, well drained (2 7-ounce jars)

2 tablespoons frozen orange juice concentrate

2 tablespoons lemon juice

2 teaspoons prepared Cajun seasoning

This sauce can be made up to 1 week in advance if stored in the refrigerator in an airtight container. It freezes up to 3 months.

1. In a blender or food processor fitted with a metal chopping blade, puree the chili sauce, roasted bell peppers, orange juice concentrate, lemon juice, and Cajun seasoning.
2. Pour the sauce into a 1 or 2-quart pot. Just before serving, heat over medium heat 4 to 5 minutes until slightly thickened and gently bubbling. Serve immediately

Approximate Nutrients Per Serving of Entire Meal

Total Calories 675	Protein 32 g / 19%	Carbohydrate 119 g / 70%	
Total Sugar 29 g / 11%	Fat Total 8 g / 11%	Saturated Fat 1 g / 2%	
Cholesterol 168 mg	Sodium 1,653 mg	Fiber 11 g	Calcium 150 mg

Orange Teriyaki Tuna Kushiyaki with Sticky Rice and Japanese Cucumber Salad

In Japanese "kushi" means skewer and "yaki" means grill. I first tasted kushi yaki when I was seven years old at Mrs. Mary Shimizu's home in southern California. Still a close family friend, Mrs. Shimizu introduced me to her traditional Japanese cuisine with meals similar to this one. Most teriyaki sauce recipes are extremely high in sodium. To cut the sodium in half, I substituted frozen orange juice concentrate and orange marmalade for half of the usual amount of soy sauce and used reduced sodium soy sauce for the other half. I hope you enjoy this easy lower sodium version of Mrs. Shimizu's dinner as much as I enjoyed creating it.

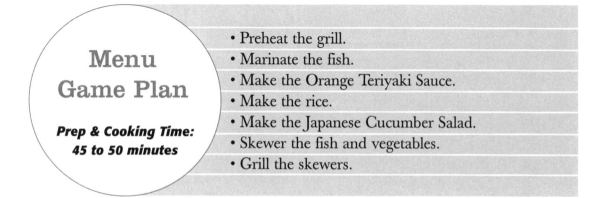

Menu Game Plan

Prep & Cooking Time: 45 to 50 minutes

- Preheat the grill.
- Marinate the fish.
- Make the Orange Teriyaki Sauce.
- Make the rice.
- Make the Japanese Cucumber Salad.
- Skewer the fish and vegetables.
- Grill the skewers.

Cook's Notes

Daikon radish, also known as Japanese radish, is large, white and carrot shaped. Its mild, slightly juicy sweet taste and crispy texture make it a perfect addition for a variety of dishes. Grated, thinly sliced, slivered or diced, daikon radish gives texture and lively flavor to salads, salsas and relishes. Sliced into thick rounds, it makes crispy dippers on hors d'oeuvre platters. Marinated overnight in a tasty vinaigrette, it becomes a delicious pickle for antipasto platters. Daikon radish also retains it shape and texture when cooked in stir-frys, stews or soups. For the freshest daikon, choose very firm radishes that have a smooth, almost luminous skin. Daikon will keep up to 1 week in your refrigerator if it is thoroughly dry and stored in an airtight bag.

Tuna Kushiyaki

Makes 4 servings

2 tablespoons low-sodium soy sauce

1 tablespoon frozen orange juice concentrate, thawed

1 tablespoon marmalade

1 teaspoon freshly grated gingerroot

1¼ pounds fresh tuna

2 medium navel oranges

¼ pound sugar pea pods (optional)

16 8-inch wooden skewers

Fat-free cooking spray or canola oil spray

Substitutions

Instead of tuna, substitute any other firm flesh fish such as swordfish, shark or halibut or substitute boneless skinless chicken breast, beef sirloin or extra-firm tofu slices.

1. **Preheat the grill.** If you have a grill with a variable temperature control, set it to medium-high (1 or 2 steps below high) or to about 350° to 400°F.

2. **Make the Marinade.** In a small bowl, mix the soy sauce, orange juice concentrate, marmalade and ginger with a fork. Pour into a 1-gallon freezer-weight zipper bag, 1-quart airtight container or shallow glass or ceramic (8 x 8 x 2-inch) dish. Set aside while you prepare the fish.

3. **Prepare and marinate the fish.** Cut the fish into 1 x 1 x 1-inch or 1 x 1 x 2-inch cubes, then put it into the bag or dish with the marinade. Turn the pieces to coat all surfaces with the marinade, then squeeze the air out of the bag and zip it closed or cover the container or dish. Marinate in your refrigerator for 20 minutes or up to 1 hour.

4. **Skewer and grill the kushiyaki.** Do not peel the oranges. Cut them into quarters then into 1-inch thick triangular shaped slices. Set aside. Remove the strings from the peapods.

Remove the fish from the marinade; discard the marinade unless using an infusion grill. Alternately thread the fish, orange pieces and pea pods onto 8 (2 skewer) sets of parallel bamboo skewers leaving a ⅛-to ¼-inch space between each piece of food. (See page 192 for double skewering technique.) Skewer the oranges so that the skewers first pierce the flesh then come out through the peel. Skewer the pea pods so that the skewers pierce the wide, center section of the pods so a thin side will face the grill.

Spray each kushiyaki lightly with fat-free cooking spray or canola oil spray. Grill the kushiyaki according to the Grill Times opposite or until the interior temperature of the tuna reaches the doneness you desire on an instant-read thermometer. Consult internal temperature grilling chart on page 207 for exact temperatures: 135° to 140°F for medium. The tuna is done when it is tender, evenly opaque and no longer translucent in the center.

5. **To serve,** put the cucumber salad in small bowls to prevent the dressing from mixing with the orange sauce. Place equal amounts of rice on 4 plates. Arrange 2 kushiyaki on opposite sides of the rice and drizzle 1 or 2 tablespoons of orange sauce over the fish and rice before serving. Pass the remaining teriyaki sauce around the table.

Two-Sided Contact Grill: *4 to 5 minutes for medium.*

Hibachi Grill, Combination Grill or Infusion Grill: *8 to 10 minutes for medium. Turn the skewers over halfway through the grilling time. Grills with lids may be covered halfway through the grilling time. Infusion grills with lids may be covered for the entire grilling time.*

Infusion Grill Notes: *For more intense flavor, pour the leftover marinade mixture into infusion cup. If there is not much leftover marinade, combine it with some extra soy sauce or orange juice to make ½ cup before pouring into it into the infusion cup.*

Orange Teriyaki Sauce

Makes 8 (2 tablespoon) servings

⅓   cup low-sodium soy sauce

¼   cup frozen orange juice concentrate, thawed

¼   cup orange marmalade

2   tablespoons granulated sugar

1   to 2 teaspoons finely grated fresh gingerroot

½   to 1 teaspoon prepared Wasabi* mustard (optional)

2   teaspoons cornstarch

2   tablespoons cool water

* Japanese green mustard.

This sauce will keep in your refrigerator for 3 weeks and may be frozen for up to 1 month.

1. In a small saucepan, whisk the soy sauce, orange juice concentrate, marmalade, sugar, ginger and Wasabi mustard until the sugar dissolves. (You can also mix this in a blender.)
2. Heat, uncovered, over medium heat, whisking occasionally, until the sauce begins to boil, about 5 minutes.
3. While the sauce is coming to a boil, whisk the cornstarch with the water in a small bowl until dissolved. Just as the sauce begins to boil, whisk in the cornstarch mixture. Bring back to a boil whisking constantly until lightly thickened, about 1 minute. Cover and set aside until ready to serve. If the sauce becomes too cool, reheat over low heat. Add a few teaspoons of water or orange juice if it becomes too thick during reheating.

Substitutions:
Instead of Wasabi mustard, substitute your favorite hot mustard or hot sauce to taste.

Mix & Match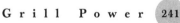
Serve the Orange Teriyaki Sauce with the main dishes from the following recipes: Mighty Maui Burgers, page 65; Cantonese Lemon Chicken Sez Me!, page 171.

Sticky Rice

Makes 4 (1 cup) servings

2   cups water

1½   cup medium grain white rice

This can be made up to 72 hours in advance of serving. Cover and reheat in the microwave on high (100%) for 4 to 5 minutes.

1. In a 3- to 4-quart pot bring the water to a soft boil. Stir in the rice. Reduce the heat to low, cover and simmer 20 minutes, or until all the water is absorbed.
2. Remove from the heat and let stand covered 10 minutes. Fluff with a fork and serve.

Japanese Cucumber Salad

Makes 4 (1 cup) servings

2   cups thinly sliced cucumber (preferably hothouse)

1   cup shredded carrot

½   cup shredded daikon radish or thinly sliced red radish

½   cup thinly sliced green onion

¼   cup seasoned rice vinegar

3   tablespoons sugar

½   teaspoon light salt

This salad can be made up to 24 hours in advance if stored in an airtight container.

1. In a 4-cup bowl, mix the cucumber, carrot, radish and green onion.
2. In a 1-cup measure or small bowl, mix the vinegar, granulated sugar and salt with a fork or small wire whisk until the sugar is dissolved.
3. Mix the dressing into the salad and set aside in your refrigerator, covered, until ready to eat.

Approximate Nutrients Per Serving of Entire Meal

Total Calories 595	Protein 41 g / 27%	Carbohydrate 104 g / 69%	
Total Sugar 27 g	Fat Total 2 g / 3%	Saturated Fat .5 g / 1%	
Cholesterol 64 mg	Sodium 774 mg	Fiber 7 g	Calcium 118 mg

(Calculated with 2 Kushiyaki, 1 cup rice, 2 tablespoons teriyaki sauce and 1 cup cucumber salad.)

Meatless

Want to add a few meatless meals to your weekly menu that look great and taste even better? Start by heating up your electric tabletop grill for the most irresistible vegetables and fruit you have ever tasted. Why are they so hard to resist? Grilled fruits and vegetables taste sweeter because the high heat of the grill caramelizes their natural sugars. High heat also sears in appetizing grill marks while allowing fruits and vegetables to remain appealingly bright and crisp, yet cooked through. When vegetables and fruit look and taste this good, everyone will want to eat more. And that is a plus because adding more plant foods to your diet (fruits, vegetables, grains, starches and beans) will give you some extra health insurance.

Researchers have not determined whether it is the fiber, vitamins, minerals, or phytochemicals abundant in plant foods that help fight cancer, diabetes, heart disease and high cholesterol levels. (Phytochemicals, found only in plant foods, are completely different elements from vitamins, minerals and fiber. Foods rich in complex carbohydrates contain hundreds of these chemicals, which scientists believe may be powerful inhibitors of carcinogens.)

What they have found consistently in research dating back to the early 1970's is people who eat the most fruits, vegetables and grains have the lowest risk of cancer, diabetes and heart disease. That is why the American Heart Association, American Cancer Society, National Osteoporosis Foundation, American Diabetes Society, American Dietetic Association and American College of Sports Medicine all suggest eating a minimum of 5 fruits and vegetables per day.

Grill Your Way to Five-a-Day

Whether you like Italian, Middle Eastern, Thai, Indian or American Southwestern cuisine, I have created a menu to suit your tastes. Better yet, you can eat your daily fruit and vegetable requirement in just one of my meatless meals because each menu in this chapter includes 5 or more fruits and vegetables.

If making a meatless meal is still too experimental for you, try grilling your side-dish vegetables instead of steaming or boiling them. For some ideas, use the Vegetable and Fruit Grilling Chart on page 244 to help you grill just about any vegetable or fruit to perfection. Looking for a little different side dish than plain grilled vegetables? How about grilled vegetable and fruit kebabs? I have included kebab-skewering techniques for each vegetable and fruit because they are fun to make and eat, and are especially appealing to vegetable resistant kids and adults. If you are cooking for kids, invite them to skewer their own veggie kebabs. Offer a dipping sauce, either one of my sauce recipes in the book or a bottled salad dressing, and you might be pleasantly surprised at finding empty skewers at the end of the meal.

- Choose vegetables and fruit that are ripe yet firm. If they are too ripe and have very soft flesh, they may fall apart as they grill.
- Watch the grill carefully if grilling very ripe fruit because they take less time to reach doneness.
- Leaving on the peel or skin helps many fruits and vegetables keep their shape and prevents them from falling apart when grilling.
- The following vegetables are better steamed, sautéed or stir-fried because the tender outer leaves get burned on the grill before the inside is cooked: brussels sprouts, broccoli, cauliflower, cabbage or Bok Choy.

1. Preheat the grill to the highest setting.
2. Spray vegetables with nonfat cooking spray or brush with olive oil. Spray fruit with non-fat cooking spray, or brush with melted butter or margarine mixed with some honey or maple syrup (about 1 tablespoon butter or margarine to 1 teaspoon honey or maple syrup).
3. Grill according to the times in the chart. To prevent overcooking and to create grill marks, turn once halfway through the grilling time.

Grilled Vegetable Chart

Vegetable	Special Preparation Instructions	Grilling Time
	Always spray or baste with vegetable oil or fat-free cooking spray before placing on the grill. See page 192 for double skewering technique.	Hibachi, Combination and Infusion Grills: Turn halfway through the grilling time
Asparagus: choose thick, mature stalks	Grill whole. Peel stems, if desired. (See page 167). For kebabs: Cut into 2- or 3-inch lengths. Double skewer so the length is at a right angle to the skewers, piercing through the widest part.	Two-Sided Contact Grill: 5 to 6 minutes. Hibachi, Combination or Infusion Grill: 10 to 12 minutes.
Carrots: choose carrots at least 1 inch in diameter in the thickest part or thick ready-to-eat baby carrots	Before grilling, precook to tenderize: Cut large carrots into 1-inch-thick pieces, either lengthwise or in rounds. Microwave covered with 1/2 cup hot water 5 minutes on high (100% power) or until fork-tender but still firm. Steam or boil 5 to 7 minutes. Drain well. For kebabs: Cut large carrots into 1-inch-thick rounds. Use ready-to-eat baby carrots right out of the bag. Double skewer 1-inch rounds through the outside skin rather than through the center so carrots will lie flat on the grill. Double skewer ready-to-eat carrots at a right angle to the skewer.	Two-Sided Contact Grill: 6 to 7 minutes. Hibachi, Combination or Infusion Grill: 12 to 14 minutes.

Vegetable	Special Preparation Instructions	Grilling Time
Cherry Tomatoes: choose firm tomatoes about 1 inch in diameter	Remove the stem to prevent it from burning. Grill cherry tomatoes whole, they are too small to slice. For kebabs: Double skewer through the stem end of the tomato.	Two-Sided Contact Grill: 3 minutes. Hibachi, Combination or Infusion Grill: 6 minutes.
Corn: choose ears no longer than 6- to 8-inches long so they will fit on the grill	Remove husks, silk, and stem ends. Precook to tenderize: Microwave covered with 1/4 cup hot water 5 minutes on high (100% power) or steam 5 to 7 minutes. Grill whole.	Two-Sided Contact Grill: 4 to 5 minutes. Hibachi, Combination or Infusion Grill: 8 to 10 minutes turning every 2 minutes to evenly brown all sides.
Eggplant: choose Japanese or large globe	Slice Japanese eggplants in half lengthwise; slice globe eggplants across the meridian into 1-inch-thick slices. For kebabs: Cut Japanese eggplants into 1-inch-thick rounds. Cut globe eggplants into 1-inch cubes. Double skewer Japanese eggplants through the outside skin rather than through the center so they will lie flat on the grill. Double skewer globe cubes through the center.	Two-Sided Contact Grill: 6 to 8 minutes. Hibachi, Combination or Infusion Grill: 12 to 15 minutes.
Fennel: choose larger bulbs	Whole: Cut off and discard round stems and feathery leaves. Reserve some leaves for garnishing your dish. Leave the stem intact. Depending on the size of the bulb, slice lengthwise into halves or quarters. For kebabs: Leave the stem intact and cut into 1-inch-thick slices. Double skewer so all pieces are facing in the same direction.	Two-Sided Contact Grill: 5 to 8 minutes. Hibachi, Combination or Infusion Grill: 10 to 15 minutes.
Green Onions: choose large onions	Whole: Cut off the root ends as close to the white part of the onion as possible. Leave about 3 inches of green above the white part of the onion and cut the remaining green part off (use the discarded green ends for another recipe). For kebabs: Cut off the root ends as close to the white part of the onion as possible. Cut into 3-inch lengths from the root end. Double skewer so the length is at a right angle to the skewers, piercing through the widest part.	Two-Sided Contact Grill: 3 to 4 minutes. Hibachi, Combination or Infusion Grill: 6 to 8 minutes.

Vegetable	Special Preparation Instructions	Grilling Time
Jicama	Peel and cut into 1-inch slices, or 1-inch cubes for kebabs. Precook to tenderize (optional): Microwave covered with 1/4 cup hot water 3 minutes on high (100% power). Steam 5 to 7 minutes. Drain well before putting on the grill. For kebabs: Double skewer through the center of the cubes.	Two-Sided Contact Grill: 5 to 6 minutes. Hibachi, Combination or Infusion Grill: 10 to 12 minutes.
Button Mushrooms: choose mushrooms with caps at least 2 inches in diameter	Either remove the stems and grill the caps whole or cut in half through the stem and cap. For kebabs: Leave the stem intact and slice in half. Arrange the mushroom pieces so they are all facing the same way. Run double skewers so they pierce the stem ends first than come out through the caps.	Two-Sided Contact Grill: 4 to 5 minutes Hibachi, Combination or Infusion Grill: 8 to 10 minutes.
Onion: medium or large, any type	Grilled Rings: Cut across the meridian into 1-inch-thick rounds. For kebabs: Cut into 1-inch cubes. Double skewer through the center to hold the layers together.	Two-Sided Contact Grill: 7 to 10 minutes. Hibachi, Combination or Infusion Grill: 14 to 20 minutes.
Bell peppers, red, yellow, orange, green	Cut in half to remove the seeds and stem, then cut lengthwise or across the meridian into 1-inch-thick slices. For kebabs: Cut into 1-inch squares. Double skewer through the center so pieces are at a right angle to the skewer.	Two-Sided Contact Grill: 6 to 8 minutes. Hibachi, Combination or Infusion Grill: 12 to 16 minutes.
Potatoes: this applies to sweet potatoes or yams, thick-skinned potatoes, like russet, or thin-skinned potatoes like red, white, Yukon	If grilling sweet potatoes, peel them. If grilling thick-skinned potatoes like russet, you can either peel them or leave the skin on. Leave the skin on thin-skinned potatoes. Cut larger potatoes into 1-inch cubes. Cut smaller potatoes into 1-inch-thick rounds, or in half. Precook to tenderize before grilling: Microwave 5 to 6 minutes covered with 1/2 cup hot water on high (100% power) or until fork tender but still firm. Steam or boil 7 to 8 minutes. For kebabs: If potatoes are large, cut into 1-inch-thick cubes. If the potatoes are small either cut them into rounds, or if petite, slice them in half. Double skewer cubes through the center. If grilling rounds with the skin left on, skewer through the skin so they lie flat on the grill.	Two-Sided Contact Grill: 4 to 5 minutes. Hibachi, Combination or Infusion Grill: 8 to 10 minutes.

Vegetable	Special Preparation Instructions	Grilling Time
Squash (summer, crookneck, pattypan or zucchini)	Cut smaller squash lengthwise into 2 equal halves. Cut larger squash into 1-inch-thick rounds or half moons. For kebabs: If small, cut into 1-inch-thick rounds. If large cut into 1-inch-thick half-moons. Double skewer through the skin so they lie flat on the grill.	Two-Sided Contact Grill: 5 to 8 minutes. Hibachi, Combination or Infusion Grill: 10 to 15 minutes.
Squash (winter, acorn, butternut or kabocha)	Cut off the stem end. Cut the squash in half and remove the seeds. Peel smooth-skinned squash like butternut. Do not remove the peel from uneven skinned squash like acorn squash. Cut thick-fleshed squash like butternut squash into 1-inch-thick slices, cubes or rounds. Cut thinner-fleshed squash like acorn squash into 1-inch half-moons. Precook to tenderize: Microwave covered with 1/2 cup hot water 7 to 9 minutes on high (100% power) or until fork-tender but still firm. Steam or boil 5 to 7 minutes. For kebabs: Double skewer cubes through center. Skewer half moons first through the inside flesh, then out through the peel side.	Two-Sided Contact Grill: 6 to 8 minutes. Hibachi, Combination or Infusion Grill: 12 to 15 minutes.
Sugar Peas (Snow Peas, Sugar Snap Peas)	Remove strings by snapping off the stem end of the pod and pulling off the string. Snow peas have strings on one side along the top of the pod. Sugar snap peas have strings on both sides so you have to snap off both ends to remove both strings. For kebabs: Double skewer through flat side of the pod in the middle.	Two-Sided Contact Grill: 3 to 5 minutes. Hibachi, Combination or Infusion Grill: 8 to 9 minutes.
Tofu: use extra-firm	Drain well and wrap in several layers of paper towel to absorb excess moisture. Cut into 1-inch-thick slices. For kebabs: Cut into 1-inch-thick cubes. Double skewer through the center of the cube.	Two-Sided Contact Grill: 6 to 8 minutes. Hibachi, Combination or Infusion Grill: 12 to 16 minutes.
Water Chestnuts: choose whole canned water chestnuts	Drain well and wrap in several layers of paper towel to dry. For kebabs: Double skewer through the center.	Two-Sided Contact Grill: 5 minutes. Hibachi, Combination or Infusion Grill: 10 minutes.

Fruit	Special Preparation Instructions	Grilling Time
	Always spray fruit with nonfat cooking spray, or brush with melted butter or margarine mixed with some honey or maple syrup before placing on the grill. About 1 tablespoon honey or butter mixed with 1 teaspoon honey or maple syrup.	Hibachi, Combination or Infusion Grill: Turn halfway through the grilling time.
Apple: any tart, firm variety such as Fuji, Braeburn, Granny Smith, Cortland, Gravenstein, Rhode Island, Greening, Macintosh, or Pippin	Leave peel on. Cut the apple in half. Remove the seeds with a melon baller then use a paring knife to remove the stem ends. Slice into 1-inch-thick half moons. For kebabs: Double skewer through the flesh then out through the peel so that slices lie flat on the grill.	Two-Sided Contact Grill: 5 to 6 minutes. Hibachi, Combination or Infusion Grill: 10 to 12 minutes.
Apricots	Cut in half and remove pits. Grill cut side down first, until grill marks appear before turning over. For kebabs: Double skewer so that cut side will lie flat on the grill.	Two-Sided Contact Grill: 3 to 5 minutes. Hibachi, Combination or Infusion Grill: 6 to 10 minutes depending on the ripeness.
Banana: choose medium size	Leave peel on. Slice lengthwise in half. Grill cut side down until grill marks appear. No need to turn over. For kebabs: Leave skin on and slice into 1-inch-thick rounds. Double skewer through the peel so slices will lie flat on the grill.	Two-Sided Contact Grill: 3 to 5 minutes. Hibachi, Combination or Infusion Grill: 6 to 10 minutes.
Figs: fresh	Cut in half lengthwise. Grill cut side down until grill marks appear. For kebabs: Double skewer parallel to the cut side so pieces will lie flat on the grill.	Two-Sided Contact Grill: 2 to 3 minutes. Hibachi, Combination or Infusion Grill: 4 to 6 minutes.
Kiwi	Wash thoroughly to remove excess fuzzy pieces from the peel. Leave peel on. Slice in half, grill cut side down until grill marks appear. For kebabs: Slice stem ends flat then cut into 1-inch-thick rounds. Double skewer parallel to the cut sides through the peel so slices will lie flat on the grill.	Two-Sided Contact Grill: 5 to 6 minutes. Hibachi, Combination or Infusion Grill: 10 to 12 minutes.
Melon: such as cantaloupe or honeydew	Cut in half and remove the seeds with a spoon. You can grill cantaloupes with rind on or peeled. Quarter, then cut into 1-inch-thick slices. For kebabs: Rind on: Cut into 1-inch-thick half-moons. Double skewer melon through the flesh then out through the rind. Peeled: Cut into 1-inch-thick cubes. Double skewer through the center of the cubes so all pieces lie flat on the grill.	Two-Sided Contact Grill: 2 to 3 minutes. Hibachi, Combination or Infusion Grill: 4 to 5 minutes.

Fruit	Special Preparation Instructions	Grilling Time
Oranges and Grapefruit	Leave the peel on. Slice stem ends flat. Cut in half then slice into 1-inch-thick half moons. For kebabs: Double skewer through the flesh first then through the peel so the slices will lie flat on the grill.	Two-Sided Contact Grill: 3 to 5 minutes. Hibachi, Combination or 1-inch Grill: 6 to 10 minutes.
Papaya: choose fruit that is firm but on the verge of being ripe; the color of the skin will be a combination of yellow and green	Leave the peel on. Cut in half and remove the seeds with a spoon. Either leave each half intact, or cut off the stem ends and slice into 1-inch-thick half moons. To grill halves: Grill the cut side until grill marks appear. For kebabs: Leave the skin on and cut into 1-inch-thick half-moons. Double skewer through the flesh first then through the peel so that the slices will lie flat on the grill.	Two-Sided Contact Grill: 2 to 4 minutes for riper fruit; 5 to 8 minutes for less ripe fruit. Hibachi, Combination or 1-inch Grill: 5 to 8 for riper fruit; 10 to 15 for less ripe fruit.
Peaches and Nectarines: choose ripe but firm fruit; if they are too soft, they will fall apart on the grill	Leave the peel on. Cut in half and remove pits. If small, grill halves intact. If they are large, slice stem ends flat then slice into 1-inch-thick half moons. For kebabs: Double skewer half-moons through the flesh first then through the peel so that the slices will lie flat on the grill.	Two-Sided Contact Grill: 2 to 6 minutes for riper fruit; 3 to 4 for less ripe fruit. Hibachi, Combination or Infusion Grill: 5 to 6 minutes for riper fruit; 7 to 8 for less ripe fruit.
Pears: choose firm varieties such as Asian, Anjou, Bosc, Bartlett, Comice or Seckel	Leave peel on. Cut in half then core with a melon baller. If pears are small, grill halves intact. If pears are large, slice stem ends flat then slice into 1-inch-thick half moons. For kebabs: Double skewer 1-inch-thick half-moons through the flesh first then out through the peel so that slices lie flat on the grill.	Two-Sided Contact Grill: 5 to 6 minutes. Hibachi, Combination or Fusion Grill: 10 to 12 minutes.
Pineapple	Leave the rind on. Slice stem ends flat. Slice lengthwise into quarters then slice each quarter into 1-inch-thick triangles. For kebabs: Double skewer through the flesh first then out through the rind so that the slices will lie flat on the grill.	Two-Sided Contact Grill: 5 to 6 minutes. Hibachi, Combination or Infusion Grill: 10 to 12 minutes.
Plums: choose plums that are not too ripe, any variety	Cut in half and remove the pit. Grill sliced side down until grill marks appear. For kebabs: Double skewer so that cut sides are flat against the grill and are all facing the same way.	Two-Sided Contact Grill: 2 to 3 minutes for riper fruit; 3 to 4 for less ripe fruit. Hibachi, Combination or Infusion Grill: 5 to 6 minutes for riper fruit 7 to 8 for less ripe fruit.

Want an easy way to arm yourself against disease? Try grilling some marinated tofu or using textured soy protein as a substitute for ground meat in your burgers. A trail of evidence links diets rich in soy foods to reduced risk of osteoporosis, hormone-dependent cancers like breast and prostate cancer, heart disease, diabetes, episodes of PMS and menopausal hot flashes. That's because soy rich foods contain a unique combination of plant compounds called isoflavones. Isoflavones, found in the vegetable protein in soybeans, are a natural plant form of estrogen 500 to 1,000 times weaker than human estrogen. Researchers have found that isoflavones may be the chemicals responsible for blocking cancer-causing substances, protecting against heart disease, preventing bone loss and warding off PMS and menopausal symptoms. Numerous studies have proven that the fiber in soy can help control diabetes and hypoglycemia and lower blood cholesterol and triglyceride levels.

Tofu Grilling Tips

Best tofu for grilling. I used firm or extra-firm organic tofu to develop the tofu recipes in this book. I do not suggest trying to grill the Japanese silken tofu as it will fall apart on the grill because it is too soft and gelatinous. This type of tofu is terrific in other types of recipes such as floating in soups, pureed in sauces, puddings, pie fillings, dressings, or chopped finely for sandwich or pasta fillings.

Preparation for water packed tofu. If you use water packed firm or extra-firm tofu, you must express excess water before trying to grill it. To do that, wrap the tofu in 3 to 4 layers of white paper towel, place it on a plate, then place another plate on top of the tofu. Put something heavy on the upper plate like a 1- or 2-pound can or a bag of rice. Allow the weighted tofu to stand for a minimum of 10 minutes or up to 1 hour. If you keep the weight on the tofu longer than 30 minutes, you may want to change the paper towel as the first batch will become very wet. The longer the tofu is under the weight, the more water gets expressed.

Grill tofu uncovered. If you own a grill with a lid, I do not recommend grilling tofu with the lid on. It will prevent the outside of the tofu from browning or becoming crispy. Tofu contains a lot of water, which will not evaporate if cooked in a covered, moist environment.

Marinating tofu. I don't recommend marinating tofu in plastic bags because even firm tofu is delicate and can fall apart. It is best marinated in a square dish or airtight container.

Fetadillas and Mixed Tomato Salad with Herbed Vinaigrette

For centuries, Mexican cooks have prepared quesadillas, cheese and chili-filled tortillas, on a hot greased griddle or in deep fat. This menu shows you how to use your tabletop grill to make these half-moon shaped goodies without using any excess fat. Just for fun, I transformed this Mexican snack food into a light Mediterranean-style main dish. I renamed it Fetadillas because instead of white Mexican "queso" (cheese in Spanish), they are filled with Greek-style feta cheese, Kalamata olives, and roasted bell peppers. For an easy and chic light lunch or dinner, serve them with my colorful mixed tomato salad with Lemon-Herb Vinaigrette.

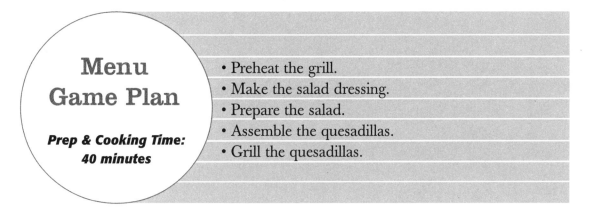

Menu Game Plan

Prep & Cooking Time: 40 minutes

- Preheat the grill.
- Make the salad dressing.
- Prepare the salad.
- Assemble the quesadillas.
- Grill the quesadillas.

Cook's Notes

Notes

Feta cheese has withstood the test of time. This white crumbly cheese originated in Greece thousands of years ago and is, to this day, Greece's most popular domestic cheese. A fresh, non-aged cheese, feta is traditionally made with sheep or goat milk, but commercial brands are often made with cow's milk. Whether plain or herbed, a good quality feta should have a crumbly, yet soft texture with small holes and taste simultaneously salty, sharp and tangy. One ounce of feta has about 6 grams of fat. But it is so flavorful, you don't have to use much. Some manufacturers pack feta in brine or olive oil to prevent it from dehydrating. As you will see in this recipe, as feta is heated it becomes soft but retains its shape. Feta is always on my weekly shopping list because I like to have it on hand to crumble on salads or to serve cubed as impromptu an hors d'oeuvre with cured olives.

Fetadillas and Tomato Salad

Serves 4

Fetadillas

4   8- or 10-inch low-fat flour tortillas

1   cup crumbled feta cheese

⅔   cup fire roasted peppers from a jar, cut into strips

8   Kalamata or cured Mediterranean style olives, pitted and cut into quarters

2   teaspoons coarsely chopped fresh dill

2   teaspoons coarsely chopped fresh oregano leaves

1   tablespoon thinly sliced green onion

Salad

8   to 12 butter lettuce leaves

2   medium tomatoes

1   cup cherry tomatoes, cut in half

¼   cup thinly sliced radish

¼   cup thinly sliced red onions

1. **Preheat the grill** to the highest setting.

2. **Fill the Fetadillas.** Lay the 4 tortillas on a flat surface. Sprinkle ½ of each tortillas with equal amounts of the feta cheese, fire roasted peppers, olives, dill, oregano and green onions.

   Fold the empty side of each tortilla over the filled side to make a half moon.

3. **Grill the fetadillas.** If you have a small grill, grill each fetadilla separately. If you have a large grill, put 2 or more fetadillas on the grill simultaneously.

4. **To serve,** arrange equal amounts of lettuce, tomato, radish, cucumbers and onions on 1 side of 4 dinner plates.

   Let the fetadillas rest 1 to 2 minutes before slicing each in half into 2 triangles. Put both halves on each of the 4 dinner plates next to the salad. Drizzle the salad with 1 to 2 tablespoons of the Lemon Herb Vinaigrette or one of your favorite dressings just before serving.

Grill Times

Two-Sided Contact Grill: *4 minutes.*

Hibachi Grill, Combination Grill or Infusion Grill: *8 minutes. Carefully turn the fetadillas halfway through the grilling time, using 2 large spatulas. If your grill has a lid, do not cover because the fetadillas will get soggy from the steam buildup.*

Mix & Match ▸ Serve the salad with either of the main dishes in the following menus: Pita the Great Lamb Burgers, page 92; Grilled Greek Tuna, page 208.

Lemon Herb Vinaigrette

Makes 8 (2 tablespoon) servings

¼ cup lemon juice

¼ cup seasoned red wine or white wine vinegar

½ cup olive oil

¼ teaspoon pressed garlic

1 tablespoon finely chopped fresh oregano or 1½ teaspoon dried

1 tablespoon finely chopped dill or 1½ teaspoon dried

½ teaspoon granulated sugar

Light salt and freshly ground pepper to taste

The dressing will keep up to 3 weeks if refrigerated in an airtight container.

In a blender, puree the lemon juice, vinegar, olive oil, garlic, oregano, dill, sugar, salt and pepper to taste. Pour into a 2-cup airtight container.

Substitutions:
If you don't want to make my dressing from scratch, substitute your favorite bottled vinaigrette.

Approximate Nutrients Per Serving of Entire Meal

Total Calories 333	Protein 10 g / 12%	Carbohydrate 37 g / 44%
Total Sugar 6 g	Fat Total 16 g / 44%	Saturated Fat 7 g / 18%
Cholesterol 25 mg	Sodium 795 mg	Fiber 12 g Calcium 173 mg

Portobello Sandwiches with Basil Parmesan Oven Fries

The first time I sank my teeth into a portobello mushroom "steak" was in a small well-known restaurant in Florence, Italy, called Pennello. Wedged around a small table with my husband John and my longtime friend Theresa Tomasetti, a native Tuscan, we dined on a variety of delightful antipasti followed by the luscious seafood risotto of the day. Full and happy, I asked Theresa about dessert choices. "We're not done yet," she said, just as a waiter arrived with a dinner plate covered with an enormous mushroom cap. Theresa insisted we sample this delicacy. "It tastes like a steak but it's heart-healthy—no cholesterol, low in calories and fat," she said. With no further prompting, we happily devoured the entire portobello—delicious!

Although Italians eat their grilled portobello mushrooms without buns, I like to serve mine between two slices of lightly toasted fresh Italian bread or on sourdough rolls topped with grilled veggies, fresh basil, and fresh mozzarella.

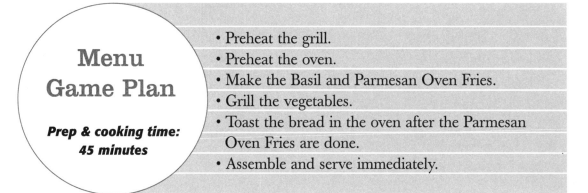

Menu Game Plan

Prep & cooking time: 45 minutes

• Preheat the grill.
• Preheat the oven.
• Make the Basil and Parmesan Oven Fries.
• Grill the vegetables.
• Toast the bread in the oven after the Parmesan Oven Fries are done.
• Assemble and serve immediately.

Cook's Notes

Notes

Portobello mushrooms are a cultivated variety of Italian field mushrooms that grow as large as dinner plates. Brown in color and meaty in flavor, many connoisseurs compare a perfectly grilled portobello to filet mignon.

Select firm, plump mushrooms with feathery gills and caps with no bruises. Avoid mushrooms with shriveled caps and stems, and stay away from slimy mushrooms. Even though many chefs insist that washing mushrooms with water makes them soggy, the amount of water absorbed is infinitesimal compared with the amount of dirt and bacteria that can accumulate on the outside of a mushroom. I always rinse my mushrooms under cool running water. Don't let mushrooms sit in water, though, or they will get waterlogged.

Portobello Sandwiches

Serves 4

2   tablespoons extra-virgin olive oil

2   tablespoons balsamic vinegar

2   teaspoons pressed garlic

4   medium portobello mushrooms (each about 5 inches in diameter)

1   medium red, yellow or orange bell pepper

1   medium red onion

Nonfat or olive oil cooking spray

1   6- or 8-ounce ball fresh or processed low-fat mozzarella

8   slices Italian or sourdough bread (from a large, round loaf) or 4 round Italian or sourdough rolls, split

12 to 16 fresh basil leaves

4   tablespoons nonfat or low-fat mayonnaise

1. Preheat the grill to the highest setting.

2. Preheat the oven to 450°F.

3. Prepare the baste. In a 1-cup bowl or measure, thoroughly mix the olive oil, balsamic vinegar and garlic with a fork.

4. Prepare the vegetables for grilling. Remove the stems from the portobello mushrooms with a small sharp knife. Reserve the stems for another recipe. (Keep them in the refrigerator wrapped in a paper towel in a zippered bag for up to a week.) Slice the bell pepper into 8 strips, each about 1-inch wide. Peel and slice the onion. Cut the onion into 4 slices, each about 1-inch wide.

5. Grill the vegetables. If your grill is small, grill the onions first, then the bell peppers. Keep them warm on a covered platter while you grill the portobellos. If your grill is large, grill every-thing simultaneously. Lightly spray the onions and the bell pep-per slices with cooking spray. Using a basting brush, baste mushrooms on both sides with the balsamic vinegar mixture. Grill according to the times below or until tender.

6. Toast the bread and melt the cheese. Slice the bread, then slice the mozzarella into 4 rounds, each about 1/2-inch thick. Put the bread on a baking sheet, then place cheese on the top half of each slice or roll. When the vegetables are halfway grilled, place the baking sheet on a rack situated in the middle of the preheated oven. Bake until the cheese begins to melt, about 3 to 5 minutes.

7. To serve, spoon even portions of the oven fries on 4 plates. Place a toasted bread slice or roll bottom on each plate and top with a tablespoon of mayonnaise, then the portobello mushroom. Top the mushroom with some grilled pepper slices and onions. Place the other slice of bread or top of the roll, cheese side up, beside the potatoes and top with 2 or 3 fresh basil leaves. Serve immediately, allowing diners to assemble their own sandwiches.

Grill Times

Two-Sided Contact Grill: *Portobellos: 8 to 9 minutes / onions 7 to 10 minutes / peppers 6 to 8 minutes.*

Hibachi Grill, Combination Grill or Infusion Grill: *Portobellos: 15 to 16 minutes / onions 14 to 20 minutes / peppers 12 to 15 minutes. Turn the vegetables halfway through the grilling time. Grills with lids may be covered halfway through the grilling time. Infusion grills with lids may be covered for the entire grilling time.*

Basil Parmesan Oven Fries

Makes 4 (1 cup) servings

⅓ cup nonfat or low-fat garlic croutons

4 medium-sized baking potatoes, scrubbed, skin left on

1 large egg white or ¼ cup egg substitute

¼ cup finely chopped fresh basil or 2 tablespoons dried

2 teaspoons pressed garlic

1 teaspoon light salt or to taste

½ teaspoon freshly ground pepper

½ cup shredded Parmesan, Romano or Asiago cheese

Nonfat or canola cooking spray

1. Preheat oven to 450°F.

2. Crush the garlic croutons (see instructions on page 46).

3. Slice the potatoes into ½-inch thick wedges.

4. In a 4-cup mixing bowl using a fork or wire whisk, thoroughly mix the egg white, basil, garlic, salt and pepper. Add the potatoes, then the crushed croutons. Using your hands, toss the potatoes to evenly coat with all the ingredients.

5. Place the potatoes in a single layer on a nonstick baking sheet. Spray lightly with oil cooking spray. Bake 20 minutes until potatoes are crisp and golden brown. Turn potatoes over halfway through the baking time. You may have to break them apart with a spatula because the coating sometimes makes the pieces stick together.

6. Sprinkle with the shredded cheese, then bake an additional 5 minutes until cheese begins to melt. Remove the baking sheet from the oven. If not ready to serve, cover the baking sheet with aluminum foil to keep the potatoes warm.

Approximate Nutrients Per Serving of Entire Meal

Total Calories 678	Protein 33 g / 19%	Carbohydrate 101 g / 57%
Total Sugar 14 g	Fat Total 19 g / 24%	Saturated Fat 6 g / 9%
Cholesterol 23 mg	Sodium 1,082 mg	Fiber 16 g	Calcium 609 mg

Middle Eastern Veggie Wrap with Heavenly Hummus

"Hummus has two meanings in Arabic," explained my friend, Rafih Benjelloun, executive chef and owner of Imperial Fez, a Moroccan restaurant in Atlanta, Georgia. The word describes the chickpea bean as well as a dip made of pureed chickpeas, garlic, lemon juice and sesame seed paste (tahini). "In Arabic," said Rafih, "we say that chickpeas are the milk of Mother Earth. That's because the rich, life-giving nutrients they contain (protein, carbohydrates, calcium, iron and folate) can sustain infants unable to digest milk as well as can restore a person close to starvation." A symbol of abundance for centuries, chickpeas are an integral part of gracious Middle Eastern dining. "When we entertain," said Rafih, "we honor our guests with a feast for their eyes as well as for their palate and chickpeas are always on the menu in one form or another." Honor your family and guests by serving my abundant Middle Eastern Wraps as an open-faced display.

Menu Game Plan

Prep & Cooking Time: 40 minutes

- Preheat the grill.
- Prepare the vegetables.
- Make the Heavenly Hummus.
- Grill the vegetables.
- Assemble the wraps.

Cook's Notes

Eggplant is usually served as a vegetable, but it is really a fruit believed to have come to the West by way of India! The first plants to arrive in Europe bore bitter fruit that was thought to cause insanity. Eggplants come in shapes and sizes ranging from the diminutive round Thai eggplant, to thin, oblong Asian eggplant, to the large truncheon-shaped Western eggplant. Colors also vary from shades of green to purple and white. When purchasing eggplants for the grill, choose firm fruit with smooth, evenly colored skin. No matter which variety you grill, cut the pieces 3/4-inch to 1-inch thick. I suggest leaving the skin on when grilling eggplant because it helps hold the center together as it becomes soft.

Middle Eastern Wrap

Serves 4

2   small Asian egg plants or 1 small globe eggplant

2   small zucchini

1   small mild onion

2   small bell peppers, red, yellow or orange

Nonfat or olive oil cooking spray

Light salt, freshly ground pepper and cayenne pepper to taste

4   large 10- to 12-inch low-fat flour tortillas

8   Romaine lettuce leaves (inner leaves preferable)

2   cups Heavenly Hummus (see recipe page 261) or 2 cups of prepared hummus

1   small tomato, cut into thin half moons

¼   cup thinly sliced cucumber (preferably hothouse)

4   tablespoons crumbled Feta cheese

12 to 16 Kalamata or cured black olives, pitted

1. Preheat the grill to thehighest setting.

2. Prepare the vegetables. Cut the stem end off of the eggplant(s). If using Asian eggplants, slice them in half lengthwise. If using a globe eggplant, slice it into 1-inch thick rounds.

Cut the stem end off of the zucchinis and slice them in half lengthwise. Peel the onion and cut off the stem end. Slice the onion into 1-inch thick rounds.

Cut the bell peppers in half lengthwise and pull out the seeds and stem. Slice the pepper lengthwise into 1-inch thick strips.

Put the vegetables in a 3- or 4-quart mixing bowl, coat them with cooking spray and toss with the salt, pepper and cayenne to taste.

3. Grill the vegetables. If you have a small grill, grill the vegetables in batches. If you have a large grill, grill them all at the same time. Set the grilled vegetables on a plate, and don't worry about keeping them warm as they come off of the grill. This wrap tastes wonderful with room temperature vegetables.

Grill the vegetables according to the Grill Times opposite until they are tender, a little over half their size when raw, and have distinct grill marks. Do not overgrill. Vegetables contain a lot of water, particularly eggplants and zucchini. If they are grilled too long, the water will evaporate and leave the vegetables limp and looking as if they are about to disappear.

4. To serve, place 1 tortilla on each of 4 dinner plates. With the palm of your hand, press down on the spine of each of the Romaine lettuce leaves so they lie flat. Place 2 lettuce leaves down the center of the wrapper, leaving a few inches on the bottom free.

Spoon ⅓- to ½-cup of Heavenly Hummus on top of the lettuce. Artfully arrange equal amounts of the grilled vegetables, tomato, cucumber and olives on top of the Hummus.

Sprinkle 1 tablespoon of feta cheese over each wrap.

Serve the wraps open-face for a beautiful presentation. Instruct diners to wrap the bottom portion of the wrap up first, then fold the right side of the wrap over the left. The top of the wrap will be open as they pick up the wrap to eat.

Grill Times

Two-Sided Contact Grill: *Eggplants 6 to 8 minutes / zucchini 5 to 6 minutes/ onions 7 to 10 minutes / bell peppers 7 to 8 minutes.*

Hibachi Grill, Combination Grill or Infusion Grill: *Eggplants 12 to 15 minutes / zucchini 10 to 12 minutes / onions 14 to 20 minutes / bell peppers 12 to 15 minutes. Turn the vegetables halfway through the grilling time. Grills with lids may be covered halfway through the grilling time. Infusion grills with lids may be covered for the entire grilling time.*

Heavenly Hummus

Makes 10 (¼ cup) servings

1 15-ounce can low-sodium garbanzo beans, liquid drained

1 8¾-ounce can low-sodium garbanzo beans with liquid

¼ cup tahini made from roasted sesame seeds or ⅓ cup creamy natural peanut butter

2 to 3 teaspoons pressed garlic

1 teaspoon light salt

¼ cup lemon juice

½ teaspoon ground cumin

⅛ to ¼ teaspoon cayenne pepper

½ cup thinly sliced green onions

Make this delicious spread up to 1 week in advance.

1. In a food processor fitted with the metal chopping blade or in your blender puree the garbanzo beans, tahini, garlic, salt, lemon juice, cumin, and cayenne until smooth.
2. Add in the green onions and pulse to coarsely chop.
3. Scrape the Hummus into a 3-cup bowl or airtight container, cover and refrigerate until ready to use.

Substitutions:
If you don't wish to take the time to make your own hummus, purchase it pre-made in the cheese or ethnic section of your grocery store.

Approximate Nutrients Per Serving of Entire Meal

Total Calories 380	Protein 15 g / 15%	Carbohydrate 57 g / 57%
Total Sugar 8 g	Fat Total 12 g / 28%	Saturated Fat 3 g / 7%
Cholesterol 9 mg	Sodium 1012 mg	Fiber 20 g Calcium 168 mg

(Calculations include low-fat flour wrap, ⅓ cup Heavenly Hummus and 3 Kalamata olives.)

Arizona Sunrise Grilled Pepper and Roasted Corn Salad with Chipotle Pepper Dressing

My first visit to Arizona a couple of years ago shattered my greenhorn fantasy of dinner in the Wild West. For years I imagined sitting around a campfire watching purple twilight sweep distant mesas while devouring hearty portions of chuck wagon grub on tin plates…like the cowboys did in my favorite 1960's TV show "Rawhide." Boy was I off base! While interviewing chefs in Scottsdale, Arizona for an article on Southwest cuisine, I had the opportunity to sample some of the finest cuisine in the world. The cooking style in Scottsdale is being transformed from exclusively Southwest to international by a demanding clientele of over 6 million visitors a year. My Arizona Sunrise Salad is a tribute to the creative Scottsdale chefs I met who are reinventing Southwest cuisine using classical cooking techniques. Arranged like a French "salade composé" (composed salad), crispy grilled bell pepper and jicama spears become rays around a glorious yellow Arizona sun of roasted corn kernels. Drizzled with my chipotle pepper salad dressing, you'll experience Arizona heat even if you make this salad on a cold winter's day.

Menu Game Plan

Prep & Cooking Time: 45 minutes

- Preheat the grill.
- Steam the jicama (optional).
- Pan-roast the corn.
- Prepare the salads.
- Grill the pepper and jicama.
- Make the dressing while the vegetables are grilling.

Cook's Notes

The Aztec name for chipotle peppers, "chil-poct-li" or, literally, "pepper-smoked", is still used to this day around the world to describe these delicious, smoke-dried jalapeño peppers. Contemporary chefs use these chipotle peppers to impart their unique smoky-hot flavor to every type of recipe imaginable…sauces, marinades, dips, salad dressings, etc. You can purchase these dried, ground or canned in a spicy tomato sauce called "adobo". Leftover canned peppers and sauce may be frozen in an airtight container for up to 1 year.

Grilled Pepper and Roasted Corn Salad

Serves 4

1 small jicama

2 medium bell peppers, red, yellow or orange

6 cups mixed salad greens or 1 10-ounce bag pre-washed lettuce

2 cups frozen petite corn

1 cup shredded or thinly sliced carrots

1 cup grated sharp low-fat cheddar cheese

½ cup thinly sliced green onion

½ cup roasted unsalted pumpkinseeds

Nonfat or canola oil cooking spray

Light salt and pepper to taste

8 to 12 tablespoons Chipotle Dressing (see recipe on page 262)

Low-fat tortilla chips

1. **Preheat the grill** to the highest setting.

2. **Precook to tenderize the jicama for the grill.** (Optional step.) Peel the jicama then cut it into 1 x ½ x 3-inch pieces.

On the stovetop, put a steamer basket into a 3- to 4- quart pot with a tight fitting lid. Fill with water to cover the bottom of the pot but not rising above the bottom of the basket. Cover and bring to a boil over high heat. Add the jicama and steam, covered, about 5 to 7 minutes, or until slightly tender. Put jicama in a strainer to drain. Let rest about 5 to 10 minutes until cool enough to handle. You can also grill the jicama raw for a super crispy version.

3. **Pan-roast the corn kernels** while the jicama is steaming. Defrost the corn in a strainer under cool running water. Drain well.

In a dry 10- or 11-inch nonstick skillet over high heat, constantly stir the corn kernels until lightly browned. Remove the pan from the heat and allow to cool, about 5 to 7 minutes.

4. **Prepare the bell peppers.** Cut the peppers in half and remove the seeds and stem. Slice each half lengthwise into 1-inch thick strips.

5. **Grill the bell peppers and jicama.** Put the peppers and jicama in a large bowl and coat them with cooking spray and light salt and pepper to taste as you toss them.

Grill the jicama and peppers according to the Grill Times on page 262 until light grill marks form. Both vegetables should be cooked through yet tender-crisp. Jicama contains a lot of water so the grill marks will be light.

6. **To serve,** place equal amounts of the lettuce on 4 dinner plates to form a bed. Put equal amounts of the roasted corn on top of the lettuce in the center of the plate to form a 2- to 3-inch wide mound. Sprinkle equal amounts of the carrots around the corn. Sprinkle the shredded Cheddar cheese around the carrots. Alternate the grilled peppers with the grilled jicama on top of the cheese and carrots around the corn like spokes of a wheel. Sprinkle with the onion and pumpkinseeds. Drizzle with 2 to 3 tablespoons of Chipotle Dressing and serve immediately with tortilla chips.

Grill Times

Two-Sided Contact Grill: *Peppers and jicama 7 to 10 minutes.*

Hibachi Grill, Combination Grill or Infusion Grill: *Peppers and jicama 14 to 20 minutes. Turn the vegetables halfway through the grilling time. Grills with lids may be covered halfway through the grilling time. Infusion grills with lids may be covered for the entire grilling time.*

Chipotle Dressing

Makes 8 (2 tablespoon) servings

¼ cup seasoned red wine vinegar

½ cup nonfat or low-fat mayonnaise

½ cup nonfat or low-fat sour cream

½ to 1 teaspoon canned chipotle pepper in adobo sauce

Light salt and freshly ground pepper to taste

In a blender, blend the vinegar, mayonnaise, sour cream and chipotle pepper until smooth. Season with salt and pepper to taste. Refrigerate in an airtight container for up to 2 weeks.

Substitutions:
Instead of chipotle peppers substitute equal amounts of canned diced green chili peppers or canned diced jalapeño pepper plus a few drops of liquid smoke to taste. You can also substitute 1 to 2 teaspoons of chili powder plus a pinch of cayenne and a few drops of liquid smoke to taste.

Mix & Match

Serve this salad with any of the main dishes in the following menus: Tortilla-crusted Burgers, page 69; Cowboy Kebabs, page 147; Oasis Pitas Suffed with Aromatic Turkey Tenderloin, page 189; Adobo Tofu Steaks, page 267.

Approximate Nutrients Per Serving of Entire Meal

Total Calories 312	Protein 22 g / 27%	Carbohydrate 45 g / 55%	
Total Sugar 11 g	Fat Total 7 g / 18%	Saturated Fat 3 g / 8%	
Cholesterol 13 mg	Sodium 503 mg	Fiber 8 g	Calcium 333 mg

(Calculated with low-fat cheddar cheese and 2 tablespoons of Chipotle Dressing made with nonfat mayonnaise and nonfat sour cream.)

Stinson Beach Grilled Veggie Salad with Sundried Tomato Balsamic Dressing

Stinson Beach is located about an hour north of San Francisco. My husband and I enjoy walking along this rejuvenating 7-mile stretch of sand several times a month. Afterward, our feet tired but our minds refreshed, we often have dinner at a tiny café that offers a delicious salad like this one.

This salad can be made ahead. The dressing will keep up to a month if stored in an airtight container in the refrigerator. You can grill the vegetables up to 24 hours in advance if you store them covered in the refrigerator.

Menu Game Plan

Prep & Cooking Time: 45 minutes

- Preheat the grill.
- Preheat the oven (if toasting the nuts).
- Steam the baby artichokes (optional).
- Marinate the vegetables.
- Make the salad dressing.
- Toast the nuts.
- Prepare the lettuce and fresh vegetable bed.
- Grill the vegetables.
- Assemble the salad.

Cook's Notes

Notes

Balsamic Vinegar: This mellow sweet vinegar, whose origins date back to early eleventh century Italy, varies in flavor and in price according to how it is made. There are two types of balsamic vinegar: traditional balsamic vinegar (aceto balsamico tradizionale), the most expensive, and industrial (industriale), less costly. Traditional balsamic vinegar cannot contain caramel or wine vinegar and must be made within either the Modena or Reggio Emilia provinces of Northern Italy. It is produced using an ancient process of aging and mellowing wine in a series of casks made of different woods. Industrial balsamic vinegar is a blend of high-quality wine vinegar, young, traditionally made balsamic vinegar and caramel.

Grilled Vegetable Salad

Serves 4

Balsamic Marinade

3   tablespoons walnut oil or
     extra-virgin olive oil

¼   cup balsamic vinegar

1   teaspoon pressed garlic

½   teaspoon light salt

Grilled Vegetables

4   baby artichokes (optional
     when not in season)

½   cup very hot tap water

1   medium zucchini

2   portobello mushrooms,
     about ½ pound each

3   small bell peppers, red,
     yellow, orange

2   large or 3 medium carrots

1   small bulb fennel

Salad

6   to 8 cups mixed field greens

½   cup pecan or walnut halves

¼   cup thinly sliced green
     onions

4   ounces goat cheese

Sundried Tomato Balsamic
     Dressing (see recipe
     on page 266)

1. **Preheat the grill** to the highest setting.

2. **Preheat the oven to 325°F.**

3. **Steam the baby artichokes** (optional step). Trim off any discolored ends of the artichoke stems, leaving about an inch of stem on each artichoke. Put a steamer basket into a 2 or 3-quart pot with a tight fitting lid. Fill with water to cover the bottom of the pot but not rising above the bottom of the basket. Cover and bring to a boil over high heat. Add the artichokes and steam, covered, about 6 to 7 minutes, or until tender. Remove artichokes with tongs and put on a rack to cool and drain.

4. **Make the marinade.** Whisk all the marinade ingredients in a 1-cup measure. Reserve 3 tablespoons of the marinade for artichokes.

5. **Marinate the vegetables.** Slice the zucchini, mushrooms and peppers into 1-inch thick pieces. Cut the carrots into 2- or 3-inch long, ½-inch thick pieces. Trim the stem and fluffy leaves off of the fennel and slice it into quarters. Place the vegetables in a gallon zippered freezer bag or a 4-quart airtight container. Pour the marinade over the vegetables and seal the bag or container, then shake gently to cover all vegetable surfaces with the marinade. Set aside for 10 minutes or up to 1 hour in the refrigerator.

6. **Toast the pecans or walnuts** (optional step). Place the nuts on a nonstick baking sheet and bake in preheated oven for 4 minutes until lightly browned. When done, put pan on a cooling rack and cool nuts to room temperature

7. **Grill the artichokes.** Cut each cooled artichoke in half. Use a basting brush to coat each artichoke with the reserved marinade, and then grill according to the Grill Times opposite. When done, set grilled artichokes aside on a plate to cool to room temperature.

8. **Grill the remaining vegetables** according to the Grill Times and methods opposite. When they are done, either put them on the prepared salad, or set them aside on a plate to cool to room temperature before storing in the refrigerator.

9. **To serve,** arrange equal amounts of the mixed field greens on 4 dinner plates. When the vegetables are grilled, arrange them on top of the greens. Sprinkle each salad with equal amounts of green onions and toasted nuts. Cut the goat cheese into 8 equal pieces. Place 2 pieces on each salad. Drizzle with 2 to 3 tablespoons of the dressing and serve immediately.

Two-Sided Contact Grill: Artichokes 2 1/2 minutes / zucchini, mushrooms, bell peppers, carrots and fennel 6 to 7 minutes.

Hibachi Grill, Combination Grill or Infusion Grill: Artichokes 5 minutes / zucchinis, mushrooms, peppers, carrots and fennel 12 to 14 minutes. Turn all vegetables halfway through the grilling time. Grills with lids may be covered halfway through the grilling time. Infusion grills with lids may be covered for the entire grilling time.

Infusion Grill Notes: For a more intense flavor, mix 1/2 cup balsamic vinegar with 1 tablespoon pressed garlic and pour it into infusion cup before preheating grill.

Substitutions:
If baby artichokes are unavailable, use water-packed canned artichokes and do not grill them.
Instead of soft goat cheese, substitute equal amounts of feta, or blue cheese.

Variation:
Beefy Stinson Beach Salad: Marinate 1 1/4 pounds skirt steak in 1/4 cup of the marinade. Grill the meat after you finish grilling all of the vegetables, cut across the grain into 1/2-inch strips and add to the salad.

Sundried Tomato Balsamic Dressing

Makes about 10 (2 tablespoon) servings

½ cup walnut oil or extra-virgin olive oil

¼ cup balsamic vinegar

¼ cup lemon juice

½ teaspoon pressed garlic

1½ teaspoons sugar

½ teaspoon light salt

2 tablespoons chopped fresh basil or 1 tablespoon dried

3 tablespoons chopped oil packed sundried tomatoes

This dressing will keep up to 2 weeks if refrigerated in an air-tight container.

Put all the ingredients in the blender or food processor and blend until smooth. Pour the dressing into a serving pitcher or container and set aside until serving time.

Nutrition Notes:

Nutritionally this is one of the higher fat salads in this book. But the fat, most of which comes from the nuts and oil, is mostly monounsaturated and polyunsaturated, the good-for you fats that have been proven to help fight heart disease. The day you plan to make this salad, balance your fat calories by eating lower fat foods for the rest of your meals.

Approximate Nutrients Per Serving of Entire Meal

Total Calories 447	Protein 16 g / 13%	Carbohydrate 45 g / 37%	
Total Sugar 16 g	Fat 26 g / 49%	Saturated Fat 6 g / 11%	
Cholesterol 13 mg	Sodium 662 mg	Fiber 14 g	Calcium 199 mg

Adobo Tofu Steaks and Grilled Polenta with Avocado and Orange Salsa

In Spanish, "adobar" means to season or pickle. The Spanish explorers introduced adobo sauce to their New World conquests as a means of preserving meat. Originally a mixture of salt and vinegar, each area that the explorers occupied adapted the recipe using local ingredients. In the Caribbean, adobo sauce is flavored with sour orange juice, garlic, cumin and/or vinegar and oregano. In the Philippines, adobo sauce might include coconut milk, annato seed, garlic and vinegar. My favorite is the Mexican version seasoned with pureed smoky chipotle chilies , garlic, oregano, cinnamon and orange juice. Although this marinade is traditionally used for meat, poultry or shellfish, I found that it is just right for turning bland tofu into a spicy delight. Dense pieces of grilled polenta, reminiscent of the cornmeal fillings used in Mexican Tamales, make a perfect partner for the adobo-flavored tofu. For added flavor, rub the polenta with a bit of the adobo sauce just before putting it on the grill. The delicious Avocado and Orange Salsa not only cools the fire of the adobo sauce but turns this meal into a colorful fiesta.

Menu Game Plan

Prep & Cooking Time: 45 to 50 minutes

- Preheat the grill.
- Make the Adobo Marinade and marinate the tofu.
- Make the salsa.
- Grill the polenta and tofu.

Cook's Notes

Notes

Polenta was originally a Roman porridge that was made from barley and millet. In fact, when the ancient Romans said polenta they meant pearl barley. Corn made its way from the New World to Northern Italy shortly after 1500, but Italians didn't begin using it for polenta until the 18th century. In order to put this polenta on the table in record time, I suggest using precooked polenta. Polenta from scratch has to be made several hours before grilling. If it has not been allowed to cool sufficiently, it falls apart on the grill. When I want to grill homemade polenta, I usually prepare it in the microwave 24 to 48 hours in advance then refrigerate it. I have found that refrigerator-cold polenta is easier to cut and keeps its shape better during grilling.

Adobo Tofu Steaks and Grilled Polenta

Serves 4

Tofu

1   pound extra-firm tofu

1   16-ounce log ready-to-eat plain polenta

Nonfat or canola oil cooking spray

Adobo Marinade

3   tablespoons cider vinegar

3   tablespoons orange juice concentrate

1   whole canned chipotle chili with sauce

1   tablespoon pressed garlic

2   tablespoons tomato paste

1/4   teaspoon ground cinnamon

1/4   teaspoon oregano

1/4   teaspoon black pepper

1/8   teaspoon ground cumin

1/2   teaspoon light salt

Low-fat or nonfat sour cream

1. **Preheat the grill** to the highest setting.

2. **Make the marinade.** In a blender puree the cider vinegar, orange juice concentrate, chipotle chili, garlic, tomato paste, cinnamon, oregano, pepper, cumin, and salt.

3. **Marinate the tofu.** Slice the tofu into 8 (1/2-inch) thick steaks. Pour the marinade into a shallow dish or shallow, airtight container large enough to accommodate all of the tofu pieces in 1 layer. Place the tofu in the marinade and turn it so all sides are coated with the marinade. Cover tightly and refrigerate for 20 minutes or up to 48 hours.

4. **Grill the polenta and tofu.** On small surface grills, grill the polenta first, and then immediately grill tofu steaks. As the polenta comes off of the grill, keep it warm until serving time on a serving platter covered with aluminum foil.

   If your grill is large enough to hold the polenta and tofu at the same time, grill both simultaneously.

   Spray each slice of polenta and each tofu steak lightly on both sides with cooking spray. Place on the grill and cook according to the Grill Times below until grill marks appear, and the polenta and tofu are heated through.

5. **To serve,** put 2 tofu steaks and 2 pieces of polenta on each of 4 dinner plates. Spoon 1/4- to 1/2-cup salsa over the tofu, then garnish with a dollop of sour cream and a sprig of fresh cilantro. Serve immediately.

Grill Times

Two-Sided Contact Grill: Polenta and tofu 6 to 7 minutes.

Hibachi Grill, Combination Grill or Infusion Grill: Polenta and tofu 12 to 14 minutes. Turn the polenta and tofu halfway through the grilling time. Do not grill covered. This will prevent the outside of the tofu from becoming crispy. Tofu contains a lot of water, which will not evaporate if cooked in a covered, moist environment.

Mix & Match

Serve the Adobo Tofu Steaks with any of the side dishes: Black Bean Salsa Salad, page 71; Corny Cheddar Cheese Grits, page 125; Rootin' Tootin' Texas Tabouli, page 149.

Avocado and Orange Salsa

Makes 6 (½ cup) servings

1 cup diced avocado

1 cup diced navel orange

1 cup seeded, diced ripe tomatoes

⅓ cup thinly sliced green onion

⅓ cup finely chopped fresh cilantro

¼ cup canned diced green chili pepper or jalapeño pepper

1 teaspoon sugar

3 tablespoons fresh lime juice

This recipe can be made up to 3 days in advance.

1. In a 2-quart mixing bowl, using a rubber spatula, mix the avocado, orange, tomatoes, green onion, cilantro and chili peppers.
2. In a 1 cup bowl or measure, mix the sugar and lime juice with a fork until sugar is dissolved.
3. Pour the lime mixture over the salsa and fold in with the spatula. Allow to chill in the refrigerator for at least 20 minutes before serving.

Super Easy Microwave Polenta

Makes 4 (1 cup) servings

4¾ cups or 2 16-ounce cans fat-free chicken stock

1¼ cups white or yellow coarse polenta grind cornmeal

½ teaspoon garlic powder or 1 teaspoon pressed garlic

½ teaspoon light salt (optional)

Nonfat or canola oil cooking spray

This recipe can be made ahead and frozen in airtight containers for up to 2 months. Defrost overnight in the refrigerator, or in the microwave for 10 minutes on low (30% power), before grilling or, if you don't want to grill it, reheat for 4 to 6 minutes on high (100% power).

1. Pour the broth into a 2-quart microwavable pot, and microwave, covered, 8 to 10 minutes on high (100% power) or until boiling.
2. Stir the cornmeal into the broth and microwave, uncovered, 18 to 20 minutes on high (100% power), stirring every 5 or 6 minutes until all the cornmeal is hydrated and the mixture is very thick. If the polenta becomes too dry, stir in ¼ cup hot water at a time. Microwave for 1 to 4 minutes after each addition.
3. Liberally spray the inside surfaces of a 1- or 1½-quart loaf pan with cooking spray. Use a rubber spatula to scrape the cooked polenta into the pan then smooth the surface of the polenta to make it even. Lightly cover the pan with plastic wrap to keep the polenta moist yet let the steam escape. Set aside on the counter to cool to room temperature, 45 minutes to 1 hour.
4. Tightly cover the dish, then chill the polenta in the refrigerator for 2 to 48 hours. To remove the polenta from the dish, hold a plate firmly over the dish and turn over to release the polenta. Cut into 1-inch thick pieces and spray all surfaces lightly with cooking spray before placing on the grill. Follow the grilling instructions on page 276.

Approximate Nutrients Per Serving of Entire Meal

Total Calories 270	Protein 13 g / 19%	Carbohydrate 37 g / 52%
Total Sugar 13 g	Fat Total 9 g / 29%	Saturated Fat 1 g / 4%
Cholesterol 0 mg	Sodium 547 mg	Fiber 5 g Calcium 215 mg

(Calculated with 4 ounces tofu, 4 ounces polenta and ½ cup of Avocado and Orange Salsa.)

Stuffed Crunchy Pes-To-Fu

"Pesto" literally means pounded in Italian. But for Italian cooks, pesto means any food that is pounded to a paste with a mortar and pestle. I learned to make basil pesto during a summer music program I attended in Florence which was held in a restored fourteenth-century villa in Fiesole, a small hilltop town just outside of Florence. Instead of spending afternoons studying my latest aria, I would study what the villa's cook was preparing for dinner. One afternoon I found her standing at a large wooden table, a giant stone mortar in front of her. With movements choreographed by years of practice, she alternately added pine nuts, walnuts, big bunches of fresh basil, garlic cloves, olive oil and grated Parmesan cheese while twirling the pestle to grind everything into a smooth paste. "I am making pesto for the pasta tonight," she explained, giving me a small spoonful on a piece of crusty bread to taste. As I rolled the aromatic concoction around my tongue, I closed my eyes and hummed in gustatory ecstasy. Delighted, the cook laughed and told me that I could have some more if I would sing a real aria for her.

Although no true Italian cook would serve tofu with pasta al pesto, I couldn't resist adding it to this menu. My crusty grilled tofu, infused with an orange flavored marinade and filled with mozzarella cheese and sundried tomatoes, makes a perfect nontraditional accompaniment for this classic pasta dish.

Menu Game Plan

Prep & Cooking Time: 50 to 60 minutes

- Preheat the grill.
- Marinate the tofu.
- Make the pesto.
- Make crushed croutons.
- Cook the pasta.
- Stuff the tofu while the pasta is cooking.
- Mix the pesto with the cooked pasta.
- Grill the stuffed tofu and bell peppers.

Cook's Notes

Notes

In Italy, basil is a sign of love. It was believed that when a man gave a woman a sprig of basil, she would fall in love with him and never leave his side. The Greeks honored this highly fragrant herb with the name "basilikon" meaning "royal". Used profusely in Mediterranean, as well as Thai, Laotian, and Vietnamese cuisines, basil is available in over 60 varieties. The leaves may be purple, red, or green and the taste varies according to the variety with hints of cinnamon, lemon, orange, chocolate, anise, thyme or clove. Store fresh basil for up to 3 days in the refrigerator wrapped in paper towel in an airtight bag or container. Wash it just before using.

Stuffed Crunchy Tofu and Grilled Peppers

Serves 4

Tofu

1   pound extra firm tofu (about 4 x 3 x 2-inch) cut into 4 pieces (about 3 x 2 x 1-inch)

2   medium bell peppers, red, yellow or orange

Orange Pepper Marinade

½   cup frozen orange juice concentrate, thawed

1   tablespoon pressed garlic

1   teaspoon lemon pepper

½   teaspoon light salt

Sundried Tomato Stuffing

2   tablespoons chopped, oil-packed sundried tomatoes

1   tablespoon chopped basil,

2   ounces low-fat mozzarella, shredded

1. Preheat the grill. If you have a grill with a variable temperature control, set it to medium-high (1 or 2 steps below high) or about 350° to 400°F.

2. Marinate the tofu. Cut the tofu into 4 equal pieces about 3 x 2 x 1-inches. Express the excess liquid according to instructions on page 276. With a small sharp knife, slit a 2-inch long (1½-inch deep) pocket down the middle of 1 of the 3-inch long sides. Leave about ½ inch of solid tofu on each side of the slit. In a shallow dish or shallow airtight container large enough to accommodate all of the tofu pieces in 1 layer, use a fork to thoroughly mix the orange juice concentrate, garlic, lemon pepper, and salt. Place the tofu in the marinade and turn it so all sides are coated. Cover tightly and refrigerate for 20 minutes or up to 48 hours.

3. Make the filling and stuff the tofu. In a food processor fitted with the metal chopping blade or in a blender, combine the sundried tomatoes, basil and mozzarella until finely chopped.

Remove the tofu from the marinade and hold it in 1 hand, slit side up. Lightly press the outer edges of the tofu to open the slit about ¼-inch.

Using a small spoon, gently stuff about 1 tablespoon of the stuffing into the pocket. Place stuffed tofu on a clean plate. Repeat with the remaining pieces of tofu.

Note: This is a messy process. Don't panic if the tofu slightly breaks open as you stuff it. Just gently press it together and place it on the plate. As it grills, the melted cheese filling combined with the crispy egg-based coating will keep the tofu in 1 piece.

4. Prepare the bell peppers. Cut the peppers in half lengthwise and remove the seeds and stems. Slice each half lengthwise into 1-inch thick strips.

5. Grill the bell peppers. Put the peppers in a large bowl and coat them with cooking spray, light salt and pepper to taste as you toss them.

Grill the peppers according to the Grill Times opposite until dark grill marks appear on the peppers and they are cooked

Crouton Crust

1 cup low-fat or nonfat garlic croutons

½ cup egg substitute or 2 large eggs, whisked

¼ cup cornstarch

Nonfat or olive oil cooking spray

1 recipe Creamy Basil Pesto Pasta (see recipe page 274)

Fresh basil leaves

through yet tender-crisp. Keep the grilled peppers warm on a covered platter until serving time.

6. Coat the tofu with the crust and grill it. Crush the garlic croutons following one of the methods on page 46.

Put the crushed croutons in a shallow glass dish and place it next to the grill. In a 1-cup bowl or measure, whisk the egg substitute or whole eggs with the cornstarch. Pour it in a shallow glass dish and place that next to the plate containing the crushed croutons.

Place the can of cooking spray nearby but not directly next to the hot grill. Dip each piece of stuffed tofu into the egg mixture to coat all sides and then into the crushed croutons to coat all sides.

Spray both large sides of the tofu with the cooking spray and place on the grill. Grill according to the times and methods below until the filling melts and the outer crust becomes crunchy.

7. To serve, put equal amounts of pasta on 4 dinner plates. Put 1 piece of tofu on top of the pasta and surround it with grilled bell peppers. Garnish with fresh basil leaves and serve immediately.

Grill Times

Two-Sided Contact Grill: Peppers 7 to 10 minutes / tofu 7 to 8 minutes

Hibachi Grill, Combination Grill or Infusion Grill: Peppers 14 to 20 minutes / tofu 14 to 16 minutes. Turn the peppers and tofu halfway through the grilling time. Do not grill covered. This will prevent the outer coating of the tofu from becoming crispy. Tofu contains a lot of water, which will not evaporate if cooked in a covered, moist environment.

Variations

If you are in a hurry, the tofu tastes delicious over ¾ pound of pasta mixed with your favorite tomato based low-fat pasta sauce. Made this way, the menu will be less caloric, about 632 calories per serving.

Mix & Match

Serve the Stuffed Crunchy Tofu with any of these side dishes: Pasta of the Gods Salad, page 210; Quick Spinach Sauté, page 114; Portobello Mushrooms with Lemon Cream Cappellini, page 178.

 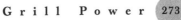

Creamy Basil Pesto Pasta

Makes 4 (1 cup) servings

¾ pound dried pasta, any shape such as fusilli, elbows, shells, bows

½ cup low-fat or nonfat sour cream

1 cup fresh basil

¼ cup fresh parsley, packed

¼ cup finely chopped green onion

¼ cup shredded Parmesan cheese

3 tablespoons each walnut pieces, pine nuts and sliced almonds

½ teaspoon to 1 tablespoon pressed garlic

½ teaspoon light salt or to taste

Freshly ground pepper to taste

1. Bring 10 cups of water to a boil in a 4- to 5-quart pot. Put the noodles into the boiling water. The water will stop boiling. When it comes back to a boil, start timing and cook the noodles for 10 to 12 minutes until al dente (meaning "to the teeth" in Italian, or cooked but slightly chewy).

2. While the pasta is cooking, make the pesto. In a food processor fitted with the metal chopping blade or in a blender, puree the sour cream, basil, parsley, green onion, Parmesan cheese, walnuts, pine nuts, sliced almonds garlic, salt and pepper.

3. Scrape the pesto into the bottom of a 3-or 4-quart mixing bowl. Just before the pasta is done, whisk 1 to 2 tablespoons of the pasta cooking water into the pesto to heat it.

4. When the pasta is done, drain well in colander. Put the pasta on top of the pesto. Using a large rubber spatula, fold the pesto into the hot pasta until evenly distributed. Serve immediately.

Substitutions

If you don't want to use the variety of nuts called for in this recipe, use just pine nuts.

For a more traditional, higher fat pesto, substitute ¼ cup extra-virgin olive oil plus ¼ cup salted butter for the sour cream.

If you don't feel like making my pesto sauce, substitute a 7-ounce container (about ¾ cup) of premade reduced-fat pesto mixed with ½ cup low-fat or nonfat sour cream.

Approximate Nutrients Per Serving of Entire Meal

Total Calories 717	Protein 37 g / 20%	Carbohydrate 96 g / 52%
Total Sugar 22 g	Fat Total 22 g / 27%	Saturated Fat 5 g / 6%
Cholesterol 11 mg	Sodium 581 mg	Fiber 7 g Calcium 459 mg

Taj Mahal Tofu Steaks with Pineapple Express Rice and Cucumber Raita Salad

My peanut-crusted Taj Mahal Tofu Steaks transform "the white, tasteless stuff" into a crunchy delight worthy of a place on a Raja's menu. The thick, curry flavored peanut crust fools your palate with its deep-fried flavor. Instead of cooking it in hot fat, though, the high heat of the electric grill bonds the seasoned cornstarch, egg, peanut and breadcrumb mixture to the tofu. Choose a sweet-hot mango chutney to enhance the flavor of the spicy crust. Served with cooling Cucumber Raita Salad and a heaping helping of Pineapple Express Rice, this menu will satisfy even the most ardent "I love to hate tofu" people.

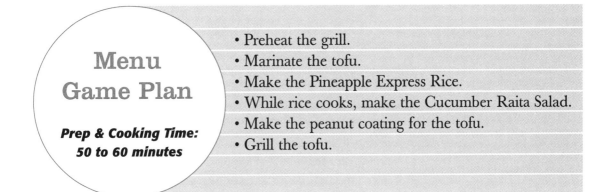

Menu Game Plan

Prep & Cooking Time: 50 to 60 minutes

- Preheat the grill.
- Marinate the tofu.
- Make the Pineapple Express Rice.
- While rice cooks, make the Cucumber Raita Salad.
- Make the peanut coating for the tofu.
- Grill the tofu.

Cook's Notes

Notes

Chutney is used both as a condiment and a sauce in traditional Indian cuisine. Its characteristic hot, sweet and sour taste comes from its exotic ingredients. The base, usually a combination of fresh and dried fruits or vegetables, is seasoned with herbs, spices, chili peppers, sugar and sometimes nuts, seeds, and vinegar. Although most of us are familiar with the bottled, jam-like chutneys, there are an infinite variety of fresh chutney recipes that range in texture from smooth to chunky. Each Indian cook has their own repertoire, based on seasonal fruits and vegetables, which they prepare daily. To save time, I suggest using the jamlike kind, but broaden your horizons by trying some of the more unusual flavors now available such as lime chutney.

Tofu Steaks

Serves 4

Tofu

1 pound firm or extra-firm tofu

Marinade

3 tablespoons plain yogurt

2 egg whites or ¼ cup egg substitute

2 tablespoons finely minced gingerroot

2 tablespoons pressed garlic

½ teaspoon granulated sugar

2 teaspoons curry powder

½ teaspoon salt

½ cup cornstarch

Coating

⅔ cup dry roasted peanuts

½ cup dry breadcrumbs

1 jar chutney, mango or your favorite flavor

Nonfat or canola oil cooking spray

Fresh or canned mango, peach, nectarine, or papaya slices

Fresh mint leaves

1. Preheat the grill. If you have a grill with a variable temperature control, set it to medium-high (1 or 2 steps below high) or to about 350° to 400°F.

2. Marinate the tofu. Cut the tofu into 8 (about ½-inch thick) "steaks" Put 3 layers of paper towel in a shallow pan large enough to accommodate the tofu in one layer and lay the tofu on the paper towel. Put 3 layers of paper towel over the tofu and gently press with the palm of your hand to express some of the water in the tofu. If the towel becomes too wet, discard it and use another paper towel. Let the tofu rest, covered with the paper towel, as you make the marinade. In a 2-cup bowl, whisk the yogurt, egg whites, ginger, garlic, sugar, curry powder, salt and cornstarch to make a thick paste. Carefully remove the tofu and paper towels from the pan. Return the tofu to the pan in a single layer. Using a spatula, scrape the paste onto the tofu. With your fingers, smear the paste over all sides of the tofu. Cover tightly with plastic wrap and refrigerate for 20 minutes or up to 48 hours.

3. Make the breadcrumb and peanut crust. Using a food processor fitted with a metal chopping blade or a blender, chop the peanuts until medium fine. Be careful not to overprocess, or they will start to form peanut butter. Mix the peanuts in a shallow dish with the breadcrumbs and place next to the grill.

4. Coat the tofu with the crust and grill it. Put the dish containing the marinated tofu next to the plate containing the crushed peanuts. Place the can of cooking spray nearby but not directly next to the hot grill. As you gently lift each piece of tofu from the marinating pan, the paste may come off of the bottom side of the tofu. As you turn it over smear it back on before dipping each piece of tofu into the peanut mixture to coat all sides. Spray both large sides of the tofu with cooking spray and place on the grill. Grill according to the times and method opposite until the outer crust becomes crunchy.

5. To serve, put equal amounts of rice in the middle of each plate. Put 2 Taj Mahal Tofu Steaks on either side of the rice. Surround the rice with some slices of mango, chutney, and the Cucumber Raita.

Variation:
If you would like to serve this peanut-crusted tofu with a sauce, try it with the Lemony Peanut Sauce (page 146).

Two-Sided Contact Grill: *7 to 8 minutes.*

Hibachi Grill, Combination Grill or Infusion Grill: *14 to 16 minutes. Turn the tofu halfway through the grilling time. Do not grill covered. This will prevent the outer coating from becoming crispy. Tofu contains a lot of water, which will not evaporate if cooked in a covered, moist environment.*

Substitutions:
The coating for the tofu is moderately spicy to appeal to a wide range of tastes. If you want more heat, use 1 tablespoon of curry powder. You can also add a dash of ground cayenne and 1/8 teaspoon ground cardamom if you want even more heat and flavor.
For the peanuts substitute equal amounts of ground pistachios, cashews, blanched almonds or macadamia nuts.

Pineapple Express Rice

Makes 4 (1 1/3 cup) servings

1 1/4 cups white long grain rice

2 1/4 cups water

1 tablespoon light butter (optional)

Light salt to taste

1 20-ounce can pineapple chunks or tidbits in natural juice

1/3 cup thinly sliced green onions

To compliment the stronger flavors of the peanut crusted tofu and the raita, I chose to season this basic rice and pineapple recipe lightly—with only butter, salt and green onions. It can be made up to 48 hours in advance of serving and frozen in an airtight container or freezer bag for up to 2 months. Defrost and reheat in the microwave to serve.

1. In a 2- or 3-quart pot with a tight fitting lid, bring the water, butter and salt to a rolling boil over high heat. Stir in the rice, bring back to a rolling boil, then cover and immediately reduce the heat to low. Simmer until all the liquid is absorbed, about 20 minutes.
2. While the rice is cooking, put the pineapple in a medium strainer over a 3 or 4 cup bowl to drain the juice. Use the juice for another recipe or to drink.
3. When the rice is done, remove the pot from the heat, uncover and quickly put the drained pineapple and green onion on top of the rice. Re-cover immediately and let stand for 10 minutes. Just before serving, use a rubber spatula to fold the pineapple and green onions evenly into the rice. To keep the rice warm until serving time, do not lift the lid. If the rice becomes too cool, transfer it into a microwavable casserole and reheat, covered, in the microwave for 2 to 4 minutes on high (100% power).

Mix & Match

Pineapple Express Rice also tastes great with the following main dishes and sauces: MacNut Crab Cake Salad, page 223; Thai Me a River Tofu Satays with Curried Coconut Basil Sauce, page 279; How's Bayou? Louisiana Shrimp and Orange Brochettes, page 235.

Cucumber Raita

Makes 8 (¼ cup) servings

1   cup plain low-fat yogurt

2   tablespoons finely chopped fresh mint or 1 tablespoon dried

¼   teaspoon ground cumin seed

⅛   teaspoon cayenne pepper

½   teaspoon salt

Freshly ground pepper to taste

⅓   cup thinly sliced green onion

½   cucumber (preferably hothouse)

This refreshing salad can be made up to 24 hours in advance of serving if refrigerated in an airtight container. It can also be served as a side dish to grilled meat, poultry or fish.

1. In a 2-cup bowl, mix the yogurt, mint, cumin, cayenne, salt, pepper to taste and green onion with a fork.
2. For hothouse cucumbers: These cucumbers do not require peeling or seeding. Dice the cucumber into small pieces, or grate it, either manually or using your food processor fitted with the medium grating disk.

For regular cucumbers: First peel the cucumber, then cut it in half lengthwise. Using a small spoon, scoop out the seeds, then either dice it into small pieces, or grate it, manually or using your food processor fitted with the medium grating disk.
3. Mix prepared cucumber into the yogurt sauce. Cover tightly and refrigerate until ready to serve.

Approximate Nutrients Per Serving of Entire Meal

Total Calories 695	Protein 34 g (19%)	Carbohydrate 106 g (59%)
Total Sugar 18 g	Fat Total 17 g (22%)	Saturated Fat 4 g (5%)
Cholesterol 6 mg	Sodium 742 mg	Fiber 8 g Calcium 269 mg

Thai Me a River Satays with Curried Coconut Basil Sauce over Jasmine Rice

One taste of the luscious Curried Coconut Basil Sauce that adorns this menu transports me back to my first trip to Bangkok, Thailand in 1970. I was 16 years old and touring the city with my 72-year-old Grandmother Lil and my 11-year-old sister, Emilie. Bangkok was once known as the Venice of the East because the city revolves around the massive Chao Phraya River, which runs through its center. Our guide convinced us that the best way to tour the city was on the water in a long tail boat. To make sure our tour included as many sites along the river as possible, he maneuvered our small craft at breakneck speed from golden roofed palace to glittering temple. At lunchtime, Grandma Lil simply had had enough. It was hot and sticky. Sensing her dissatisfaction, our guide slowed the boat in front of a very plain looking building reassuring us that it was one of the most beautiful restaurants in the area. Skeptical, we climbed onto the restaurant's rickety dock, walked into its foyer and were momentarily speechless. We had escaped the daily bustle of the river to a garden paradise where the enticing aroma of exotic food competed with the perfume of the flowers. Sitting at one of the tables hidden among the peaceful large-shade trees, we sipped ice tea and feasted on a menu much like this one. Once you taste the jade green sauce, you may make this menu your escape to paradise, too.

Menu Game Plan

Prep & Cooking Time: 50 to 60 minutes

- Preheat the grill.
- Marinate the tofu.
- Make the Jasmine Rice.
- Make the Curried Coconut Basil sauce.
- Prepare the skewers.
- Grill the skewers.

Cook's Notes

The distinct flavors of Thai, Indonesian and Malaysian curry dishes come from a variety of colorful curry pastes. Made from a blend of aromatic spices, herbs and vegetables, each curry paste derives its predominant color from a main ingredient—green curry paste from fresh green chilies, red curry paste from dried red chilies and yellow curry paste from tumeric. Making curry pastes from scratch is not difficult, but can be time-consuming. I suggest using curry paste from a jar because its flavors are authentic and it is very convenient for quick dinners.

Tofu Satays

Serves 4

1 pound extra-firm tofu

8 large button mushrooms about 2 inches in diameter

2 teaspoons pressed garlic

1 tablespoon grated gingerroot

2 tablespoons Thai fish sauce, soy sauce or teriyaki sauce

¼ cup light coconut milk

2 medium sweet onions such as Maui, Walla Walla or Vidalia

16 8-inch bamboo skewers

Fresh cilantro

Fresh papaya, pineapple or navel orange slices

Nonfat or canola oil cooking spray

Substitutions:

If you are not a fan of tofu, substitute boneless skinless chicken breasts, pork tenderloin or any firm fleshed fish. The green curry sauce tastes great with them all.

1. **Preheat the grill** to the highest setting.

2. **Prepare the vegetables.** Cut the tofu into 1 x 1 x 1-inch cubes. Cut the button mushrooms in half. Place the tofu and mushrooms in a 1- or 2-quart shallow dish or airtight container.

3. **Make the marinade.** In a 1-cup bowl or glass measure, mix the garlic, ginger, fish or soy sauce and coconut milk with a fork or wire whisk.

Pour the marinade over the tofu and the mushrooms. Turn them so that all sides are evenly coated with the marinade. Cover tightly with plastic wrap or a lid and refrigerate for 20 minutes or up to 24 hours.

4. **Prepare the skewers.** Slice the onions in half, then cut them into (1-inch thick) chunks. Remove the tofu and mushrooms from the marinade. Discard the marinade. Alternately thread the tofu, mushrooms and onion onto 8 sets of (8-inch) double bamboo skewers leaving a ⅛- to ¼-inch space between each piece of food. (See page 192 for double skewering technique.) To allow the mushrooms to lie flat on the grill, skewer them so that the parallel skewers pierce first through the stem, than out through the cap.

5. **Grill the skewers.** Spray each skewer lightly with cooking spray before placing on the grill. Grill the skewers according to the times below until grill marks appear on the tofu and it becomes crispy around the edges.

6. **To serve,** spoon equal amounts of rice onto the center of 4 plates. Arrange 2 skewers on 1 side of the rice. Garnish the opposite side with fresh papaya, pineapple, or navel orange slices. Top the rice with ¼ cup of the coconut basil sauce and sprinkle with the fresh cilantro. Serve immediately.

G r i l l   T i m e s

Two-Sided Contact Grill: *5 to 6 minutes.*

Hibachi Grill, Combination Grill or Infusion Grill: *10 to 12 minutes. Turn the skewers over halfway through the grilling time. Do not grill covered. This will prevent the outside of the tofu from becoming crispy. Tofu contains a lot of water, which will not evaporate if cooked in a covered, moist environment.*

Jasmine Rice and Petite Peas

Makes 4 generous (1 cup) servings

1½ cups Jasmine rice

3 cups water

1 cup frozen petite peas or frozen shelled edamame (green cooked soy beans)

You can make this recipe ahead but leave out the peas until reheating the rice just before serving. Refrigerate the rice for up to 2 days, or freeze up to 2 months in an airtight container or a zippered freezer bag.

1. Rinse rice in a fine mesh strainer under cool running water for a few minutes until water runs clear.

2. In a 2-quart pot with a tight fitting lid, mix the rice with the water.

3. Bring to a boil, cover and reduce heat to a simmer. Cook 20 minutes, or until all of the liquid has been absorbed. Remove from heat.

4. While the rice is cooking, put the peas or edamame in a strainer and hold it under cool running water until the vegetables are thawed. Drain well.

5. Just after you remove the rice from the heat, lift the lid and put the drained peas or edamame on top. Do not mix into the rice. Cover immediately and let stand 5 to 10 minutes to cook the peas or edamame. Stir with a fork to fluff up the rice and mix peas in before serving.

Curried Coconut Basil Sauce

Makes 8 (¼ cup) servings

1½ cups canned light coconut milk

¼ to 1 teaspoon green curry paste, to taste

½ cup nonfat chicken broth or canned vegetable broth

2 tablespoons fish sauce or low-sodium soy sauce

2 tablespoons brown sugar

¼ cup fresh basil leaves, packed or 1 tablespoon dried

2 tablespoons cornstarch

Substitution
If you can't find green curry paste, you can substitute ½ teaspoon ground curry powder and ⅛ to ¼ teaspoon cayenne pepper.

This sauce is so good that many people want more than ¼ cup—that's why there's enough for everyone to have a double portion. Leftovers will keep in the refrigerator for 2 days or can be frozen for up to 2 months. Thaw and reheat the sauce in the microwave.

1. In the blender, puree, the coconut milk, curry paste, chicken broth, fish or soy sauce, brown sugar, basil and cornstarch until smooth.
2. Pour the sauce into a 2-quart sauce pan and whisk constantly over medium-high heat until mixture is at a slow boil, then thickens, about 4 to 5 minutes. Remove the pot from the heat, and cover to keep it warm until the satays are ready. If it becomes too cool, reheat in the microwave.

Approximate Nutrients Per Serving of Entire Meal

Total Calories 480	Protein 20 g / 17%	Carbohydrates 77 g / 64%	
Total Sugar 8 g	Total Fat 10 g / 19%	Saturated Fat 1 g / 2%	
Cholesterol 0 mg	Sodium 804 mg	Fiber 4 g	Calcium 144 mg

Index

Menu Index